The Education
of
Lieutenant Kerrey

ALSO BY GREGORY L. VISTICA

Fall from Glory: The Men Who Sank the U.S. Navy

The Education
of
Lieutenant Kerrey

GREGORY L. VISTICA

THOMAS DUNNE BOOKS

ST. MARTIN'S PRESS

NEW YORK

THOMAS DUNNE BOOKS.
An imprint of St. Martin's Press.

www.stmartins.com

ISBN 0-312-28547-7

First Edition: January 2003

10 9 8 7 6 5 4 3 2 1

To my mother, Barbara (1925–2001),
may she finally rest in peace.
And, once again, to my wife, Joan,
and the girls: Rachel, Hannah, and Grace

Acknowledgments

THIS WAS NOT AN easy story to write. It brought out good emotions, painful emotions, and a great struggle to understand the complexities of truth. This project only reinforced my belief that there is no higher calling for a journalist than the honest pursuit of the truth. I've had tremendous help on this undertaking from many people. I'm indebted to my colleagues at *60 Minutes II* for their support—Dan Rather, Jeff Fager, Patti Hassler, Matt Richman, and especially Tom Anderson, who wrestled through the same soul-searching as I did when we broadcast this story in 2001. Tom is a very good journalist who brought great skill and foresight to the Kerrey story. It was because of the inquisitiveness of Derek Williams in Vietnam that this became an even better story. Kyle Crichton, Adam Moss, and Bill Keller of *The New York Times*, were steadfast supporters and great editors of the Kerrey story that first appeared in the *Times Magazine*. My agent, Jay Acton, instinctively knew that there was much more to the story than a magazine article. Jay realized how important it was for the history of Vietnam to tell the Kerrey story in book length. He was right, and I thank him for his brains, his friendship, and his tireless advocacy on my behalf. Tom Dunne at St. Martin's Press is more than just a great editor—he's a saint with unmatchable patience and book sense. Sean Desmond's skillful handling of the manuscript and his insightfulness brought important depth to the book.

Many people gave their time and ideas, and I thank them. Bill Turque brought his great talent as a writer and editor to this project. Jim Stevenson's insistence on moral clarity was invaluable. I'm grateful for John Weisman's guidance and to Mike Walker at the Navy archives, Betty Medsger, Marshall Windmiller, Dale Andradé, Rich Boylan at the National Archives, and many SEALs, whom I'd like to mention but for their good, do not. Two SEALs, however, deserve to be named for their courage and devotion to the truth: Larry Bailey, who read the manuscript and demanded accuracy and honesty in this story, and Clint Major, who was the first SEAL to publicly call for an investigation. As always, Lucy Shackelford was a great and fun research assistant who is the best at what she does. All of these people made this book better than it ever would have been if I had had to go it alone.

Area of Detail

VIETNAM

CAMBODIA

NHA TRANG
Medal of Honor mission

CAM RANH BAY
Hoffmann's Headquarters

Mekong River

SAIGON

BEN TRE

VUNG TAU
Swift boats kept here

VINH LONG
Song Co Chien River
TRA VINH

THANH PHU DISTRICT
free-fire zone

THANH PHONG
site of massacre

SOUTH CHINA SEA

N

0   100 Miles
0   100 Kilometers

Map by James Sinclair

Prologue

MAY 14, 1970, SHOULD have been the greatest day of Bob Kerrey's life. At precisely eleven o'clock that morning the young Navy lieutenant was standing in the East Room of the White House, summoned by the president of the United States to receive the nation's highest award for valor—the Medal of Honor. He shifted uneasily, trying to relieve the pain from his new ill-fitting wooden leg. Earlier that morning, while dressing in his tan uniform, his surgically shaped stump, which still bled almost daily, was so swollen he could barely fit it into his prosthesis. His face was dotted with beads of sweat, and inside he was a tangle of emotions. There was a bit of pride and some joy—the occasion warranted at least that. But mostly what Lieutenant J. Robert Kerrey felt was guilt and grief.

The military band had struck up "Hail to the Chief" and the honor guard stood at attention when President Richard Nixon arrived to begin the ceremony. Kerrey watched his commander in chief work his way toward him, smiling and shaking hands with some of the bravest veterans of Vietnam, if not of American history. It would soon be Lieutenant Kerrey's turn to embrace the one man he "hated most on earth."

Kerrey had contemplated using his White House visit to make a public stand against the war. He had told confidants that he "didn't want the damn medal" and was not even certain he would shake the president's hand. Kerrey blamed Nixon for his mental anguish. It was Nixon's war that made him do the unthinkable. It was Nixon's war that had taken half of his leg and left him haunted by nightmares. His defiance would be seen as a shameful act of insubordination, but Kerrey was angry, confused, and still emotionally and physically fragile from his wounds. He felt he had every right to speak out. But before he challenged his president in front of the world, his father, James Kerrey, imparted some old-fashioned advice to his son: "Don't do something dumb that you're going to regret all of your life."

The president took great pride in honoring Medal of Honor recipients. Nixon was known to tear up at these ceremonies, his usually stolid demeanor overcome by patriotic sentiment. These were his men-of-war, warriors willing to make the ultimate sacrifice and die for their country. Faithful, honorable men who had gone above and well beyond the call of duty. Each had given something of himself—either in body or spirit—that was irreplaceable and for a cause that, by 1970, great segments of the public, like the young Bob Kerrey, had turned against.

That Kerrey was even considering such a bold protest was in itself remarkable. He came of age after World War II, raised on the Great Plains, in a Nebraska family that cherished traditional American values. "This boy grew up patriotic, raised in an America flush with victory and certain beliefs," Kerrey said. "He never doubted that his country and its leaders were right and good. For him, patriotism was never a choice. It was simply an instinct." When the young Bob Kerrey grew older and departed for Vietnam as a twenty-five-year-old naval officer, he felt as if he could breathe fire. "I was ready to go at Hanoi with a knife in my teeth," he said.

Kerrey chose perhaps the most arduous and dangerous of all military specialties, the Navy's SEALs—elite commandos trained to fight from the sea, air, and on land. Over the years they became cultural icons, lionized in the press for their daring missions and portrayed as fearless, calculating killers by Hollywood. The luster always stayed with Kerrey.

In fact, his second combat mission in the war, which led to his Medal of Honor, would become, in retrospect, a well-polished memory. The secret raid on an island in the Bay of Nha Trang began flawlessly but ended in disaster when Kerrey's team lost the element of surprise—the most critical requisite for commando operations. An exploding grenade would cost him the lower part of his right leg. And while Kerrey spent months in a Philadelphia Navy hospital learning to walk again, the president, now standing just a few feet from him, promised but never delivered an end to the war. The country seemed to be spiraling out of control. Two weeks before his trip to the White House, Nixon had ordered the invasion of Cambodia. Ten days before the ceremony, National Guard troops had opened fire on students at Kent State University in Ohio, killing four and injuring nine. The Cambodian adventurism and the campus bloodshed both enraged him.

Despite his misgivings about Nixon, Kerrey yielded to his father's wishes. He had decided to at least show up, even though he regarded the ceremony as part patriotic pageantry and part political theater to boost an unpopular war. "I felt like I was being used, you know, flagged," Kerrey said, "to take the edge off this horrible experience. The right thing in 1968 was to negotiate an end to the war. We'd have gotten a hell of a lot more in 1968 than we got in 1973. And Henry Kissinger gets a Nobel Peace Prize for the damn thing? What shame does he have? And likewise with Nixon and other political leaders."

Nixon was now addressing the East Room audience. "I am very honored to welcome this group here in the East Room of the White House this morning and particularly because this is one of those occasions that is one of the really mountaintop experiences for a president of the United States," he said. "The Medal of Honor has been described many times, and there are no words that can add to the grandeur of that medal, what it means to those who receive it. I will simply say that when we think of this great country of ours . . . we think of it as the land of the free. We should all be reminded that it could not be the land of the free if it were not also the home of the brave. Today we honor the brave men, the men who, far beyond the call of duty, served their country magnificently in a war very far away, in a war which is many times not understood and not supported by some in this country."

The president then began to decorate the other medal recipients, smile, say a few words, and consecrate their bond with a handshake. As Kerrey waited his turn, he looked like a young man at the height of his glory. But inside, he was tormented, and in his darkest moments he even thought of himself as a coward. It wasn't so much the loss of his leg that had soured him. It was his first combat action in the war, a secret raid in the Mekong Delta just weeks before his Medal of Honor mission, that somehow had gone horribly wrong. "For me, what I lost in 1969 wasn't a leg. What I lost was an innocence. I had now done something that I never dreamed possible that I could do."

Nixon faced Kerrey, who stiffened to attention. Their eyes met, Nixon smiled, congratulated the Navy lieutenant, and pinned the bright blue sash that held the distinctive medallion around Kerrey's neck. Their hands clasped and in a moment it was over. All Kerrey would jokingly remember was Nixon's bad breath. But he was now a certifiable American hero and the first Navy SEAL to win the Medal of Honor for a combat action in Vietnam.

This is not a biography of J. Robert Kerrey. It is a story about war, memory, and the terrible corrosive power of secrets.

Above all, it's about the courage to confront past sins. It chronicles the struggle of one man's search for forgiveness and how a brotherhood of warriors, trained like few others to do battle, have lived with the legacy of one terrible night.

For on that first mission in Vietnam, Lieutenant Kerrey and his unit committed, as he later put it, an "atrocity."

Kerrey carried his secret through three decades of what was, by all appearances, a storybook existence: war hero, self-made millionaire businessman, governor, and a United States senator. Dashing and quick-witted, the national press dubbed him "the JFK of the plains." During his term as governor of Nebraska (1982–86) journalists took to calling his executive mansion "Cornhusker Camelot." As a senator (1988–2000), he carried in his laptop computer a video clip of President Kennedy challenging the nation to put a man on the moon before the end of the sixties, displaying it during presentations to prod his listeners to dream big.

He was glamorous enough to date a movie star (Debra Winger) and close enough to his midwestern roots to sit for hours with a suicidal farmer and talk him out of pulling the trigger. He quietly visited amputees in hospitals and cut insurance red tape so that maimed children could receive the prostheses they had been denied. He was a romantic who could cite Emily Dickinson's poems and short stories by Flannery O'Connor or move an election night crowd to tears by singing "And the Band Played Waltzing Mathilda," the Australian ballad about the World War I slaughter at Gallipoli. He was also a wiseacre with a taste for off-color jokes and a flair for searing put-downs. "Santorum," he once quipped about an especially unpleasant Republican Senate colleague from Pennsylvania, "isn't that Latin for asshole?"

Kerrey was, in a way, a modern day Jimmy Stewart in *Mr. Smith Goes to Washington*. Stewart was the only person Kerrey ever wanted to be photographed with, and he kept the small framed snapshot on a bookcase behind the desk in his Senate office. Like Jefferson Smith, Kerrey thought of himself as an outsider, the clear-eyed citizen taking on the establishment. "Yeah, there were times when I acted a bit like a renegade," Kerrey said. "There are times I'd almost intentionally take on issues that were unpopular because I feel it's necessary for somebody to do that."

Kerrey had come to Washington wanting to accomplish great things. His impassioned speeches on the floor of the Senate soon won him a reputation as an engaging orator and deep thinker. And though he said he really didn't want acceptance by the clubby Georgetown set, his celebrated story brought him into a world always looking for the fresh new face in power. He dined in the homes of grandees where he could be counted on to liven up the discussion with a joke or a provocative opinion. One evening with Colin Powell and Sally Quinn, the doyenne of A-list Washington, Kerrey spoke passionately about how he accepted the Medal of Honor only for others who had sacrificed so much more then he. As a military man, General Powell was moved close to tears by Kerrey's eloquence.

But the burdens of his secret were never far from the surface. He was often cold and unpredictable, prone to black moods and flip-flops on the issues. So erratic was his behavior that reporters took to calling him "Cosmic Bob," a nickname he hated. Kerrey's struggle with the demons of memory made it difficult for him to trust and quick to withhold. He had few truly close friends. "The only people who knew Bob were the people in the SEALs," said June Levine, a University of Nebraska professor who first met him years ago when he was struggling with his memories of Vietnam. Like a character in a Shakespearean tragedy, he often seemed to be engaged in a compulsive and desperate search for redemption, but incapable of accepting resolution. "I carry memories of what I did, and I survive and live based upon lots of different mechanisms," he said.

When I first uncovered Kerrey's secrets about Vietnam and confronted him in December 1998, he acknowledged that he had done something unspeakable but didn't tell the complete story. He seemed to live in fear of the hard facts and said he wasn't sure what the real truth about his mission was. Ultimately, he concluded it would be better to cooperate in the public disclosure of his role and accept the consequences. Kerrey's intention in acknowledging what happened, he said, was to use his experience as a teaching tool. He was convinced that America's elite special forces will likely confront similar situations while fighting terrorism in hot spots around the world.

It is difficult to know with certainty what Kerrey's motives were. And it is even harder to know with full confidence what really happened that night in Vietnam three decades ago. Kerrey's own accounts were often so tangled with contradictions and laced with grief and guilt that it was hard to press him. Was this real or an act to win sympathy? Perhaps a little of both. My challenge was figuring out what was true—or as close to the truth as it was possible to get.

The Education

of

Lieutenant Kerrey

Chapter One

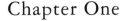

IT WAS TIME TO put the grandchildren to bed.

Bui Van Vat and his wife took the three youngsters to a small bunker dug into the earth in the back of their thatched hut. It had been awhile since the Americans, the "devils with green faces," had come brandishing guns and asking a lot of questions. They had shown up out of nowhere, stayed for several hours, then left. There was little reason for Vat or the other villagers to believe they would return to tiny Thanh Phong. But then again, why had they come in the first place? The bunker, hard to see in the blackness of the night, offered some security—just in case the men with guns reappeared.

The grandparents said good night to the children: a boy not yet nine; his sister, who was about a year older; and the eldest girl, who was approaching thirteen. Throughout the hamlet—in the flatland marshes of the Mekong Delta about seventy-five miles south of Saigon—the nightly routines of dousing cooking fires and putting children to bed were underway. In a group of huts not far from Vat's hooch, twelve-year-old Bui Thi Luom and her fifteen relatives—a few women and lots of children—were climbing into their own underground bunker, one big enough to sleep two dozen people.

Perhaps tonight would be quiet again, the way it had been for much of the war.

Thanh Phong lay in an area the generals had decided to call a "secret zone." For this village it was a peculiar name, because there was nothing all that secret about it. "Remote" was a more accurate description. Thanh Phong was about as far away from the war as one could get while still being in it. The only real access was from the South China Sea and then up the Song Co Chien River, past beaches and the sandy dunes that gave way to thickets of mangroves marking the hamlet's southern border.

It had been, for the most part, untouched by either war or progress except for the occasional bombs from Phantom jets or shells lobbed in from bigger Navy ships prowling the coast (thus the bunkers). The village was essentially left alone. So impoverished that it didn't get electricity until the late 1980s, there was no real town center, just the simple hooches with thatch for their roofs, where poorly clothed children and their families slept on the hard ground. There was no school and there were no young men of fighting age. They had either left to join the ranks of the Vietcong or fled before being conscripted into the government of South Vietnam's army. The place was populated solely by older men like Bui Van Vat and women and children. They numbered about 150 at most and spent the day tending to their rice crops or eking out a living by fishing or crabbing.

But on this night in February 1969, the war would change Thanh Phong forever. The "devils with green faces" were coming back. They were doing what they did best—hiding in the darkness and waiting for the right moment to strike.

Lieutenant Robert Kerrey sat in the darkness, watching, waiting, and nerving himself for the task that was coming. The SEALs had slipped over the sides of the Swift boat shortly before midnight and quietly and quickly came ashore on the outskirts of Thanh Phong. Their jungle fatigues blended with the brush, as did their faces—painted green with black stripes in various zigzags running down their cheeks and around their eyes and on their noses. Some wore bandanas or stockings pulled tight over their hair and tied in the back. They did look like devils. But underneath the uniforms and warpaint, they were seven boys-next-door who grew up in the suburbs and small towns across America.

They carried a small arsenal with them: antiarmor weapons, grenade launchers, large- and small-caliber automatic rifles, 9mm Smith & Wesson pistols, and nearly 1,500 rounds of ammunition. Knives and hand grenades hung from their belts, including "Willie Peter," phosphorous grenades used to root out or kill people hiding in bunkers or hooches.

It meant they would have the edge in firepower over virtually any opposition they encountered. But this was little comfort to Kerrey. The twenty-five-year-old squad leader "was really frightened, frightened of the unknown. The idea that a man trained in a SEAL team is somehow a cold-blooded killer and doesn't worry about anything, doesn't have any elevated blood pressure and accelerated pulse," Kerrey said, "I think is a false idea." On first impression, Kerrey did not strike a commanding presence. He spoke in a high-pitched tone, and his military-issue fatigues looked as if they didn't fit. His haircut was odd for a military man—long and shaggy on top and very short on the sides. He liked to tell jokes about parrots and told his teammates he dreamed in cartoons. But there was a real toughness under the gentle facade. He and his team had trained hard for moments just like this one. They had to— only two of the seven squad members had seen combat. And one of the greenhorns was their leader. If Kerrey didn't get it right, he could get himself and his men killed.

The squad had practiced this kind of mission hundreds of times during SEAL training back in San Diego and had laid some ambushes since arriving in Vietnam only a few weeks before. (The ambushes, mostly in safe territory, never amounted to anything.) But Thanh Phong was different.

Here they had real intelligence about a real target: a Vietcong political leader who was supposed to be attending a meeting in the village.

Kerrey was told the Communist official would almost certainly have armed guards. That meant a good chance of a firefight, a prospect that sent fear running throughout his body. As he sat in the darkness, sweating profusely, he felt as if he was back in high school, slogging through football practice in Lincoln, Nebraska, when his team scrimmaged twice a day in the sticky summer heat.

What worried Kerrey was the prime requirement of command—keeping his men alive. The thought of losing even one of them was too dreadful to dwell on. Lieutenant Kerrey had come to love his men, and they had come to see him as a father figure, even a protector who cared only for their well-being. As they sat waiting to move out, all Kerrey could do was pray that things would go according to plan.

The Swift boat that brought them, under the command of Lieutenant William Garlow, had pushed back off the beach and into the river. It would quietly motor away and await the SEAL team's radio call to extract them, hopefully when their mission was accomplished.

Now the SEALs were all alone. For a while, they sat and waited, letting their eyes adjust to the darkness, and listening for anything that sounded out of place: the bark of a frightened dog or a slight rustling in the brush from someone trying to move undetected.

William Tucker, the rear security man, had heard about these long pauses in a patrol, waiting in enemy territory for a guerrilla to pop out from nowhere, guns blazing. The silence and darkness coupled with fear could play tricks on your mind, Tucker knew, particularly after dropping a few tabs of readily available speed to keep alert. Another SEAL once told him he saw Captain Marvel all dressed up in his comic strip uniform, coming down a canal on a surfboard. Tucker imagined the big leaf next to him was really a Vietcong fighter.

Certain that their entry had not been observed, Kerrey gave the signal to move out.

Mike Ambrose, a handsome, well-built petty officer from Illinois whom Tucker called "the mouth" for his cockiness, took the lead. Behind him was Gerhard Klann, the best operator in the group. He looked like the quintessential German: a fair-haired blond who stood 6'3", lean at the waist, and broad shouldered. Kerrey and Lloyd "Doc" Schrier, the stoic medic, were right by him. Next came more rookies, a radio man and grenadier, followed by Tucker in the rear. A Vietnamese SEAL tagged along to interpret.

Ambrose crept in the shadows toward the first hooch he could see. His gaze came to a stop on an old, unarmed man sitting outside an isolated hooch.

It was Bui Van Vat.

Ambrose felt a quick rush of adrenaline. The SEALs hadn't planned on anyone in the hamlet being awake at this hour. And this was certainly not the right hooch. There were no guards, nothing that would signify that somebody important was inside. Perhaps the man was a forward sentry, but he carried no weapon.

So far, Kerrey's men hadn't been spotted. They could try to creep past the old man in silence. But eight men carrying weapons and sundry gear were bound to make some noise. Bui Van Vat could wreck the mission.

The SEALs faced a stark choice: Should they kill him and anyone inside the hooch and continue their operation deeper into the village, or should they abort? That would look bad on their first big mission. "To tie them up and leave them in place puts the entire operation at risk," Kerrey said. The SOPs—the standard operating procedures drilled into Kerrey—spelled out exactly what to do. "Kill the people we make contact with or we have to abort," Kerrey said.

It was the lieutenant's call.

William Garlow was a meticulous officer who liked a clean and orderly ship. In his spiral-bound calendar, under Tuesday, February 25, 1969, he had jotted down "SEAL insertion." Below that in the same box was "troop insertion," a reference to another operation in the region that night. At about the same time he was moving Kerrey's unit into position, a small fleet of other Swift boats were transporting one hundred Vietnamese troops to a major search-and-destroy mission in An Nohn, a village close to Thanh Phong.

Garlow was queasy about raids to take out villages. Carrying out orders to prosecute the war was one thing. But indiscriminate violence was not something he thought appropriate. The destruction of a family's home pained him, filling him with a sense of injustice. Garlow rationalized it as a necessary part of the war, but he didn't have to like it; he just had to follow orders. Before destroying a village, he did his best to insure that it was empty. Then his boat's gunners would take aim at the hooches and launch a few phosphorous rounds, exploding the homes into balls of fire. As far as he knew, he wasn't killing anybody, and that was just fine by him. Sending a hooch up in flames had become an American calling card. Infantry units that rolled through a suspect village used cigarette lighters to ignite the thatch roofs that quickly engulfed entire homes, usually while helpless families stood by and watched. The practice, caught by television cameras and shown in the living rooms back home, appalled many Americans.

Garlow's calendar was both a ship's log and a reminder of how many days remained before he could return stateside. On the twenty-third of February, two days before he picked up

Kerrey's team, he wrote the number "80" and circled it—eighty days in country. This was also the first time he had written the word "SEAL" in his 1969 calendar, but Garlow knew what the commandos were in Vietnam to do—intelligence collection, assassinations, and abductions or, in the euphemism chosen for such deeds, "neutralizations."

The object was to terrorize the civilians and get them to cooperate with the Vietnamese government and quit aiding the enemy Vietcong. "You're not successful in a war unless you do hideous, awful things. It is hell on earth," Kerrey said. "Violence to the maximum for the purpose of trying to get the enemy to surrender." Though the SEALs were few in number, their reputation as fierce warriors, capable of appearing out of nowhere, had spread throughout the Mekong Delta.

It was past midnight when Garlow slowly motored toward the beach to extract the Navy men. While his sailors manned the boat's two .50-caliber machine-guns, the seven SEALs and the Vietnamese interpreter came running out of the shadows and quickly climbed aboard. Garlow revved the engines and pointed the bow out of the river and toward the South China Sea. The SEALs had moved to the stern of the boat, where crewman William O'Mara, an Irishman from the Bronx, eyed them and couldn't help feeling that something was wrong. None of the commandos had been shot or wounded, but they were all oddly subdued. "I knew something was up. They were really quiet. It was eerie," O'Mara recalled. He had heard gunfire and figured they had been in some kind of engagement, but other than that, he couldn't explain their peculiar behavior. SEALs were normally pumped up after a mission. "No way," he said, "not this night they weren't."

Once in open water, Garlow set a course for the Coast Guard cutter *Point Comfort*, which was standing by to whisk Kerrey and his men some three hundred miles back up the coast to Cam Rahn Bay, where their senior operational commander had his headquarters. Later, Garlow went to the radio room to call in his status. One of the SEALs accompanied him to send his own message, that the mission had been completed with no friendly casualties.

Around 4:30 that morning, Kerrey's team boarded the *Point Comfort*. As the ship cut through the water, the events of the night began to torment Kerrey. "I knew something really bad had come from me," he said. "I had perpetrated something just terrible. At that moment, you feel like what just happened is you've been possessed by something really evil, and you've acted on it. You've done it. You've let yourself go in a way that you never dreamed possible."

Kerrey hung over the ship's railing, vomiting and "howling like a dog" into the wind.

With terror in his eyes, he screamed, "Jesus, what have we done!"

Chapter Two

———————■———————

TWENTY-EIGHT YEARS LATER, in May 1997, the telephone rang at my desk in the Washington bureau of *Newsweek* magazine.

The caller was a retired Navy captain who had spent his entire career in the SEALs. He had done a tour in Vietnam about the same time as Bob Kerrey, commanding a platoon in the Mekong Delta. His last posting was at SEAL headquarters in Coronado, California, a secure oceanside compound on the shores of the azure Pacific and across the bay from San Diego. The job gave him access to a trove of sensitive information, from personal performance records to histories of operations in Vietnam. It made him one of the few people who had a good grasp of the truth about SEAL activities, not the Hollywood-inspired images of warriors laying in wait for a prey, sucking air through thin reeds while hiding in shallow marshy water. He'd heard and seen enough that he grew to show disdain for medals, believing they often ended up pinned to an undeserving chest. He was a realist when it came to retelling stories from Vietnam. War was hell, SEALs did good, SEALs did bad. It was mostly good, but the bad he felt should not be covered up.

He was spending his retirement from the Navy as a combination historian, sleuth, and bounty hunter. He joined several of his retired SEAL colleagues who had created a database with the names of every person who had ever made it into and graduated from Basic Underwater Demolition/SEAL (BUD/S) training. It was a way to organize information for reunions and correspondence. But the real purpose was to root out imposters, the frauds who claimed to be SEALs, often with fictitious decorations, to impress a girlfriend or get a job. When they caught a phony, the confrontation was usually by e-mail, sometimes by telephone, or in a personal visit. It was not at all pleasant. More often than not, coercive language or perhaps even veiled threats of bodily harm were enough to get the job done. At last count, they had outted several thousand charlatans.

I had known the captain well for many years and trusted his information. It is why I left a telephone message which prompted his return call.

"I'm kicking around doing something on Bob Kerrey," I said. "What do you know about him?" I had made the same request of other SEALs I knew, all of whom delivered the same canned response: "Great guy . . . a stand-up fellow . . . good SEAL . . . I liked him very much."

At the time, Kerrey was making rumblings about running for president again, taking on Vice President Al Gore in the 2000 Democratic primaries. During his last campaign, in 1992, he steered as far as he could from the details of his war record, never venturing beyond a cursory description of his Medal of Honor mission and saying "I killed people," which seemed to be a reasonable talking point for a Navy SEAL who saw combat in Vietnam. But after nearly two decades in public life, his war record consisted of little else. There had to be more. What kind of operations had he gone on? If he had indeed killed before, how many times? With a knife or a gun? Did he feel remorse?

The captain did not regard Kerrey as an imposter. But he was troubled by his acceptance of the Medal of Honor.

"You know, he should not have won the Medal of Honor," he said in a matter-of-fact way.

"What? What do you mean?"

"He was first put in for a Bronze Star, and it was upped to the Medal of Honor."

This was not news. The story had cropped up in 1992 and quickly disappeared because there was a plausible explanation. The initial information supporting a Bronze Star was probably incomplete, later revised to offer a more complete account of the dangers Kerrey faced. The captain's skepticism notwithstanding, nobody in the press corps was ready to question Kerrey's bravery. Nonetheless, I made a note to check on it.

Then, in his southern drawl, the captain dropped the real showstopper. Senator Kerrey had been on a mission that went very badly, he said, and what happened "has been kept secret ever since."

"I have a hard time believing that," I said. It seemed highly unlikely to me that a man in public life for so long—a presidential candidate, no less, could successfully conceal such a big secret. "If it was so bad," I said, "it would have gotten out."

It felt like another half-baked conspiracy rumor. Still, I had to consider the source. The man on the other end of the line had a set-in-stone scorn for such stories. If he thought something was there, I had to take him seriously.

And while the SEALs were professionals, they could also be renegades—covert cowboys who operated by their own rules. In 1968, the chief of naval operations sent Roy Boehm, one of the founders of the SEALs, on a fact-finding trip to the Mekong Delta, not far from where Kerrey operated. Reports had trickled back to Washington about a troublesome platoon. What Boehm found was something out of *Apocalypse Now*, a SEAL squad where the men had cut their hair into Mohawks and were terrorizing and abusing peasants. Boehm sacked the skipper and put an enlisted man he knew in charge. It wasn't long before the new squad leader was killed by his teammates in a friendly-fire accident. The SEALs also were deeply involved in the Phoenix program, an intelligence collection effort created by the CIA that mutated into a fairly brutal assassination campaign.

Not all the SEALs who went to Vietnam served in Phoenix. Some performed missions for it without being told where the orders came from. But the connection was strong enough that, before long, the entire community was stuck with a reputation as a cadre of cold-blooded killers.

Kerrey's image as a war hero and statesman had always seemed unassailable. But now, a respected Vietnam veteran and fellow SEAL was raising the unthinkable.

"I had a SEAL who worked for me, and he came to me and said, 'Captain, I got to tell you something, get something off of my chest.' He was on Kerrey's squad. Told me all about the killing. He was a really good kid and a helluva SEAL."

"What's his name?" I asked.

"Gerhard Klann," the captain said, adding that he didn't want to see anything bad happen to him, or to Kerrey, for that matter. Even so, he said, "I believe Gerhard. He's never once changed his story in all these years." The captain said it was more then a dozen years since he first heard it.

"Where did this take place?"

"Somewhere in the delta," he said.

I hung up the telephone, my thoughts racing from disbelief to excitement over a potentially huge news tip. I also realized that I needed to exercise extraordinary care. At stake was the reputation of a man thought not only to be honorable but even a truth teller in a town full of spin doctors.

The closest Bob Kerrey had ever come to killing anybody before Vietnam was in high school.

He was a runty sixteen-year-old, barely weighing one hundred pounds. But he was in the lawn and garden section of Bob's Supermarket in Lincoln, Nebraska, beating the tar out of a much bigger classmate. Kerrey had wrestled the boy to the ground and was on top of him, banging his classmate's head onto the concrete floor when he heard an alarmed shopper scream, "Call the police!" The shriek was enough to snap Kerrey back to reality. He knew trying to crack open the kid's skull was not a good thing to do, but he was in a fight and thrashing his opponent any way he could came almost instinctively to him. Kerrey reluctantly let go and stood up, thinking it wiser to back off before the authorities arrived. But his opponent was not about to give up. He grabbed some pruning shears from a nearby shelf and squared off for another go.

Kerrey thought he would do what he had seen the good guys pull off countless times in the movies and take the weapon away. But the boy lunged forward and before Kerrey could dodge him, the kid drove the steel tip of the shears deep through his side.

When the sheriff showed up, Kerrey was taken away in a patrol car to the hospital. He was lucky. Had the shears gone in a few inches deeper, they would have punctured his heart. The doctors sewed Kerrey up and released him to the police who threw him into the county jail on assault charges.

Elinor Kerrey posted bail for her son. She was not ready to accept the sheriff's version of events that her third oldest boy, with his crew cut, soft skin, and diminutive size, was the out-of-control villain. She believed Bob's story: He was sticking up for his older brother Jim, who was incapable of defending himself. Jim, the oldest of the Kerrey children, had been born mentally retarded, due in part, his mother believed, to a difficult delivery. The family had sent him off to a special boarding school in Philadelphia hoping that more experienced teachers and mental health experts would improve the quality of his life. But Jim's letters home hinted at difficult times there, and his parents traveled by train to the school to see for themselves. The conditions they found were deplorable. Health and hygiene were so bad that Jim was sleeping in his own excrement. They brought him right home.

Having Jim around spurred some mixed emotions among Kerrey and his siblings. It could be confusing and embarrassing to watch a grown teenager behave like a small child. He suffered from epilepsy, and the medication he took cut the blood flow to his gums, causing his teeth to fall out. It embarrassed but also pained Bob Kerrey that his older brother "had a very troubled life," and he was not about to let anybody torment him, even if it meant defending him with his fists.

Kerrey got a less sympathetic hearing when he returned from jail. His father, James, who sided with the cops, regarded his son as the thug who picked the fight. Kerrey senior soon came around to his wife's view, but the sting of the unfair reprimand lingered for years into adulthood, and young Kerrey never forgot who first came to his defense. "My mother saw injustice right at the moment," Kerrey said.

Propriety and image were important to James Kerrey, and it was probably one reason why he was quick to judge his son. Lincoln was a city known as a peaceful and especially safe place to raise children, a reputation that remains today. And Bethany, the suburb where the Kerrey's lived, was a small and devoutly religious community. "My father and mother were not what I called Bible-thumpers or anything like that," Kerrey said. "But we were a deeply religious family." Bailing a juvenile delinquent son out of jail, if only for a minor fistfight, ran against the town's puritanical grain.

Kerrey was not a wild-eyed rebel, but like most precocious adolescents, he could be reckless. In grade school, he helped form Lincoln's benign version of a "gang." They called themselves the "Angles" because they misspelled "Angels" on the barn that served as their clubhouse. Later, he and his friends would pick fights at high school football and basketball games, and they would pull risky stunts. When a local creek flooded, Kerrey, never a strong swimmer, would jump into the fast-flowing current and try to grab a pylon on a bridge downstream as he rushed by.

Winters were long and harsh, with temperatures typically below freezing as wind swept across the the Great Plains. But for Bob Kerrey and his chums, the weather was merely an opportunity for more mischief. Before they could legally drive, they would "borrow" a car, he said, from one of the boys' homes, tie a rope to the bumper, and ski behind it. Other times they would ride behind the car on a garbage can lid, sliding around corners on icy roads.

They set up a daredevil sled course just outside the city, using a rope tied between two trees as a brake. Barreling down the icy hill at up to fifty miles per hour, they'd grab the rope to stop their flight downhill. But the first boy to do so did a full flip, flew thirty feet into the air, and broke his arm. Things got worse in the hospital. Just before this accident, Kerrey and his friend had broken into their high school chemistry lab and stolen enough materials to make an outlaw lab in Kerrey's home. In the hospital, the boy with the broken arm bragged to the nurse about their caper. She was not amused. Her husband was the chemistry teacher.

Kerrey never lost his boyish interest in a good joke or pranks. Writing in *Esquire* magazine, Martha Sherrill told how Senator Kerrey caused a stir among her guests at a New York dinner party. One woman had been recounting the story of her blind date with a television producer named Michael Epstein and wondered out loud if she should initiate a call to him.

"So where does this guy live?" Kerrey asked.

"Brooklyn," the woman, Barbara Feinman, replied.

Kerrey excused himself to use the telephone, only to reappear rattling off addresses. "Is that East Tenth? Or Elmwood . . . or Second Street . . . or Hicks?"

"You bastard! Stop him!" Feinman yelled as a giggling Kerrey slipped back into the kitchen. "He's calling Michael Epstein!"

This was the Bob Kerrey friends knew: impulsive, unpredictable, always ready to push the envelope. What no one in their wildest imaginings suspected was that the envelope might stretch all the way to allegations of murder.

Chapter Three

————————■————————

Bob Kerrey was already out of bed when the bell tower near his apartment at 6th and Pennsylvania Avenue chimed six times. He strapped on his artificial leg, the one he used with a running shoe, and began his five mile morning jog down the Washington Mall. The sun was at his back, but still low in the sky, chasing the shadows on the ellipse and slowly turning the Jefferson Memorial and Washington Monument to luminous white. Kerrey knew the path by heart. It led to the Vietnam Memorial, with the names of all those "dead boys," as he called them, etched into black marble that rose out of the ground like a giant tombstone. This was a place of sanctity to Kerrey, a place where "you have to be steely-eyed," he said, "if you really want to avoid sobbing like a baby."

Most of his days in Washington started this way, a run down to the Vietnam wall and back. After a shower he headed for the Hart Senate Office Building on the north side of the Capitol, to begin a typically packed schedule. On this day, June 18, 1998, it included a 12:30 luncheon with the political reporters at *Newsweek*'s Washington bureau, located just a block from the White House on Pennsylvania Avenue.

By 11 A.M. the caterers had prepared *Newsweek*'s conference room for Kerrey's arrival. On normal working days, when a VIP was not expected for lunch, reporters sat around a large round table eating their take-out sandwiches and reading the morning papers, while trading Washington or industry gossip. But by mid-morning, the caterers had set the table for Kerrey with a white linen cloth, china, and silver. The senator's seat faced a wall of sliding glass doors opening onto a balcony with a commanding southern exposure: the lush green expanse of the Mall, the playful curls of the Potomac River, the New York shuttle gliding in and out of Reagan National Airport, and, on clear days, George Washington's home at Mount Vernon.

Inside, along the walls, were reminders of more recent history. Above a worn love seat, was an enormous photograph of President Ronald Reagan on graduation day at the Naval Academy, smiling broadly while giving a high-five to a black midshipman. On other walls throughout the bureau hung a patchwork of *Newsweek* covers spanning many years of great news events and news makers. There were the wives of presidents and of course the Kennedys, John and Bobby; covers featuring CIA men, politicians like Newt Gingrich under the headline "The Quitter"; and war—from Vietnam to the Persian Gulf, which Senator Kerrey had voted against. Kerrey had yet to grace *Newsweek*'s cover.

When Kerrey arrived, he was escorted down a long hall, examining various magazine covers along the way as he glided past my office. Until that day I had never before seen him in person. Yet I felt as if I knew him better than most of the reporters who would be dining with him and hoping he would be his typical unpredictable self, the one who rarely uses a five-second delay before saying what he thinks. It had been a little over a year since my phone conversation with the captain, and I had spent a lot of it poking into Kerrey's background, trying to understand him—his fears, his passions, his loves, his hatreds—anything that might shed light on what had happened to him in Vietnam. I tried to read everything he read—books like *The Meadow* and *The Foreseeable Future*, authors such as Albert Camus, Ken Kesey, Pat Conroy, Cormac McCarthy, and scores of other titles and poems that he mentioned as his favorites. I examined his speeches and statements on the Senate floor, poured over old reports in the Navy's historical archives, interviewed friends and many Navy SEALs—even some from his unit who were willing to discuss Vietnam.

I assumed that word of my inquiries had gotten back to him. Kerrey's network of acolytes was wide and deep, and the SEALs were a tight, secretive community of men who looked after each other. They had little love for the press. Journalists looking for interviews almost always needed a reference from a trusted friend before a SEAL said one word. If Kerrey knew what I was up to, there was a chance he might confront me at lunch, tell me his war record was none of my damn business. Then again, as unpredictable as he was, he might just as easily tell all. As he walked past me in the hallway there was no way to read his face or judge his mood.

His looks were rather normal, and he would have been lost in a crowd if not for his well-known face. At fifty-five, he was still boyishly handsome, his hair graying at the temples and worn stylishly long. He was not a big man physically, a few inches under six feet tall with a slight but firm build. "Astronaut size" is how one reporter summed up his physical stature. His eyes, soft and blue, had taken on "a new depth" since the war, his sister once said, a look that seemed to flick back and forth between fear and remorse. His most distinguishing feature, however, was not visible. But as Kerrey walked past my office, I could hear the soft *pffft* from his prosthesis when it touched the ground. It gave him a noticeably different gait that he always tried to hide and only rarely spoke about publicly. "Suddenly, for the first time in my life, I was different. I was unable to change it. I was unable to disguise it. I was unable to pretend that it was not so. So now I walk with a limp that I cannot hide no matter how hard I try.

I had to learn, and it was a wonderful thing to learn, that being different is good, that being different from other people is a good thing."

Watching him turn the corner into the conference room, I was well aware that Kerrey was indeed very different. He was not just a complex politician, but a war hero who, if Gerhard Klann's story had any merit, might be considered by some to be a war criminal. But as far as I was concerned, until the evidence overwhelmingly proved otherwise, the tip from my SEAL captain was just a rumor, and the man in the conference room was a distinguished U.S. senator who had been awarded the Medal of Honor for gallantry.

I waited ten minutes or so, to give the senator and the correspondents time to settle into their rituals of give-and-take before heading back to the conference room. When I walked in, they were all chatting like old school chums. A courteous Kerrey stood and came over to greet me.

"Bob Kerrey," he replied to my own introduction in a kind of high-pitched, singsong voice. Eyes fixed on mine, he grasped my hand tightly and pulled it toward his gut, bringing us within inches of each other. The few seconds of his embrace seemed to last a minute or two, then he smiled and let go. It felt far more intimate than a politician's usual autopilot greeting. I couldn't help feeling that he was sizing me up, and sending a message: He knew that I knew.

The rest of the journalists in the room were oblivious to our coded exchange. None of them were aware of my investigation into Kerrey's background and I was not about to bring it up at the luncheon. Reporters were terrible at keeping secrets. Besides, Kerrey was a favorite of the Washington press corps—the result of a careful, ongoing courtship the senator artfully managed himself, without much assistance, or interference of a press aide. Kerrey had developed relationships with some of the country's most influential journalists, many of whom had covered Vietnam and viewed him as a hero beyond serious reproach. He wielded an almost mystical power over the Washington media elite. "I saw Jim Lehrer fall in love with him on the television," said Kandra Hahn, a member of Kerrey's gubernatorial campaign staff who was later rewarded with a state cabinet post.

Part of it was simply that they loved his story: Handsome war hero turns politician and gets the movie star as his girl. How he coped with his wound only garnered him more admirers. When the doctors said he would never again drive a car with a clutch, Kerrey insisted on using one with a manual transmission anyway. Ed Howard, a reporter who covered Kerrey for the Associated Press in Nebraska, said a "tight-ass Lutheran nurse told Kerrey in the hospital, 'If you're looking for sympathy, it's between shit and syphilis [in the dictionary] where it belongs.'" Kerrey was not a whiner, Howard said. After leaving the hospital in October 1969, instead of hobbling around feeling sorry for himself, he began a physical fitness regimen that started with swimming, then progressed into regular jogging. He finished the 1983 Lincoln Marathon with a prosthesis that rubbed his still-tender stump raw.

That old-fashioned ruggedness was fused with a quirky, self-deprecating humor that many journalists found refreshing. *Meet the Press* host Tim Russert, an unabashed Kerrey fan, once asked, "Are you not concerned that if you cut a deal with the Republicans, President Clinton will saw your limb off?"

"Oh, that's a terrible metaphor," Kerrey said, not missing a beat, "since somebody's already sawed one of them off." When an apologetic Russert attempted to follow up, Kerrey interjected: "If you don't saw off my limbs." On CNN, the late Rowland Evans said to Kerrey, ". . . isn't it obvious, just between us grown-ups here, that the Republican strategy—" Before Evans could finish, Kerrey quipped, "Where are the grown-ups?"

Much of the national political press yearned for another Kerrey presidential campaign in 2000. Some saw the Kennedy magic in his style. Kerrey never discouraged the comparison, although the parallels (Harvard-educated, Irish-Catholic aristocrats versus middle-class heartlanders with state school degrees) were few. For much of his life, Kerrey believed he was Irish, too, only to learn a few years ago that his bloodlines were English. The original family name had been "Kerry" until his great-grandfather moved from England to America and added an extra "e." Kerrey was Catholic, but only after converting in the late 1990s from Congregationalism.

And Nebraska was a long way from Massachusetts. Natives poked fun at their bland, corn-fed stereotype, but they also valued it. "We're not the first to grab onto anything, whether it's a hula hoop or whether it's a political problem," one of Kerrey's high school teachers explained to Karen Tumulty, then a reporter with the *Los Angeles Times*. A wealthy Nebraskan on the Republican National Committee, Duane Acklie, told commentator Morton Kondracke, "come to think of it, most people in Nebraska are typically pretty dull."

Nebraskans knew they could indeed be staid old cornhuskers, but shrewd ones at that. How else to explain Johnny Carson, billionaire Warren Buffett, and one of the nation's highest literacy rates? An old Kerrey friend, Lincoln newsman Dick Herman, put it simply, "we're self-reliant people."

Kerrey never lost that sensibility.

Joseph Robert Kerrey was born on August 27, 1943, in a hospital named after William Jennings Bryan, Nebraska's prairie populist. His father never liked the name Joe and preferred to call his son Bob, after a favorite relative. He grew up in a family-oriented home down the street from a public library on a block lined with lilac bushes, played the trumpet and piano, had a paper route, was a Boy Scout (didn't make it past second class), and still remembers the name of the grade-school girl he gave his first kiss to: Geraldine. "Oh, you know, it was great, it was very happy times," Kerrey recalled.

Kerrey, his three sisters, and three brothers, grew up in Bethany, a white middle-class enclave on the north side of Lincoln, Nebraska's capital city. The statue gracing the capitol dome, of a man sowing seed, left little doubt of the state's ethos: hard work, no flash, no nonsense. "In my world, a great celebrity was somebody who got their name in the *Lincoln Journal* or *Lincoln Star*," Kerrey said. The closest thing to a community vice was football. When the University of Nebraska Cornhuskers played at home in Lincoln, the stadium became the third largest city in the state. The most notable person in Nebraska was the football coach, whose name recognition topped even that of the state's popular politicians. One legendary coach, Tom Osborne, used his popularity to campaign successfully for Congress.

Bethany scarcely existed before the late nineteenth century. That is when farmers sold out to real estate speculators who in turn found an eager buyer in the Nebraska Christian Missionary Alliance, which consisted primarily of the Disciples of Christ denomination. The church elders built Cotner Christian College, which closed its doors because of financial problems in 1933. At its peak, half of the denomination's overseas missionaries were graduates of Cotner. The church land soon developed into a fast-growing residential suburb attracting devout Christians eager to escape higher real estate prices in posh south Lincoln.

At the end of World War II, Kerrey's father settled in Bethany after serving as a G.I. in Japan. A captain in the Army Air Corps, he was to be part of the American invasion force, but after the atomic bombing of Hiroshima and Nagasaki, James Kerrey's duty was with U.S. occupation forces in Japan. He saw opportunity in Lincoln, the center of the state's political life, and in tiny Bethany, with its block-long business district, which included a drugstore, a doctor's office, a grocery store, a barbershop, and a library. The Bethany community shunned alcohol and tried to keep the town "dry" for years. (As a businessman in the 1970s, Bob Kerrey had to fight hard for a liquor license for his bowling alley.)

James Kerrey became a crafty and respected entrepreneur in Bethany who tried his hand at a number of business ventures, some successful, some failures. "My father was thrilled anytime he could buy something cheap," Kerrey said. "My poor mother would come home and my father had gotten a real bargain on four cases of No. 10 pickles. So we'd be eating pickles forever." James Kerrey bought a lumberyard with the help of Larry Price, a wealthy Bethany businessman who saw Kerrey as a quick study and promising partner. The senior Kerrey branched out into the hardware and construction business, and built everything from bowling alleys and light industrial centers to residential homes.

But like many fathers of that era, James Kerrey found it difficult to develop a close bond with his children. "If you would have asked me when I was sixteen or seventeen I would have told you he sort of was embarrassing to me," Kerrey said. "He didn't dress very cool." He was not a conversationalist nor one to complain. "His two-word motto to any response in life was, 'No problem.' No matter what it was, 'Gee, I was walking down the street and ran into a lawn mower and both my arms and legs were cut off. 'No problem.' I had cancer. 'No problem.'"

It was many years before Kerrey ever knew much about his father's background. What he learned helped him come to a better understanding of who James Kerrey was. It wasn't until she was on her deathbed in 1978 that Elinor Kerrey told him about his father's difficult childhood. James was two and a half, and his younger brother John was only one, when their parents died in Tennessee within a year of each other. The boys were sent to Chicago to live with Frances "Fannie" Potter, an aunt much older than the Kerrey boys, and her daughters, Jessie and Eva. Fatherless and exceedingly poor, the boys got by on hand-me-downs. The happiest day in James's life, Elinor said, was at age twelve when he bought new boots with money he saved from delivering newspapers in Chicago.

After a boyhood devoid of love, Kerrey found it difficult to connect with his own children. The only anchor he had, his brother John, was taken away in high school for starting fistfights. He was handed over to a male relative to learn some discipline.

James Kerrey rarely, if ever, mentioned his brother to his children. The first memory Bob had of his uncle came at ten, when he broke into a closet and opened an old war chest. Inside, he found a black-and-white photograph of a man who looked remarkably like a Kerrey. "I took it to my father, and I thought he was going to beat me," he said. "I mean, he just grabbed it away from me."

His mysterious uncle had a brief life as a hobo, traveling across the United States in the 1930s by train. He joined the Army and was shipped to the Philippines in 1940, where he was serving on General Douglas MacArthur's staff when the Japanese overran American positions. Kerrey said his uncle escaped from the Bataan death march and fought with Philippine guerrilla forces until he disappeared before World War II ended. Bob Kerrey knew none of this until he was a candidate for the U.S. Senate in the early 1980s. By that time James was dying of cancer, and Bob would come regularly to the hospital to sit with him, reading an occasional poem. As James Kerrey faded, he left one wish with his son: find out how Uncle John had perished. Honoring the promise, Kerrey has spent years piecing together the story, which he included in a memoir completed in the spring of 2002.

It was Elinor Kerrey who provided the children with emotional support. Bob Kerrey adored his mother. She had grand dreams for her life but ultimately surrendered them to the realities of American womanhood in the 1940s. "My sister kept her journal," Kerrey said. "She wanted to be an actress; she wanted to go into performing, not a movie actress but a stage actress. She had real ambition. She had a great desire to travel. She had lots of dreams. But she also had this understanding that she was going to get married and have kids and that was her duty. Her family was more important than these dreams she had in her life. She was really talented. She was valedictorian of her class at Iowa State. My father, he was lucky it was only a five-year program."

Elinor had been raised in a large Iowa farm family. She met her husband at Iowa State, where she was studying to be a schoolteacher while he tried unsuccessfully to become an engineer. In 1938 they married and moved to Waterloo, Iowa, and five years later to Bethany, where James was stationed at a nearby military base. After his stint in the Army, James, with Elinor's help, began his business career in Bethany. She worked all day keeping the business books for her husband. "I don't have any doubt," Bob Kerrey said, "that my dad would have been bankrupt [without her], because he had no sense of money at all. He died without a penny. He would give it all away. He had a huge heart; he couldn't say no." Bereft of money, he left a simple note in his will: "To each of my children, I give my love."

Elinor's other job was at home—managing a household for seven children, including Jim, whose special needs had increased the burdens on the family. She mowed the lawn, washed the clothes, cleaned the windows, and did so with stoic obligation. Sometimes, in the evening, she fell asleep playing bridge with friends. "My mother did all of that and she goes back to college, when I was in college," Kerrey said. "And we took organic chemistry together. What I really had to make certain is that I at least got as good a grade as she did."

Kerrey followed his older brother John to the University of

Nebraska. "John was a real hero to me. I wanted to be like my brother John." He had it all, in Kerrey's eyes: big bruising high school fullback, good swimmer, fine runner. Although he wanted to follow John's model, childhood asthma kept him on the puny side until his early teens. "I remember the year I went over one hundred pounds. That was a major moment in my life." Despite his efforts, including a Charles Atlas program, he was never able to re-create his brother's muscular build.

Other footsteps John left were a little easier to follow. Kerrey joined his fraternity, Phi Gamma Delta, otherwise known as the hell-raising, beer-chugging Fijis. (Johnny Carson had been a member, too.) Bob Kerrey was not much of a drinker, but still a natural fit with the group. They debated Kennedy's politics and were transfixed by the television coverage of his assassination and funeral. While Kennedy would later become a political lodestar, Kerrey's politics at the time could not have been more different. He was, in fact, a Barry Goldwater Republican.

It was also with the Fijis that Kerrey got an early taste of politics. While serving as a fraternity president, Kerrey displayed a knack for cultivating strategically important friendships with several frat brothers. One was John Gottschalk, future publisher of the state's largest daily newspaper, the *Omaha World Herald*, which was generally kind to him in its editorial columns. Another college-era chum, William L. Wright, would later sit on the board of directors of the *Lincoln Journal Star* and chair Kerrey's 1982 gubernatorial campaign. (He later left the state after a savings and loan scandal.)

Kerrey adjusted well to college life, though he was uneasy around girls. While he eventually became one of Washington's hottest bachelors, Kerrey didn't automatically set pulses pounding on campus. The runty frame was gone—he'd filled out to a wiry 160 pounds—but his piercing blue eyes were lost in a thin face, with a large forehead and a long bony jaw.

He had given up the crew cut from his high school days, wear-ing his hair longer but still conservatively trimmed. But women enjoyed his sense of humor, and he soon developed a reputation as someone who was fun to be with. Soon enough, he was picked as one of the university's most eligible bachelors.

More political prizes came to Kerrey as an upperclassman. He served as vice president on the University of Nebraska's student council, and in his senior year he was chosen by secret ballot to be included in a group of campus leaders called the Innocents Honor Society. The Innocent's charter was straight-forward: Be above reproach and lead by example. But adher-ing to those standards became a problem for Kerrey. And it led to his first brush with political scandal. He was caught pocketing $380 in proceeds from advertising purchased by local merchants for display on council-sponsored student dis-count credit cards. The school newspaper editorialized that he "should be promptly removed from office." An investigation found that, at the least, "Kerrey was guilty of extremely poor judgment." He was allowed to keep the money, but only because the rules for disposing of profits were not clear. It would not be Kerrey's last episode of problems in office.

The *Newsweek* lunch was uneventful.

Kerrey took a few digs at President Clinton and Al Gore and made passing but noncommittal remarks on the question of running against the vice president in the 2000 elections. There was nothing worthy of a magazine story, certainly nothing that would be considered breaking news. (Nothing on the order of his infamous line to *Esquire* writer Martha Sherrill—"Clinton's an unusually good liar. *Unusually good,* do you realize that?" Tried as he might to say nice things about the president, his true feelings usually took over. He really did detest Clinton.)

After Kerrey said his good-byes to the *Newsweek* reporters, I walked him down the long hall toward the front door. His spokesman, brought along to clean up any slips of the tongue, tagged several feet behind.

"I've been doing some reporting on your military record," I told him, out of earshot of other correspondents. "About your time in Vietnam, your other missions, not just the Medal of Honor one."

"I know," he said. "I've been getting calls from SEALs telling me you've been calling around."

"I figured they would."

"When you're ready to sit down and talk, just give me a call," he said. And then offering another handshake before darting out the door, he added:

"You know, SEALs don't talk."

But he was wrong. Some do.

Chapter Four

———————————■———————————

ENSIGN BOB KERREY HAD slept less than fifty minutes a night for the last week. He was soaking wet, his kapok life vest so full of water it hung like a twenty-five-pound millstone around his neck. For days on end, sand and mud caked most of his body. It was in his eyes, his ears, up his buttocks, and in his nose. He had spent so much time in the cold ocean water, crawling over the picturesque dunes and mud flats around San Diego Bay, that his wet dungarees had the grit of sandpaper. His joints ached and popped, and his feet were so swollen that if he took off his boots he might never get them back on again. Exhausted mentally and physically, he had been close to delusion while paddling for hours during the nightly boat runs down toward Mexico. He was near the breaking point—just the way his instructors wanted him.

"What do you think we ought to do?" thundered Chief Bosun's Mate Vince Olivera. The massively built Mexican Indian was an instructor at the Navy's Underwater Demolition Training compound—"UDT" as it was commonly referred to in the teams—and it was his job to take raw recruits like Kerrey and turn them into Navy frogmen.

He was staring at Kerrey, giving him the "I can kill you" look that all the student "tadpoles" in Kerrey's UDT Class 42 dreaded. Olivera's big, crooked nose hung over a mouth usually full of chewing tobacco. On six-mile runs in the sand, he would stick a wad of tobacco in his cheek, clench a lit cigar, and run backward smoking and yelling all the way. His body was one big muscle, a physically fit specimen who seemed to the would-be frogmen more machine than man. He had the look of the toughest thing that ever walked the face of the earth. The students were scared to death of him. And now he was bearing down on Kerrey. Olivera was chewing him out and not giving him much of a chance to explain why the boat that Kerrey and his crew had been using had gone flat.

This was Hell Week, the fifth and toughest week of UDT training. The washout rate in this week alone could be as high as fifty percent. The most physically fit, highly educated and competent men broke down and cried as they walked away from the dream of being a Navy commando. If the tadpoles made it through Hell Week and finished the six months of underwater demolition training, they had a chance to be handpicked to try out for the SEAL teams.

Now it looked like that wasn't going to happen for Kerrey. His boat crew had been pulled out of training to answer to Olivera for their screwup. When he finished yelling at Kerrey, he yelled for the rest of the boat crew. Just standing where they were—a drab office near their barracks—filled them with doom. They lined up next to Bob, all in the same sorry-looking state as just about everybody else trying to survive Hell Week. Just being in this room made them feel defeated. This was where the instructors brought the quitters, the ones who didn't have what it took to be frogmen. Those who opted out had only to throw down their helmet and say "I quit." The failures were given their papers and sent packing. Kerrey knew he had the moxie to go on. Still, he felt practically broken. He had made it through the first four weeks of UDT training and almost all of Hell Week, and now this. He couldn't stop thinking they had washed out. "They sent us over here," he said, "and, my God, they are going to muster us out."

"What do you think we ought to do?" Olivera demanded

of the entire crew. Kerrey piped up first. As their leader, it was his job to deflect Olivera's wrath from his men.

"I think you ought to let us go out there, pump up our boat, and go do the exercise," Kerrey said quickly.

Olivera wore his poker face and didn't let on either way whether this was a good idea or not. Kerrey knew that if given a second chance, he and his boat crew could finish Hell Week and go on to the next phase in their six-month training cycle. He wanted desperately to make the cut, to be a frogman. He and his team had come this far, had made it to the last day of Hell Week—why not get a break? But there were rarely second or third chances in UDT training, even fewer in Vietnam, where the tadpoles who were lucky enough to graduate and become frogmen or SEALs were headed. Blunders could be fatal. What would happen if they made some dumb mistake out at sea and their boat went flat? The 500-pound IBS (inflatable boats small), nicknamed "itty bitty ships," were central to the mission of a frogman and a key part of the training regime. Whether running or walking, Kerrey and his crew carried the boats on their heads. That kind of burden created unusual occupational hazards. For the tallest squad members it usually meant losing the hair on the top of their scalps. The shortest man often wore a bucket to even out the load.

Their load sometimes included Olivera, who would sit atop the boat barking out insults as the students endlessly "duck-walked" around a football field with the IBS perched on their heads. They practiced beach landings in the surf, perfecting their approach to keep from being crushed between the heavy boats and the rocks. Their boats sat atop their heads while they ran the roundtrip five miles down and back to the mud-flats in Imperial Beach. The students would stack them one on top of the other, then dive off into the mud, which had the smell and feel of raw sewage. Training without the boats wasn't any easier. They would do push-ups and sit-ups in the mud with the instructors standing on their backs and stomachs. Then each boat crew had to carry around a 750-pound telephone pole. They ran in the mud with it, rolled in the mud with it, swam with it in the surf, and had to carry it through parts of the obstacle course.

They ate their lunch in the field during Hell Week, never knowing until it was too late that the instructors had planted small caches of explosives all around them. Just when the class began to relax on its short break, the devices splattered the miserable students and their food with even more mud. The instructors also placed packets of TNT in the murky waters of the "demo pit," where two wires, one about six feet above the other, stretched overhead to be slackened or pulled taut as the men tried to cross them. They walked on one wire while holding the other, and if one of the instructors yanked one of the cables, it would snap the wire and, nine times out of ten, catapult the student some ten feet into the muddy water below. To make things even more realistic, exploding packets of TNT detonated in the pit, hitting the students with pressure waves as they inched their way across the wires. Smoke, sand, and mud flew up into their faces, making it impossible to see. The rancid smell of TNT filled the air.

On the obstacle course, they crawled under the barbed wire as live ammunition crackled all around them. The course rose some sixty feet into the air and stood out on the open beach, enough so that passersby could stop and marvel as the well-built young men went through their routine. Climbing into the air, swinging on ropes, demonstrating that they were America's finest, preparing for what America did better than most anybody—wage war.

Kerrey had not just survived the demo pit and everything else the instructors had thrown at him in the last four days of Hell Week. In the system used to rank the boat crews, his team had accumulated enough points to put them in the lead.

If they finished first against the five other boat crews, they would be excused from the last night of Hell Week.

Their one final task was a grueling all-night paddle down the Pacific Coast to a point near the Mexican border and back. They had to carry their boats out of the training compound and embark from the shores of San Diego Bay, paddling north to the ritzy Hotel Del Coronado, where Tony Curtis and Marilyn Monroe filmed the movie *Some Like It Hot*, then pull their boats out of the water and carry them across the strand and rocks where they would slip into the Pacific Ocean. Lack of sleep left students delirious: Some threw their paddles into the water, thinking they were snakes; others were certain the San Diego ferry was off-loading cars in front of them. "I mean, when you're tired, you've been without sleep, and you've been without food, your mind works in funny ways," Kerrey recalled. "You'll find yourself doing things you never dreamed that you'd do."

The smart crews in Class 42 had figured out how to sleep on the way. While four men paddled, two would catch a short nap, alternating until everyone got a few extra minutes. It wasn't a lot, but just enough to recharge their sleep-drained batteries.

But now there was no way Kerrey's boat would float. That night had started normally enough, for Hell Week. The instructors had the students lie down in a field. They played soft music and warned that anybody who nodded off would have to sit immersed in sixty-degree bay water. At that temperature, the water was OK for the first few minutes, but after that, muscles quickly tighten up in knots. After fifteen minutes, the students shivered uncontrollably. It made paddling toward Mexico in the night air a frigid trip. "I figured out right in the beginning that we were all going to go in the bay anyway," Kerrey recalled, "so I just went to sleep. Sure enough, they eventually threw everybody in."

After the bay immersion, they ran as fast as they could to

their boats to head to Mexico. "We got down there and our boat is flat as a pancake. I'm the captain of the crew and I'm trying to figure out what in the hell happened here," Kerrey said. The instructors screamed at them for ruining a perfectly good IBS and blowing their assignment. As the other boat crews pushed off, Kerrey was ordered to see Olivera, who would decide their fate.

Olivera was now contemplating how to respond to Kerrey's idea.

"No," he said, with a stern look on his face. They could not pump up the boat and do the last exercise. There was no need for that. Then he became almost human, showing a bit of a smile.

"You guys won Hell Week. You can just secure for the night."

Kerrey didn't know it at the time, but the instructors had sabotaged his boat to see how he and his crew would react. "They jacked us around. It was a drill," Kerrey said. "They were masters of psychology. They had permission to do just about most anything to test how effective you would be when you were fatigued. And it was mostly mental pressure, but, yeah, the mental pressure along with the physical difficulties would cause quite a few people to say, 'I don't want to do this.'"

For a boy from Nebraska, San Diego in the summer of 1967 was paradise denied. From their barbed-wire compound they could see the sunbathers lounging on the powdery white sands of Coronado Beach and the patio deck of the Hotel Del Coronado, where beautiful young women drank margaritas. But it might as well have been on another continent. The instructors made sure of that.

Their view of the world boiled down to a few whip-cracking one-liners: "The only easy day was yesterday"; "The more you sweat in training the less you bleed in battle." Completing the grueling physical regime was all about mind over matter: "We don't mind and you don't matter."

They were teachers, mentors, and wardens bent on whatever it took to get the job done and turn a bunch of kids into warriors, and maybe save their lives in Vietnam. There were a couple dozen or so at the training camp, most of whom were enlisted men or noncoms like Olivera. It was the noncommissioned officers who made the Navy's ships run on time. They were career men with little use for some inexperienced officer fresh from Newport telling them how to do things. The NCOs outnumbered the officers twelve to two on SEAL teams, and it was pretty much the same ratio in San Diego.

On paper, Kerrey may have outranked Olivera, but in UDT training the instructors ruled. Privately, they relished the chance to make the guys with stripes on their shoulder boards suffer. If they really had it in for an officer, which was not infrequent, they would do everything in their power to make him quit. There was some deference barking out orders ("Give me fifty push-ups, you asshole, sir!"), but it served nobody's purpose to go easy on the officers. They were going to Vietnam, too, and needed to know the secrets of the frogmen.

When Bob Kerrey arrived in the summer of 1967 at the training compound, he had no real idea what to expect. He was issued a pair of boondockers, three pairs of green fatigue pants and shirts, a helmet, khaki swimming trunks, a face mask, and a snorkel and told to fall into line. From the beginning, some of his class fell afoul with Olivera and the other instructors. The bachelor officer's quarters and the barracks for the enlisted instructors were close enough that instructors could hear the trainees carping. At first, they were the usual gripes from men who had been worked too hard. But as the bad-mouthing intensified, the NCOs decided to respond. One morning, part of Class 42 was taken for a deep ocean dive.

"It was a sixty-foot dive," said Bill Hemming, a young, junior grade lieutenant. "The officers were told we couldn't wear wet suits but everybody else could. At the bottom the water was so cold that when we came up closer to the surface, the water [felt] hot. We had to do it again that night, again without wet suits. When we finished, we all jumped in cars and turned on heaters or took really hot showers."

For veterans of the fleet like Hemming, who worked out every day running and swimming at least a mile, the swims and long-distance runs in the sand were tough but doable. Of Kerrey and the other OCS graduates, well, Hemming said, "Those poor guys were in bad shape; it was a killer."

Hundreds of men had applied for Class 42—one of the largest groups in the history of the program. The United States was ramping up the war in Vietnam and the Navy needed more SEALs and demolition teams. The whole process took about eighteen months: six in underwater demolition training, then normally another year on a SEAL team before being shipped off to Vietnam. The lengthy timing kept the total number of SEALs small. Fewer than fifty were in combat at any one time. But if they did their jobs right, they could be extraordinarily effective in fighting the Vietcong and its infrastructure. If they blew it, their tours in Vietnam could be disastrous.

The naval instructors believed that it all started with a type of training that was unparalleled in its physical and mental demands. Indeed, the other services were in awe of the Navy frogmen's conditioning. When part of Class 42 went to jump school in Fort Benning, Georgia, they ran the Army trainers ragged. They carried a teammate over their heads as they ran their daily miles. Or, like Olivera, they ran backward. Their cockiness was an irritant to the more traditional Army jump masters. At night, some tadpoles snuck out of their barracks, climbed the 250-foot jump tower and hung a bed sheet with a frogman painted on it from the rigging. At dawn, the banner awaited the not-so-amused Army trainers. The day's class had to be delayed until someone climbed up the rigging and cut the pennant away.

If there was criticism of SEAL training in the Vietnam era, it was for the overemphasis on the physical aspects of it, and the minimal instruction on the intellectual side of waging war. The Army's special unit, the Green Berets, was also superbly trained for combat but spent more time learning the finer points of how to use psychological warfare to win the hearts and minds of the enemy. Green Beret units provided food, medical care, and education that helped the peasants to improve village life—and persuade Vietcong sympathizers that the U.S. really cared. While the SEALs were trained to collect intelligence on enemy fortifications, their other job, to kill or abduct their prey, terrorized the local population through fear and intimidation.

The boys of Class 42 were aggressive, patriotic, self-confident, and eager to prove their toughness. But their teachers, most of whom had already served one or two tours as commandos in Vietnam, knew that would not be enough. They wanted young men possessed with a special level of mental and physical determination that would allow them to fight in the face of madness. They were blunt realists: They were preparing men for war. Their primary job in the first few weeks was to identify the quitters—the ones who would be the weakest link in the teamwork chain—and drive them out of Class 42. The instructors were not overly impressed by the all-American athletes who breezed through training barely breaking a sweat. It was the guy who struggled to beat the obstacle course—the one way behind in ocean swims and long runs but who had the strength of character to never give up, no matter how cold, how tired, or how stressed he was—who usually made the best SEAL.

Kerrey had written home that he was not among the top finishers, in most cases falling behind his peers. "He used to come in last in the swims," his younger brother, Bill, told the *Lincoln Journal Star*. "He would write and tell me that he would barely make it. But he kept at it. That's the way he does things."

His grit could be traced back to childhood, back to Bob's Supermarket, where a scrawny, asthmatic kid was banging a larger classmate's head against the concrete floor to defend his retarded older brother. Kerrey was not the classic boy next door. He was bright and charming but could also be nasty, driven, and reckless. When his asthma was so bad that his wheezing could be heard all over the house, he was rushed to the hospital, found to be anemic, and given a blood transfusion.

He had to work extra hard to play sports and he once altered a doctor's medical report recommending nonphysical activities so he could play high school football. And despite being one of the smallest backup centers in the league, Kerrey kept at it, eventually starting in his senior year at Northeast High School (he played against Gayle Sayers). He also lettered in golf and swimming, a product of summers in a cabin on a Wisconsin lake with his father and brother John. "We went to this lake and my father promised us a sailboat as soon as my older brother and I were able to swim over to this island and back. And it's about a mile round trip. So I certainly wasn't intimidated by long distances in the water." Kerrey was not a gifted athlete when compared to his peers. The gridiron was more of a proving ground for him, a way to demonstrate that guts and determination to overcome one's weaknesses counted as much as natural talent.

Kerrey's high school and college teachers saw this will to succeed, too, not necessarily in his grades—he was an average student in high school—but in his ferocious determination. "He had a drive that was somewhat uncharacteristic for someone his age" said one of his teachers.

All of which caught the eye of SEAL instructors. He was willing to go along with the physical demands that oftentimes made little sense. "I was twenty-two years old when I made the critical, pivotal decision in my life to join the Navy. Once that decision's been made, it's 'Yes sir, no sir.' You have some moments when you sort of rise above it."

But what made Kerrey uniquely tough also made him unusually difficult. Even in college, taking orders was a problem.

Cadet Robert Kerrey was shy one boot.

The Air Force ROTC instructor at the University of Nebraska had ordered his unit to muster, and Kerrey was sure to catch hell again for yet another infraction of the rules if he showed up with the wrong shoes on. It seemed he had been in trouble almost from the day he began, much of it his own making. He hated the mindless routine and crude discipline used to sharpen a young recruit's respect for authority. He thought it overbearing and a waste of time. Kerrey had come to college to have fun, not have people yell at him. He was "always goofing off," he said, not an approach that sat well with his instructors. He spent a good amount of his ROTC time in the doghouse, working off punishments, like marching around a building the size of a city block just off campus; he totaled at least 250 hours circling the place. "I just had trouble doing what people told me to do," he recalled. "I never saw the point of all the marching and attention to your shoelaces."

He grabbed the one boot he had, laced it up, and joined the others standing at attention. The shoeless Kerrey did not look like a man who was bound for a career in the United States military, let alone a Medal of Honor several years later. He could have cared less. He did not volunteer for Air Force ROTC and had no desire to join it—he was forced to.

In 1963, two semesters of ROTC was a requirement for all male students at the University of Nebraska. By senior year,

Kerrey had fallen short in his units and was in danger of not graduating. "It was the only class I failed in school," he said. Had the university followed its regulations, it would have held up Kerrey's degree. He was determined not to let that happen. He decided not only to fix his situation but also to do away with a policy he found wrongheaded. His goal was to make ROTC an elective. Kerrey had done his homework, studying the arcane Merrill Act, where he found a loophole. It required land grant colleges like Nebraska only to *offer* ROTC courses, not to make them compulsory. Kerrey's efforts on the student council of which he was vice president, led the Board of Regents to drop the requirement. Most important, he insured that the reform was retroactive to cover his time on campus. "I wouldn't have graduated except for my successful political effort," he said. "It was self-serving, I admit."

Kerrey's political agility couldn't stop his draft notice from arriving in the mail two months after graduation in 1965.

By then he was working as a pharmacist in a small store in Iowa. He had decided on a career that promised full employment for as long as he wanted to work at it. Kerrey never explained to anybody why he selected such a quiet, low-key profession. Perhaps it was a reaction to his father's roller-coaster business career as an on-the-fly deal maker. Few jobs seemed steadier and more respectable than counting pills and filling prescriptions from eight to five. And Kerrey held the promise of being good at it. He finished Nebraska's five-year pharmacy program in four years with a high grade point average.

The draft notice told him to report to a certain address where government doctors would examine him to determine if he was fit to wear the uniform of the United States Army. Had he wanted to, Kerrey could have bypassed the military altogether. His asthma was enough to claim an exemption, but his father had taught him that duty was an important part of citizenship. The military also offered him an escape from a job he was starting to wonder about—even after only a few months. For a young man of twenty-two, standing behind a counter in a white coat dispensing blood pressure pills did not offer much in the way of adventure.

His next government letter told him he was in good health and that he would be assigned to the Army. Kerrey had misgivings about the Army, where he was now scheduled to spend the next two years. The Navy held more allure, largely because at the time he happened to be reading *The Caine Mutiny*. Herman Wouk's classic tale about a paranoid Navy captain mesmerized Kerrey. "I said, 'That's for me. I want to go overseas,'" Kerrey recalled. "It's easy to romanticize it, and it was a bit odd, I suppose."

"Since Wouk's book was about officers, I volunteered for OCS," Kerrey said, enrolling on February 4, 1967, in Officer Candidate School in Newport, Rhode Island, where college graduates had their heads shaved, then learned how to behave as gentlemen officers in the all-male wardrooms aboard warships. The Navy's enlisted men called OCS "Organized Chicken Shit," believing that it was typical of an East Coast finishing school without the boot camp training that the grunts had to suffer through. Kerrey said the ridicule was largely justified—though other naval officers remembered days of tough discipline and hard work. Kerrey joked that he learned "how to use a knife and fork," and time in Rhode Island, he said, was not much better than that spent in the University of Nebraska's ROTC program.

Kerrey was told that if he flunked out of OCS, he would be discharged and redrafted by the Army. But the threat of the infantry didn't stop him from challenging the system. After a stiff letter to his commanding officer, arguing that such a discharge would violate the terms of his agreement with the Navy, he was promoted to assistant company commander. In general, though, there was little to motivate young officers like Kerrey. The curriculum was filled with do-it-by-the-book training on everything from celestial navigation to tying knots, with a lot of polishing brass and porcelain in between. Officer candidates spent most of their time in the classroom, where lecturers would drone on about Navy customs and the importance of keeping age-old traditions. Even though he was going to end up in Vietnam, there was no instruction about how to kill somebody and when they could or could not do it under the rules of land warfare. "No, absolutely not," Kerrey said. "When you talked about the Geneva Convention, you spent more time talking about how court-martials are done." (Other naval officers remember specific training on what was allowed under the law in war.)

Kerrey did learn one thing at OCS that changed his life forever. He heard that the Navy's underwater demolition teams, the frogmen, were looking for volunteers. Their missions were the stuff of legends. In World War II they swam into shallow enemy waters to survey coastal defenses or blow up underwater barricades so U.S. forces could land troops ashore. Spirited and headstrong, they often left signs like "Welcome Marines" to show that they were the first on the beach, not the leathernecks. Frogmen operated in the Arctic Ocean in water so cold that untrained men without proper gear would have died in minutes from exposure. And they helped to train special operations teams for U.S. allies. It was daring and exciting work, popularized by Hollywood in the 1950s drama *The Frogmen*, starring Richard Widmark.

But the real draw for Kerrey and other young officers was the brand-new, still secret guerrilla force the Navy was developing to fight in Vietnam. Five years earlier, President John Kennedy was captivated by the Army's Green Berets, trained to carry out unconventional assignments behind enemy lines.

The youthful president thought it a good idea if all the services had specialized counterinsurgency units. The Navy turned to frogmen like Roy Boehm to conceive, develop, select, train, and lead an elite group of operatives who could go at the enemy from the sea, the air, and on land. They were called SEALs and they drew on the best of the frogmen to fill their ranks. They operated in small seven-man teams and quickly won a reputation as perhaps the most fearsome and physically fit warriors in the American military.

Largely because of Boehm, who was sometimes called the "first SEAL," the Navy's new special forces exuded a confidence and arrogance that intoxicated aspirants at OCS. They lived by a simple code: The "team" was paramount, and there were no individual heroes. That notion clicked with Kerrey. His high school football coach taught that teamwork built character and trust and won championships. But this was not a game. This was the real thing. Men's lives depended on everybody pulling together as a team. He was hooked.

Kerrey offered few clues as to why he'd selected such a dangerous military speciality. He could have used his pharmacy degree to get a cushy job stateside or on a clean and comfortable air-conditioned aircraft carrier with warm water for showers and three squares a day cooked in a well-stocked galley. But he might have also ended up back behind the counter with a white coat on—this time in the dispensary counting pills to sick sailors. That was the last thing Kerrey wanted. He and his OCS roommate, a friend from Nebraska, had originally wanted to be naval aviators. An eye problem kept his roommate out, so they signed up for Underwater Demolition Team training.

When asked why a young man from Nebraska volunteered for the SEALs, Kerrey said nothing of his Uncle John, or his great-grandfather, who served under Ulysses S. Grant in the Civil War. Instead, he offered humor: "I had become severely nauseous while touring a destroyer that was safely tied up at

dockside. UDT offered thrills without having to throw up."
He sometimes said he wanted to learn how to scuba dive
with a Rolex watch on and to meet women. "They give you a
watch and a blue and teal T-shirt and some khaki shorts,"
Kerrey said, "and you have pretty good liberty as long as
you're in UDT."

Perhaps the real reason could be found in looking at his
mother's life. Like young Elinor Kerrey, who had yearned for
adventure as a young woman, Bob knew that there was a
world full of risk and opportunity outside of Lincoln. She had
given up on her dream of seeing that world. He was not about
to make that same decision. There had to be something else,
something bigger." On June 8, 1967, he graduated from
OCS, receiving his ensign's commission the following day.
Nine days later he was in Coronado.

"On your backs! On your feet! On your belly! On your
feet . . ."

It was impossible to keep up with the barked orders. Kerrey's class was in the large courtyard at the training center.
The one called "The Grinder." The black asphalt sizzled
under the early summer sun, frying the hands of aspiring
SEALs as they struggled to do their push-ups. Hell Week
usually began in this space, which gained its name from the
punishment tadpoles endured there through countless hours
of calisthenics and other torture in the name of training.

One of the instructors was riding a young student. The
sailor was laboring more than most, which caught the eye of
the instructor, and now he was circling around the struggling
youngster. He stood over him, then placed his boot on the
back of the sailor's head, smashing his face into the ground,
hard enough that it broke his upper teeth.

Kerrey seethed at the casual brutality against a defenseless
recruit. He angrily confronted the instructor, and word

quickly got around Class 42. "It took balls," said Frank Czajkowski, who made it through Class 42 with Kerrey. "From
the start of training Bob Kerrey was different. He was always
cool, calm, collected, and very much in control. He took
charge of situations when the rest took a step back under the
pressure."

Kerrey's willingness to confront an instructor and stand up
for the enlisted men sent a signal that he was not a typical
Navy officer. Even sailors from the fleet, like Czajkowski, who
had little regard for most young officers, admired Kerrey for
his willingness to buck the system. In the regular Navy the
divide between the enlisted man and the officer was nearly
impossible to bridge—underscored by outlined written warnings over bulkheads where the officers lived: "Officer Country."
Those entering had better be on official business; otherwise
they had no place in the wardroom and officers' quarters.

In UDT and the teams, rank meant virtually nothing. Officers and sailors trained side by side and learned that teamwork
saved lives. During the day they struggled together, unified
in their desire to overcome the tyranny of the instructors—
enlisted men, yes, but who "had the POWER!" as Czajkowski
wrote in an e-mail. At night, when they had free time, they
partied together.

The enlisted men trying to make the cut in UDT were raw
gems, smart in a commonsense way without, for the most
part, formal educations. Kerrey never held that against them.
He may have had a diploma, but if that was removed, he was
in his own way also a commoner. Some of the enlisted men
were more confident and assertive then the others when
approaching officers like Kerrey. Michael Ambrose had a con-
temptuous and cocksure look about him, as if he were the
equal of any man, certainly the equal of any officer. "I had a
lot of ego, a lot of faith in my ability at that time," he
recalled. He had a handsome face and uneasy eyes that
focused into a penetrating stare. He wasn't too tall, about

5'9", but he had a trim muscular build, as if he had been raised surfing the waters of Southern California rather than landlocked in Illinois in a good-sized family with a father who was a veteran. Ambrose blew his knee out running the football on a scholarship in college and decided to get his military obligation "out of the way," so he enlisted in the Navy. He was assigned to the fleet but had a hard time in the strict confines of a warship. Then he met a Navy frogman in a bar. "You can be one, too," he told Ambrose, who was so taken with the man and his story of adventure, that he went as fast as he could to see a Navy recruiter.

Almost from the moment they met, they struck up a friendship that would last a lifetime. Kerrey was the funny man, the prankster who didn't take himself too seriously; Ambrose was all business, as if he didn't know what it was to smile. He and Kerrey bopped around San Diego in a red Volkswagen bus and rented a California bungalow in Imperial Beach, not far from the mudflats where they manhandled telephone poles during their UDT training. Imperial Beach, or "IB," was a scruffy, downscale cousin to Coronado, filled with biker joints, sex shops where Kerrey and his buddies went to watch "Nasty Nickels," groupies looking for a good time, and plenty of cheap beer; it was the perfect hang out for Frogmen. "We did a lot of hustling of chicks in biker bars," Ambrose said. When they weren't carousing, they hosted regular parties at their beach house to let their fellow classmates come "to chill out," or they dove for lobsters in Mexico.

For Ambrose, the good times ended quickly. He was one of the first of Class 42 to make it to the war. After graduating from UDT and partway through his SEAL training, he and several others were rushed over to Vietnam as replacements for a platoon that got shot up and lost four men. Ambrose volunteered to go, then voted himself point man for the platoon. They were a bit timid, he said, and resented him coming in with a strong dose of what he termed good leadership.

"There's a body on the line!"

The panicked scream was loud and its meaning unmistakable. A training exercise had gone bad. Somebody was drowning.

It was Friday the thirteenth of October 1967, and Kerrey's class was on San Clemente Island, a small outcropping in the Pacific Ocean about sixty miles from San Diego. It was inhabited by wild goats, a Navy caretaker, and several times a year by UDT and SEAL classes. Half of Class 42 was on the island for three to four weeks practicing combat diving techniques and learning how to blow things up underwater. Today's exercise had been delayed because of bad weather. The ocean was surging, churning up the water inside of Northwest Harbor, where the students were free diving some fifty yards offshore to an obstacle resting on the bottom. Visibility was so bad it was almost impossible to find their target underwater, which increased the danger to the students. Kerrey was upset. He thought they should scrap the exercise until the water conditions improved, but the instructor in charge, Mordecai Jones, insisted that the training continue.

Kerrey and his swim buddy, Peter Baker, were in the water with a half dozen other students when they heard the scream. They immediately dove below the choppy surface looking for their classmate. Harry Greco was tangled up in a rope, out of breath, just three feet from the surface. But where was his swim buddy, Charles McCall? The prospective frogmen were taught never to leave their swim buddies—it was the golden rule in underwater demolition training and part of a core SEAL value: No one was left behind in combat. Swim buddies became so close that they knew each other's moves underwater and could calculate the distance to and from a target in the dark by holding onto a partner's ankle and counting flipper kicks. It taught them how to navigate in the darkness of the ocean. Twenty-year-old Greco and McCall, who was twenty-three, had been together since almost the beginning of Class 42. The two men, both from northern California, had less than one month to graduate and now McCall was missing.

Wearing wet-suit tops, weight belts, and carrying knives, they had been working on the bottom of the harbor, tying off an explosive satchel to an obstacle in cloudy water. The exercise required them to free dive about twenty feet to the bottom, find the concrete obstacle, then attach the packet. It was not an easy job. The divers had to insure that no water got between the explosives and the concrete. If it did, the force of the blast would be cut down and Mordecai Jones would likely flunk them. It took time, and the task was made harder by the poor visibility. Greco had stayed down too long, trying to complete the mission. Then he drove hard for the surface, moving his arms in small circles as he'd been taught, when he apparently became tangled in the line tied from the obstacle to a buoy. In a panic, he stopped swimming and reached up for McCall, grabbing him with such strength that he pulled his swim buddy under the water. McCall could not free himself from the clutches of his partner. "McCall wasn't attached to anything and he just dropped out of sight," recalled Kerrey. "Greco hung on the line and was held there by the buoy. When we got there and we unwrapped his arm, he just sank like a rock. Baker went down and got him and pulled him up." Greco's face was puffed up, his eyes were bulging out of their sockets, and mucus filled his mask. He was dead. A few minutes later, divers operating from a boat found McCall's lifeless body, too.

Kerrey said he helped to haul the dead men up on the beach, where a Navy corpsman spent forty-five minutes trying unsuccessfully to revive them. Then the students were ordered back to their quarters, small trailers converted into makeshift bunkrooms. As the boat crews headed for their own trailers, the five instructors walked off to begin an investigation. Kerrey stood out in front of his barracks with another student, Steve Frisk, and waited for the instructors to return with orders for the rest of the day. A feeling of despair, even fear, hung in the air. It was the first time two men had drowned during an exercise. It reminded everybody just how dangerous their work was.

Frisk then saw Jones making his way slowly toward the students. He didn't care for Jones and thought he "even walked in a snidely, ambling, 'I'm on my own time' sort of way . . . the perfect lead to whatever mayhem he was going to level on the trainees." Frisk waited, not certain what to expect.

Jones stood in front of Kerrey and the class and was momentarily silent, trying to figure out what to say to the students. It was a delicate moment. "We had just seen two of our own pulled lifeless from the water, and we were exhausted," Frisk said.

Kerrey was mad. They were going off to fight a guerrilla war in Vietnam, not clear the beaches of Tarawa. "This was fighting yesterday's war," he said. He wasn't holding Jones accountable, but he felt the students needed a break. Before Jones could speak, Kerrey let loose. "Chief Jones, we don't want to listen to any of your cheap shit!"

There was an eerie silence, and even Jones, who could shout with the best of instructors, was speechless. Frisk and several others thought that Kerrey had really done it this time, that the rest of the class would suffer for his outspokenness. There would be hell to pay the rest of the afternoon doing jumping jacks and push-ups. Everyone dreaded the moment. They looked at Jones, waiting, wondering how he would respond to Kerrey, a lowly trainee in the UDT world but Jones's superior officer nonetheless.

Jones stared at Kerrey.

"You trainees fall into your trailers," he said, the usual authority in his voice drained away. Then he turned on his heel and headed back to the instructor hooches.

There was no celebration over Kerrey's dressing down of Jones. The men were still numb from the deaths of Greco and McCall. Even so, there was a feeling of camaraderie—one of their own had risked much and "stood up to an instructor when we needed it most," Frisk recalled. "Morale could have plummeted to the depths that awful day, but it was saved by Bob Kerrey."

Before training started, UDT Class 42 was winnowed from approximately one thousand applicants to one hundred and forty-nine people. Six months later, at graduation, more than half the class had washed out. Bob Kerrey and sixty-nine other men had survived. At the most, Kerrey said, only fifteen to twenty men went on to SEAL Team One. It was an endless cycle of misery, and only the most unique, the men who were not conformists, made it through. "May be the nine hundred and thirty [dropouts] did the right thing," Kerrey joked. "Yeah, it's tough. It's a very hard physical program," he said, but one that built tremendous courage and forged lasting emotional bonds among the men—bonds they could depend on in combat when their lives were on the line. It was an education in which Bob Kerrey pushed himself to his very limits—an education that he would never forget.

Chapter Five

———————————■———————————

IN JANUARY 1969, A FEW DAYS after Joe Namath and the New York Jets pulled off their Super Bowl upset of the Baltimore Colts, a small military transport plane departed the North Island Naval Air Station in Coronado. The creaky transport slowly lumbered into the sky, then banked over the white surf breaking for miles on the sandy beaches around the SEAL training compound, and headed west, past San Clemente Island. For the last year and a half, the platoon squeezed inside the cabin had spent hundreds of hours in and around these waters learning to be warriors. Now the practice sessions were over. They were on their way to do battle.

As the engines droned, Lieutenant Robert Kerrey eyed his men. Though SEAL training had hardened them, it was impossible not to see how young, even innocent they still looked. As their leader, the twenty-five-year-old Kerrey accepted the role of the old man amongst them, though others were beyond him in age. "I may have been the oldest of the group," Kerrey recalled, "but I was hardly what I call a wizened old veteran." Aboard the aircraft were fourteen SEALs, twelve enlisted men, and two officers, a diverse group in physical size, age, and most certainly in personality. Their official designation was Delta Platoon, SEAL Team One, and they were divided down the middle. Kerrey commanded Fire Team Bravo—which would soon be called "Kerrey's Raiders"—and his counterpart, Lieutenant Tim Wettack, headed the six other SEALs for Fire Team Alpha. Once in country, they would split up and operate in different parts of the Mekong Delta. "We came from all walks of life," Kerrey said. "We weren't lifting weights and we didn't have great bodies. We were trained to shoot as accurately as we could and then to carry out a very small but we thought important mission."

Ambrose. Klann. Tucker. Knepper. Peterson and Schrier. Kerrey had handpicked the six enlisted men for his team back in San Diego. In each man he was looking for that special talent that could save the entire squad in a bad scrape.

At the same time he was eyeing them for any peculiarities that might spell trouble. He wanted reliable operators who could be depended on if things fell apart. In Gerhard Klann, Kerrey found one of the best automatic weapons men in the SEAL community who was widely known as a fearsome operator, a man you wanted at your back in a firefight. He had just returned from a tour in Vietnam and was volunteering to go back on a quick turnaround. Mike Ambrose was the sneak-and-peak expert—a proven point man, nominally the most dangerous position in a platoon. Rick Knepper was a relative unknown, a quiet introvert who "was in his own little world, as a few of his teammates said, but who possessed immense physical power and great common sense." The others, Gene Peterson, Lloyd "Doc" Schrier, and William Tucker, each brought a particular skill or trait that fit into the team ethos that Kerrey envisioned for his Raiders. Fighting skills, of course, were paramount. But the ability of the men to get along could not be overlooked. In the military, it was called "unit integrity" or "unit cohesion." In layman's terms, it was simply good chemistry. And it mattered in combat.

It was a delicate task identifying young men who would do well in Vietnam, and, not surprisingly, Kerrey ended up with individuals who were, in many ways, a lot like him. Some distrusted authority, some were cutups, some drank too much, and all were prone to brawling and countless other troubles. Klann had been temporarily busted down in rank for fighting. Figuring "we were short-timers in the Navy, anyway," Klann said he and Tucker once went AWOL after a scheduled rest and recreation break. As for Ambrose, he said, "I couldn't stay out of trouble." Lloyd Schrier, the corpsman, was pretty straight, "with the skinniest legs" Ambrose said he had ever seen. Medics in the teams wanted to be seen as warriors, not just semitrained doctors. Because they didn't have to go through SEAL training, some medics felt as if they had to prove themselves in combat—a potentially dangerous attribute. But Doc Schrier fit the bill and was seen as an important asset. Peterson "walked like a girl," Klann teased good-naturedly, "the guy every platoon gets stuck with." Photographs of the diminutive Peterson taken in Vietnam caught him staring blankly into the distance with a melancholy look on his face. Others in the platoon noticed the open-ended stare, too, and knew what he was thinking. "He wasn't sure he could do it, be a SEAL in combat," said one squad mate. In the end, Peterson pulled his weight.

William H. Tucker III, "was just Tucker," a one-of-a-kind, as his teammates described him—hardly an avowed Marxist but well enough versed in anticapitalist polemic that he could easily debate his college-educated commanding officer. A laid-back boy from a rich family in Kansas, Tucker had a promising professional baseball career ahead of him when he joined the Navy to be a frogman. He had the long-legged gait of an athlete, and when he draped a bandoleer of bullets over his shoulders his dark hair and goatee made him look like Pancho Villa. And he could be just as intransigent. When the Navy tried to send him to a warship, instead of granting his request to try out for UDT as promised, he went AWOL to Mexico, staying with a local beautician he was intent on marrying. Eventually he made his way back to the United States and onto Kerrey's team.

Like Kerrey, Tucker was more willing than the others to

question authority, and he had a face that always seemed to glow with pleasure, as if he was happy at whatever he was doing. During off hours in training, he'd lay back in a reclining chair, his legs stretched forward, wearing rose-colored glasses and blasting "Purple Haze." He was a product of peace and love, and an unusual fit for the SEALs. He found American involvement in the war troubling, particularly in its harsh treatment of the peasantry and the average Vietnamese. "I would have rather stayed back to hang out with the guys and party than go out on operations," he said. "I liked the camaraderie of hanging out. But if they needed me on an operation, I would go."

Somehow Lieutenant Robert Kerrey was supposed to lead this eclectic group. The only saving grace for Kerrey was that each member of the platoon subscribed to the SEAL motto— that the team was paramount and individuality was okay off-duty, but in combat, they all depended on each other. "Trained to work as a team," Kerrey said, "and not think about themselves as much as they think about other people."

"There is no 'I' in SEAL team," Klann said. "It's a team from the word go." They thought of themselves as one unit that would live or die together. They had worked so closely that each member intuitively knew the others, knew how they thought and knew how they would react in a given combat situation. "We trained to know what each other was doing," Kerrey recalled. "And we trained to operate without having to give any voice signals. We tried to be a very close operating unit." They swam for miles under the sea together, jumped out of airplanes, got drunk together, fought in countless brawls, chased women, and teased each other with little mercy. In one year, they had come to know each other better then most of their mothers knew them. "We were all really good friends," Klann said.

Brawling and mayhem came naturally to them. The night before they left for Vietnam they got into a fight with some pilots. On the way over, with plane stops in Hawaii and Guam, Ambrose said they had gotten into some minor go-arounds. Earlier, at Eglin Air Force Base in Florida, where Delta Platoon was going through Ranger school, the Navy SEALs were to play the role of aggressors, taking on the Army's elite soldiers in a week of combat exercises. Practically before they had unpacked their gear, a fight broke out between the SEALs and the Army Rangers in a bar for the enlisted men. Two days later, five of the fourteen-man platoon snuck away to New Orleans for a bit of pre-Vietnam partying. The unauthorized road trip probably said more about Ranger readiness than SEAL discipline. It appeared that their absence had not been noticed, Ambrose was proud to say; the war games went on as if the SEALs had just been hiding in the bush somewhere.

Another time Kerrey's team started a free-for-all that so angered the mayor of Fort Walton Beach, Florida, he unceremoniously kicked them out of his town. On arrival, they found a motel room, then picked out a bar in town to serve as their watering hole. Kerrey and another officer had arranged to meet the rest of the team there. But when Kerrey came, he saw there had been big trouble: "We went to the bar and it was blacked out, the front window was busted out, lights out," Kerrey saw, with some concern. "My version of the story is we come in there, the thing is dark, there is nothing there. It was in the middle of the evening, it wasn't very late. So we drive over to the motel in a Jeep and one of the guys jumped out from behind a tree and said, 'Kill your lights, we've got a problem.' So we go in the motel room and it looked like an emergency room in a hospital, guys and gals all over the place, holding and nursing wounds. The first story we get I believe is the most accurate. Tucker is in a pool game and he gets beat in the pool game and he turns to the guy and says, 'You won the pool game but you're not gonna win the fight.' And these guys figure they're a couple of rednecks here in

Fort Walton Beach and we'll show them we're rough, tough SEAL team guys and we'll just mop the floor up with them. And guess what? The other way around. The bartender had a thirty-eight and started firing rounds in the air . . . and the first story was, 'We thought there are only five or six of them and it turned out to be fifteen or twenty of them, and they weren't bothered by the idea of picking up a pool cue and swinging at your head. We thought we were going to fight them with our hands and these guys escalated to heavier weapons.' They got driven out of the bar and we got thrown out of town."

In his own defense, Tucker said another SEAL had started the melee by biting a go-go dancer on her crotch—an account corroborated by Ambrose—which led to the biter having his skull cracked open by a beer bottle. To head off trouble, Kerrey had to smooth things over with the mayor. He was not a stickler for rules and was rarely stern with his men. Rather, he trusted his men and treated them as equals. But now they had let him down. Kerrey "was a lot more mature than all of us put together," Ambrose said. "He was a calming force for different egos. He had to take care of us. We had nothing to do but raise hell."

The long plane ride finally came to an end.

Here they were, in Vietnam, with the most distinct odors that Bob Kerrey had ever smelled, the most unusual sights he had ever seen, and the most interesting sounds he had ever heard. And the heat—it was worse then the stickiest dog days on the prairie. "It was like stepping into another world," he said. "It was like discovering women. It was a new world, the smells, the sights . . ."

His SEAL training kicked in immediately. Even on the truck ride to the Navy compound at Cam Ranh Bay, Kerrey had his men keep their M-16s out and ready. "I figured we were in a war. I figured we were gonna get ambushed along the way. All the training I had—you have to be ready, you have to be prepared. I know I had worked myself into a psychic fear of what was going to happen."

He felt silly when he saw the base, more theme park than military installation, "lit up like the Mall of America," Kerrey recalled. "There were guys on the beach with surfboards, no more a secure area than you could find in all of Vietnam."

He had promised himself that he'd do everything in his power to keep all of his men alive—and now this puzzling irony of seeing soldiers at Cam Rahn Bay with surfboards under their arms instead of weapons seemed to make that pledge meaningless. Nonetheless, his vow to protect his men was an overwhelming responsibility. As much as he wanted to, it wasn't something that he could do with complete certainty. They were SEALs, and SEALs did dangerous things in dangerous places. A single enemy ambush or a hidden booby trap could wipe out the team in the blink of an eye. They were trained to guard against such uncertainties, but they were human. And humans, in the fog of war, made mistakes.

The veterans in the group, Mike Ambrose and Gerhard Klann, would be okay. But the others could still only fantasize what combat was like and wonder how they would react when the shooting started. Would they be brave or would they cut and run? Would they overreact, lose their cool, and throw their training to the wind? Nobody could answer those questions until they engaged the enemy. Until then, they had no idea what real fear was. At their age, they felt immortal, unconquerable. "You think you're gonna live forever," Kerrey said. "The idea that you're gonna die is not something that you sit down and worry about. I didn't figure I was going to die until much later. You know, when you're young, you do a lot of crazy things."

They had all volunteered, not just to be elite SEALs but, as some recalled years later, to help their country beat back the then perceived threat of communism in Asia. Almost all of them felt it was the right thing to do and had wanted to join up before the lottery popped out their draft number and forced them to become an infantryman in the Army or, worse, a Marine rifleman—sure avenues to death in the jungle war. They may have been inexperienced, but they were well trained, well armed, and emotionally pumped up for combat.

The question was, was their commanding officer ready?

Kerrey had his own fears and doubts about the war, but as squad leader he kept these pretty much to himself. His misgivings began in the turbulent spring of 1968, as he hitchhiked from Fort Benning, Georgia, across the south, enroute back to San Diego. He was on the road when Martin Luther King, Jr., was killed. "You know, it was hard not to notice that the country was in turmoil. The Democratic convention, Bobby Kennedy's assassination. I mean, it was a terrible time. And here we were training to go to war, to fight in the Vietnam War. I remember sitting in the audience and listening to Joan Baez say, 'Say yes to the boys who say no.' I mean, that's a terrifying thought, you know, that I was gonna get excluded here somehow."

The antiwar feelings ate at him, clashing with everything he had been taught as a youth. As a child, Kerrey would go with his family on outings to the cemetery on Memorial Day and Veterans Day. His father belonged to the American Legion hall in Lincoln, one of the largest and most active in the nation, and he was a member of the Lions Club, too. While James Kerrey was no zealot, his experience as a soldier and a veteran stirred just below the surface, plainly visible to his children. "It wasn't that he told patriotic stories," Bob Kerrey said, but pride in the flag and the ideals it stood for were important in the Kerrey household.

Bob Kerrey grew up in a time of both unparalled optimism and fear. Postwar America was booming economically, but the Soviet Union had launched Sputnik and become a nuclear superpower, and a Cold War arch rival. American troops took unexpected losses in North Korea, and Francis Gary Powers was shot down in a U-2 over the Soviet Union. Senator Joe McCarthy's anti-Communist witch-hunts would ensure that no politician for decades to come would be soft on communism. In his *Weekly Reader*, a popular grade-school periodical, Kerrey read descriptions of how Communists were infiltrating the political and security systems of the United States.

But Kerrey was more influenced by the heroism depicted in Hollywood movies and stories from his high school teachers, many of whom had fought in World War II. Both helped to conjure images of himself as a warrior.

Still, when he came of age Kerrey had no burning desire to enlist. He was quite comfortable with his college deferment and felt no guilt or regret about not signing up for the new war in Vietnam. He had no romantic pangs to go off to where the action was. "I didn't even give it a lot of thought through college," Kerrey said. "I wasn't necessarily trying to avoid going to Vietnam, but I can't deny that it probably was on my mind, as well."

After graduation he settled into his new career as a pharmacist, looking ahead to a future in the medical field. At one point, he thought about changing careers to become a minister but dropped the idea. Indirectly, he had helped some friends avoid the draft "by monitoring a couple of thermometers in town with men who were trying to get their wives pregnant," he said, which would exclude them from military service. It's likely he would not have joined the military or become a Navy SEAL had he not been drafted.

Kerrey carried those moral ambiguities with him to San Diego. He was a warrior, but there was also a place in him that believed peace was the better way in Vietnam. Later that year he would walk into an election booth and vote for Richard Nixon in the 1968 presidential election, because "he had a plan for ending the war, and I believed him." Kerrey's view was that "this'd be a good one to get over in a hurry." But Nixon would disappoint him. The official line from the Pentagon was what one would expect: that the U.S. was winning the war handily. Still, the evidence that this wasn't so gnawed at Kerrey. He had gone to the big San Diego Navy hospital in Balboa Park to visit with SEALs who had been wounded in Vietnam and whose accounts of the war were at complete odds with Nixon and his generals. "These guys were telling me a sad story. There is no end here, there is no win here," Kerrey remembers. He didn't know it at the time, but Kerrey was preparing to fight in a war that his leaders considered a lost cause, both on the battlefield and at home. "The blanket of moral permission had been withdrawn," Kerrey said.

In May of 1967, Robert McNamara, the secretary of defense, wrote a classified memorandum to Lyndon Johnson recommending that Johnson should be prepared to "negotiate an unfavorable peace." That spring, the top general in Vietnam, William Westmoreland, asked to increase American force levels to 678,000 troops. Johnson had no intention of granting Westmoreland's request, nor did he accept McNamara's suggestion. Privately, Johnson knew the war was a lost cause, but publicly the president pressed on.

In January 1968 the Vietcong and the North Vietnamese Army launched the Tet Offensive, with simultaneous surprise attacks in almost every major South Vietnamese city. It only proved McNamara's point. But the new president, Richard Nixon, continued the fight. By 1969 the White House began shifting more of the responsibility for the war to the government of Vietnam. The Pentagon called it the "Vietnamization" of the war, and while everyone knew it was a fig leaf for retreat, it was a welcome one to the American troops lucky enough to be sent home early. Despite the drawdown, the war went on under Nixon. "Another twenty-five thousand or thirty thousand men" ended up with their names etched into the Vietnam Memorial because of Nixon, Kerrey said. "All that suffering, and countless Vietnamese that died."

As he left for Vietnam, Kerrey was not entirely sure who or what to believe or what would come of the war effort. He knew this much: He was no longer the wide-eyed kid in awe of power and authority. "What I did was buy into a body of a very false kind of patriotism," he said. "A very dangerous kind of patriotism. A blind, knee-jerk patriotism that says you have to do this or you're not an American."

His psychological tug of war, between blind patriotism and reality, was playing on him in subtle ways. "I could be gung ho one day," he said, "not so much [for] going to war as [it was] going into the service, for all the excitement of it, and have doubts the next."

But he also knew that when the time came to ship out, the place he wanted to be was with his teammates. "I was in my platoon," Kerrey said, "and I was going."

Chapter Six

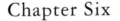

THE SUMMONS FOR LIEUTENANT Kerrey came almost immediately.

Captain Roy "Latch" Hoffmann, United States Navy, Notre Dame University student, Korean War veteran, and steadfast fighter, was not a man to put things off. He was all Navy and no-nonsense, a man who carried himself like the admiral he would later become. Stiff and gruff, with a formal military bearing, he was convinced that everything he was doing in Vietnam, everything the United States was doing, was right and just. Hoffmann's piece of the war was the waterways of Vietnam: the lengthy coast along the South China Sea and the inland rivers and canals. Wherever one of his boats could float was Latch Hoffmann's turf.

The official name for his command was CTF 115, the Coastal Surveillance Force, and he ran it like a field marshal. Hoffmann was not an officer to be taken for granted. It wasn't just that he had the ear of the top admiral in Vietnam, his close friend Elmo Zumwalt, but also that he was a commander determined to use every asset he had and a leader who demanded much of his men. He had a presence that some officers compared to that of George Patton.

He was short, a bantam rooster who preferred the field to sitting behind a desk, especially if things were hot. But, he was also a first-rate administrator, adept at tallying the numbers, or "body counts," of Vietcong his troops killed or wounded.

He carried his own M-16 into the field, along with a silver-handled revolver at his waist and a well-chewed cigar stuck into a corner of his mouth. He was given to the pep talk, pumping up the troops before they were to go into battle. What Hoffmann liked best were the Swift boats—fifty-foot aluminum-skinned crafts equipped with two .50-caliber machine-guns and twin 480-horsepower Detroit diesels. They were powerful and dangerous boats with an innocuous-sounding radio call sign: "Perky Bear."

Not all commanders were pleased to see him when he showed up, knowing full well that he expected to increase the body count, one way or the other. "He sat up high above the deck, with his rifle and revolver, and we had to go find some action for him," said William Garlow, whose Swift boat, PCF 102, had had Hoffmann aboard. "He always wanted to be where the action was."

When Hoffmann arrived in Vietnam, approximately six months prior to Kerrey's appearance in Cam Ranh Bay, there was not enough war for him. He moved quickly to change that, meeting with the admiral in charge of U.S. Pacific forces in the summer of 1968. It was his intention, he said, to ratchet up the fight against the Vietcong by loosening the rules of engagement.

His argument was straightforward enough. His troops were being shot at before they could shoot first. The "official" rules that regulated his Swift boats and other warships in the Mekong Delta were too constrictive, he said, and didn't let his men initiate fire unless they were threatened or had come under attack. That put the Swift boats in a bind, Hoffmann contended. It was hard for the boats to turn around in the narrow canals and rivers, and exits usually had to be made in reverse. This often put crews at risk when they passed near sampans and villages where guerrillas could hit them with machine-gun fire, or rockets.

Hoffmann wanted to turn the tables and let his men become the aggressors. It was really a pro forma request that went through with little resistance.

Back in Cam Ranh Bay, Hoffmann began briefing his commanding officers—including the new ones like Kerrey who had to pass before him en route to their various commands—on the changes that were afoot. "I told them you not only have authority, I damn well expect action," Hoffmann recalled. "If there were men there and they didn't kill them or capture them, you'd hear from me."

By the time Kerrey and his Raiders were on the ground, the new rules were being enforced with a vengeance. A suspect boat had only to change direction, refuse to stop, or make some other evasive or suspicious move at the sight of a Navy warship to be fired on. The Swift boat skippers had orders to open up on most anything deemed to be suspicious, sinking old junks that plied the waterways and burning villages at water's edge that supposedly harbored Vietcong guerrillas.

The new open season brought a dramatic increase in the war-fighting productivity of the Swift boats. The numbers of destroyed sampans and junks blown out of the water spiked up significantly, increasing by thirty-five percent in three months to 2,786. Another 580 were heavily damaged, a fifty percent increase. There was also a corresponding boost of sixty-four percent in the rate of enemy killed in action. On one mission alone in late January, five Swift boats entered the Song Bo De and destroyed ninety-one sampans, sixty-three structures, one bunker, two bridges, and one fish trap, and damaged another seven sampans, fifty-seven structures, and five bunkers.

But the aggressive strategy often led to mistakes and near catastrophes. Swift boats converged on one village targeted for destruction, only to find when they arrived that it was allied with the Americans and flying the South Vietnamese flag. On another occasion, boats fired their big guns into a hooch, sending its occupants diving for cover—including Colonel Carl Bernard, a senior American military advisor and winner of the Distinguished Service Cross for heroism in Korea.

Hoffmann made no apologies for the excesses caused by his hard-nosed approach. "This was war; this wasn't Sunday school," was his way of describing the mission. He laughed when an association representing Vietnamese sampans and junks sued him for financial damages resulting from what they said was a callous strategy to attack innocent boats trying to carry out their commercial ventures. In fact, the Swift boats were under orders to confiscate rice, Hoffmann said, to keep food out of enemy hands. But Hoffmann also looked the other way when his troops gave the rice right back to mothers with children.

Reports of Hoffmann's work reached all the way to the White House, which was always looking for stories affirming the illusion that the war effort was a glowing success. Hoffmann was rewarded by the president himself. "For extraordinary heroism and outstanding performance of duty during the operations against enemy forces in the Republic of Vietnam" was Nixon's somewhat inflated characterization in the Presidential Unit Citation he awarded to Hoffmann's Task Force 115. "Time and again, friendly patrol craft of swift and daring raids penetrated the enemy strongholds in the face of concentrated hostile fire to inflict extensive personnel and material casualties. Enemy vessels were intercepted and destroyed thus denying him freedom of waterways he formerly controlled."

This was the man who would be reading Kerrey's after-action reports for the next six months. At their first meeting, Kerrey was struck by his meticulous inventory of the destruction his troops had achieved. Every wall of Hoffmann's office was pasted with charts and graphs, some of them in color, recording everything from enemy killed to sampans destroyed.

To Kerrey, Hoffmann seemed to have walked out of a scene from *Apocalypse Now*. "He was a classic. Central casting. Cigar, body counts, hooches destroyed, the whole thing," Kerrey said. "He kept charts of all the action. I mean, he was the scorekeeper."

Hoffmann wanted to try something new with Kerrey's Raiders: place them on Swift boats. SEALs had been moving around the interior waterways on PBRs (patrol boats river)— smaller, slower craft that lacked the range of the Swift boats and had no real oceangoing capability. Swift boats could move the commandos more quickly into and out of remote locations to disrupt, capture, or kill the enemy.

The plan made Kerrey uneasy. SEALs were accustomed to working in small, well-defined areas, bolstered by intelligence from platoons that had already been there. The immense size of Hoffmann's command (the entire South China Sea Coast) together with the range of the Swift boats, created a whole new and somewhat dangerous operating style.

In other words, Kerrey's Raiders were going into the war zone blind.

As unsure as Kerrey was of Hoffmann, the gruff captain was not completely sold on the idea of having a squad of nearly all green SEALs. As gung-ho as he was, the last thing he wanted on his watch were a bunch of dead commandos. In a message to his boss, Admiral Zumwalt, Hoffmann suggested that Kerrey's platoon conduct operations "of a low-key nature . . . against least formidable targets for a minimum of two weeks after arrival in country."

The Raiders stayed close to home, working in Cam Ranh Bay and Nha Trang, another big Navy base just to the north. There, they interrogated a Vietcong shot while slipping through a security fence. That effort came to nothing. "He died as we were interrogating him," Kerrey said.

But new and more disturbing orders soon came down the chain of command. Ambrose recalled that Hoffmann wanted to use the SEALs as executioners—an assassination squad to do his bidding. "We were a new toy for the commodore," Ambrose said. The target was a group of monks in a nearby Buddhist monastery.

Kerrey argued to Hoffmann that such missions did not make good use of the SEALs' skills. "It was a very difficult situation, to put it mildly," he said.

The monks were believed to be drawing maps of Cam Ranh to help the Vietcong to sneak in and place explosives in strategic locations, like a munitions depot. "He wanted us to go in there and hit the monastery," Kerrey said. Hoffmann remembered the mission but said "that was an Army order."

Though the operation never took place, Kerrey had no qualms about killing the monks. His concern was about the political impact of such an act, which could turn the Buddhist community against the Americans. Still, if ordered, Kerrey believed he had the authority to carry out the execution. "If you said to me, 'Your understanding of the rules gives you permission to do it,' my answer is yes. My understanding of the rules of engagement, I would have had permission to proceed and carry out that operation."

He was badly informed. U.S. military and international law specifically prohibit killing unarmed civilians, whether they were monks or not, as well as killing soldiers in detention. To do so was considered a war crime.

Kerrey didn't see it that way, and his view was rooted in the culture of the SEALs and counterinsurgency warfare. The formal SOPs (standard operating procedures) were clear. They were warriors, and warriors were supposed to adhere to a certain code of warfare. Innocents were to be left alone.

Those were the formal SOPs. The informal ones were situational. And some, but not all, SEAL platoons saw themselves outside the traditional chain of command—and established military law. They operated on their own and in secrecy, doing what they thought they had to do to get the job done. That meant gunning down anyone who posed a threat. "Kill the people we made contact with or we have to abort the mission," is how Kerrey described what his instructors taught him. SEALs who served in Vietnam generally agree but put more emphasis on the latter part of that directive: a good number of vets said they simply walked away from assignments under such circumstances.

"I tried to kill them according to the general rules," Kerrey said, "which were not as specific as they should have been. We were given a hell of a lot more latitude then we should have been."

Assassination was clearly in the SEAL portfolio. SEAL advisers were made available to the CIA's Phoenix program, and Langley used them to train Vietnamese Provincial Reconnaissance Units, commonly referred to as the PRUs. Their mission was to terrorize the enemy through assassination and abduction of Vietcong cadre, fighters, and sympathizers. By 1968 it was common for complete SEAL platoons to operate with the PRUs.

But faced with his first assassination mission to take out the monks in a monastery, Kerrey balked. Not because he wasn't prepared to do it, but because he thought it was simply a bad idea. Kerrey prevailed, but Hoffmann took notice of his young SEAL's resistance to orders in a message to Zumwalt. "There is no question that the officer contingent of SEAL Delta Platoon know their SEAL business, but like many junior officers the requirement for carrying out specific orders and instructions does not always penetrate the first time around."

In early February 1969, Lieutenant Kerrey and his Raiders were at last on their way to "find some place to do business."

Hoffmann dispatched them south to an area they could use as a jumping-off point to the Mekong Delta. "He knew he had to put them in there one way or the other," said Paul Connolly, a Hoffman deputy responsible for Swift boat operations in the delta. "When Bob Kerrey and his enlisted SEALs came down," Connolly said, "they reported to me." His headquarters in Cat Lo were adjacent to the strategic Navy port of Vung Tau, where elements of the Swift boat fleet moored when not on patrol. About seventy-five miles southeast of Saigon, Vung Tau was a nexus of Navy activity and wartime intrigue. CIA operatives and a panoply of uniformed warriors hung out in the seaside resort telling spy stories and tales of derring-do under the watchful eyes of lustful bar girls, some whom were almost certainly VC spies.

Connolly held the rank of commander, a full grade below his prickly boss Hoffmann, who called the shots. Hoffman sent the SEALs to Cai Nuoc near the bottom of South Vietnam. Their assignment, Hoffmann wrote in his classified evaluation report to Admiral Zumwalt, was "to gain real time operational intelligence and eliminate the VC infrastructure."

The platoon loaded up a boat with construction supplies, weapons, ammunition, and their gear, and headed south to build a new home. It wasn't much, a few sheets of plywood and corrugated tin with thatch for the roof. But the little makeshift shack would be a base from where the team could now conduct their first combat sorties.

But Kerrey's time at Cai Nuoc was quickly cut short by yet another directive. Tim Wettack and his squad were to stay there, but Kerrey and his Raiders were to pack up and head north again. This time, the destination was a region where intelligence reports suggested enemy activity and the possible presence of Vietcong military leaders. "I got word they were looking for a base the VC had in the Mekong Delta," Connolly recalled.

Their new area of operation would be in the Thanh Phu Secret Zone.

Chapter Seven

———————■———————

MAJOR JAMES H. COOK, a sandy-haired Texan, didn't have much use for Vietnamese on either side of the war in the Thanh Phu Secret Zone.

As far as Cook was concerned, they were all untrustworthy, even the ones working in his headquarters as part of the military advisory Team 88, which he commanded. He had good reason not to trust them. Someone, likely an insider who knew that Cook would be attending a local cockfight, had fed that information to the Vietcong, who placed an explosive device under his seat. Only a last-minute change in Cook's schedule kept him away that day.

That was about the most dangerous thing that he had faced. It was his job to provide professional military advice to the district chief, a local south Vietnamese official much like an American mayor—except he wielded considerable power in deciding how the U.S. military would conduct itself in the eight villages under his control. In addition to providing counsel that the district chief could accept or reject, Cook also had to coordinate the State Department's pacification program, and CIA and Army intelligence.

But there wasn't much of a war in the Thanh Phu Secret Zone, and life at the headquarters was pretty much humdrum. The official journal kept by the Phoenix program's U.S. adviser (he scribbled "Light reading for those leisure hours" across the cover) also reflected the tedium of the assignment. His entries consisted of petty complaints: Vietnamese showing up late for work or not showing up at all; their taking extended and unauthorized leave, or failing to fill out the proper military forms. References to anything combat related were infrequent. One consistent notation was about his request for a transfer.

Cook wanted out, too. He was a career soldier, but he would just as soon have left Vietnam, he said, and returned to the United States. His discontent could be attributed to his MOS, or military occupational specialty—air defense expert. In the Mekong Delta there was no use for this. The Vietcong guerrillas didn't have any aircraft. Enemy action in the district had been mostly limited to snipers taking shots at the Americans who patrolled with the small number of Vietnamese troops loyal to the district chief. When shot at, the Americans retaliated with a few rounds of artillery. But it was tit for tat, never escalating into a major engagement. A really busy month, according to Cook's monthly report, was the loss of "three M-16 rifles and one .45 caliber pistol" to the enemy and the abductions of sixteen "friendly personnel" who were later released.

It was nothing like the heavy combat on the peninsula just above the Thanh Phu District in a place the generals called the Rung Sat Special Zone and to the southeast, all along the villages and canals that shot off of the Bassac River up to Chau Duc, near the Cambodian border. Several SEAL platoons had found plenty of work in the Rung Sat, which was generally considered a very dangerous place to operate. And the Navy was running myriad operations using a variety of heavily armed boats up the rivers and canals that crisscrossed throughout the delta.

The Swift boats did make occasional runs up the Song Co Chien River and into parts of the Thanh Phu Secret Zone. And the U.S. 9th Infantry had a small presence. Other that that, there was not a lot of focus. "The American military didn't care about this place and neither did the South Vietnamese in Saigon," Cook recalled. Even getting to Cook's headquarters from Saigon required endless crossings of rivers and bad roads.

If there was a center of enemy activity in the district, it was two hamlets, Thanh Phong and An Nhon, which at the very least were home to Vietcong supporters. The villages were about ten miles from Cook's headquarters. The road to Thanh Phong was narrow and dusty and became nearly impassable when frequent heavy rains turned it to mud. Nearby An Nohn was equally hard to reach. Cook was not overly concerned with these two hamlets or with the small number of Vietcong cadre who operated throughout the entire district—about 157, according to his calculations. "There are no major problems which can be foreseen at this time," he assured his superiors in early 1969. He reported that "eighty-one percent" of the district's population was under government control. It would soon increase to ninety percent, he wrote.

But a good number of Thanh Phu inhabitants, in fact, had little love for Saigon, and leaned more toward supporting the guerrillas than Cook realized. Buddhist villagers mistrusted the predominantly Catholic officials and their political aspirations—with good reason. The district chief, at American insistence, wanted the peasants to leave their land and move into a government relocation center in the main town of Thanh Phu, which was the "county seat." It was part of Washington's Strategic Hamlet program, which operated under the dubious assumption that people who refused to leave their ancestral homes had to be hostile and thus legitimate targets for attack. They even gave a name to these new targets of opportunity—"Free-Fire Zones."

Some villagers relocated, but many did not. "They weren't gonna leave and basically didn't care who was in charge," said Cook's deputy, a competent young lieutenant named David Marion, who pinned on captain's bars well before the required time in grade.

Marion was a Texan, and the Vietnamese were about as far away physically and culturally as one could get from his view of things. But he easily figured out the philosophy of the peasants in places like Thanh Phong. " 'Just leave me alone' was the basic attitude of most of the people down in that area," he said.

Part of the problem was that the incumbent district chief, who understood pro-guerrilla sentiment in the area, had struck an unofficial armistice with the Vietcong and their cadre. His straightforward message to the guerrillas—"You don't bother me and I don't bother you"—infuriated Marion. He knew the enemy had paid off the mayor to turn a blind eye to the occasional gunrunning or Communist meetings in his district. The American advisers were helpless to do anything about the bribes and watched as village after village, three quarters of the district in all, threw in with Hanoi. By day, the peasants tilled their fields and supported the government. But by night, they became sympathizers, offering to feed, shelter, and hide the few guerrillas who passed through, or to protect weapons and political literature. So secure was Thanh Phong regarded by the Vietcong, that the village served as the site for their court to settle disputes among the peasants. Marion didn't share Cook's benign view of the peasantry. He believed that the Vietcong threat was growing and that places like Thanh Phong were a lot more dangerous than the U.S. realized. "It was not a good place to be by yourself," he said.

The turning point came in late 1968, when Saigon appointed a new mayor, Tiet Lun Duc, to the Thanh Phu District. Duc was a military man, a captain soon to become a major in the Vietnamese Army, who had trained at Fort Bragg, North Carolina, home to the Army's elite airborne and Green Berets. The North Vietnamese jailed Duc, a Catholic with ten children, early in his life, and it left him with an intense hatred of anybody associated with Ho Chi Minh's revolutionaries.

Duc was determined to win back the peasants in the Thanh Phu Secret Zone, and he thought the time was right. The Tet Offensive, launched in January 1968 by the Vietcong, had been rolled back, and most of the armed guerrillas had been either killed or driven from the delta. But Duc and the Americans had different ideas how to proceed. While the new district chief wanted to wipe out the remaining Vietcong, U.S. advisers insisted on first targeting the cadre who recruited for guerrilla combat units, supplied civilian laborers, conducted propaganda, evacuated the wounded, maintained the intelligence network, provided medical support, and acted as guides for soldiers moving through the district. Eliminate the infrastructure they supplied, the Americans argued, and the guerrillas would wither away. It was always a battle with "Duck," as his U.S. advisers called him. He was eager to hunt down the Vietcong and engage in traditional military firefights. To him, the cadre was an afterthought.

Duc chose to deal with the Vietcong underground through threat-filled speeches to the villagers. "If you are my friend, you will do fine," he said on his first tour of the district. "You support me and the government of Vietnam, we get along OK. You do not, you're Vietcong, you die."

"Those were the rules," said Marion, who wrote of Duc's warnings in his journal. Marion, an infantryman, liked what he was hearing, that Duc was getting tough with the enemy.

Early on, Duc took Marion aside and announced, "We're going to make some changes." He unfolded a map of his Thanh Phu Secret Zone, Marion recalled, and spread it out to explain his new strategy. Duc drew a line down through the district, almost in a north-south axis.

"Everything east of this line, free-fire zone. Go get 'em," he told Marion.

Everything east was mostly territory thought to be populated by Vietcong sympathizers. One of the targets in Duc's free-fire zone was the sleepy little village of Thanh Phong.

Duc was not about to accept what Washington believed to be inevitable—that the war was lost. Neither was Hoffmann, who was eager to send men and Swift boats into the swamps of the Mekong Delta to help gung-ho allies like Duc. Lieutenant General Julian Ewell, the 9th Division commander, whose area of operation included parts of the Thanh Phu District was also bent on continuing the war. That February, Ewell, soon to be named American military representative to the Paris Peace talks, demanded that his troops "begin killing four thousand of these little bastards a month" not "the two thousand little bastards" they were targeting. General Ewell was known for his "body count mania" and slogans like "killing fish in a barrel." It led some of the advisers in the delta to call him the "Butcher of IV Corps," a somewhat over-rated label that spoke more to Ewell's talked-up reputation among the troops than to the reality that his body count numbers were oftentimes bloated.

Duc shared Ewell's enthusiasm for victory. Working with the CIA's Phoenix program, his agents and informants fanned out across the Thanh Phu area, collecting names of suspected Vietcong and listing them for "neutralization." But old Phoenix ledgers that recorded the missions of Duc's police forces say they were underwhelming. More often than not, his sweeps failed to apprehend or kill any targeted suspects.

At the same time, the remaining Vietcong in the district were becoming more aggressive. Shortly after Christmas in 1968, two enemy guerrillas penetrated the security perimeter of Duc's compound and, according to Cook, broke through an interior fence before a local guard spotted them and opened fire. The firefight that ensued lasted only minutes, but it did not end before a guerrilla's grenade had blown apart a hooch, taking the lives of two young grade-school children. Word quickly got around that the children were in some way a part of Duc's very large extended family.

Almost immediately after the raid, Duc gathered his men

and, with Cook in tow, headed south to Thanh Phong, where he believed the guerrillas had come from. In the rush southward, it looked to Cook like a revenge mission.

Duc's troops rounded up about 150 villagers, all women, children, and old men. He ranted to the meek assemblage, delivering one of his "You're either with us or against us speeches," as Cook described it, warning them if they continued to support and sympathize with the Vietcong, they risked death.

Cook was certain there was going to be a massacre. As the district chief threatened the crowd, his troops stood at the ready, their fingers on the triggers of a small arsenal trained on the unarmed peasants. He was a career fighting man and accustomed to seeing men with guns. But he had yet to see anything quite like the tinderbox of pent-up emotions he was now watching. And he had never seen Duc so worked up before, and he knew there was nothing he could say that might rein him in. "I thought we were going to have our first My Lai," Cook recalled years later. The soldiers "were standing there, watching Duc. Had he said anything, gave them any signal, these fellas would have shot up the place." Calmer heads prevailed, Cook said, and the group eventually returned to Thanh Phu.

But Duc's message was clear: This wasn't the end of it. Such incidents in his district would not go unpunished.

In February 1969, a few weeks after Duc's quixotic incursion, Kerrey's team was settling into its new outpost in the Thanh Phu Secret Zone. It was actually a "junk base," housing sampans the Navy occasionally used to conceal their river patrols. The place was "pretty much in the boonies," Connolly told Kerrey. They didn't grouse about the remote location or the primitive conditions, though others complained about the SEALs' bedraggled appearance. "We had this little camp set up," Kerrey said. "There was an inspection done of us, and the guy was not very happy with the way we looked. We were pretty scruffy."

Their encampment was far from a bustling citadel, but it put them among the local population from whom the SEALs needed to determine the whereabouts of the elusive Vietcong. "We met with the [district] chief," Kerrey said, and "played volleyball with the local village people there."

Kerrey also made contact with the NILO—the Naval Intelligence Officer—in Vung Tau who was to be the official clearinghouse for information, none of it very good. Nonetheless, Kerrey was obligated to incorporate it into whatever plans he was developing for his missions. The best intelligence came from the local officials with whom the SEALs were trying to ingratiate themselves. The village elders could identify (or accuse wrongly) the Vietcong. Once identified, the names of suspects made their way onto the Phoenix program's black lists. More than a dozen villagers in Thanh Phong were suspected of being part of the Vietcong infrastructure and placed on the Phoenix advisers' list at Cook's district headquarters.

It's doubtful Kerrey saw the actual names, but he knew enough about the lists in general to realize they could be a death sentence. "It was assassination," he said. "Somebody put somebody on a list, it could be a family on a list, they are on the list, they're dead."

From their new location, the SEALs began prowling at night, setting up ambushes and attempting to collect their own tips that could lead to more fruitful missions.

Their first armed sallies yielded nothing of value. Partly to blame was the lack of any hard-core Vietcong guerrillas. In February 1969, the Thanh Phu District was not the nest of enemy activity it would later become. The other likely factor for their initial poor showing was inexperience. Though Gerhard Klann and Mike Ambrose were savvy combat veterans, the five other squad members were still green and prone to misreading signs of the enemy. Even so, each foray shortened the learning curve and added to their confidence.

By February 13, nearly a month after arriving in Vietnam, Kerrey's team had yet to fire a shot in anger, or make much headway in interrogating the villagers in the Thanh Phu Secret Zone.

That was about to change.

At 11:30 that morning Kerrey's unit boarded a Swift boat and headed for Thanh Phong in search of Vietcong cadre. Despite intelligence reports of enemy presence, the hamlet was safe for a daytime visit. According to their reports, the team spent the next several hours "searching hooches and bunkers" and "interrogated fourteen women and small children from two hooches." Satisfied that no males were present or nearby, they let the residents go, departed, and set an ambush on the outskirts of the village that was uneventful.

The Raiders hopped back on their Swift boat and left at 6 A.M. the next morning. They returned later that evening at 10 P.M. to the area but this, too, was a bust. In their report they blamed "lost radio 'comm.' and an extremely dense coconut grove." The radio wasn't working and they feared getting lost. The squad was pulled out by boat again the next morning, February 15, at 1:30 A.M., and radioed their bad luck to Connolly in Cat Lo: two visits to Thanh Phong and no signs of an enemy leader or Vietcong activity.

But Kerrey and his men would have a third chance at Thanh Phong. Planning was underway for a major nighttime attack on nearby An Nohn to be carried out on February 25. An armada of Swift boats would transport more than one hundred South Vietnamese troops for a search-and-destroy mission. That same night Kerrey's Raiders would return to Thanh Phong. Naval intelligence said a meeting of senior enemy leaders was to take place there that evening. The team was assigned a "take-out" mission, as in, "Come out with me, or you die," said Captain Marion, who would soon replace Cook as senior military adviser to Duc. "He either comes out with you as a prisoner or you kill him. That's what a take-out mission is." The order was "No matter who you came across," Klann said, "bring back anybody if you think they're gonna be of any intelligence worth, or eliminate them."

In Kerrey's eyes, it was a dangerous mission. If the intelligence reports proved valid and a Vietcong rendezvous was underway, his Raiders could encounter stiff resistance. Back in San Diego, instructors warned Kerrey against getting his small SEAL team in a fight they could not win. "Be careful not to engage a unit that has such overwhelming force that you have no chance to get out alive," he said of his training. While the only occupants of Thanh Phong they had encountered in their last visit were unarmed peasants, that was in daylight. Kerrey knew that operating at night often meant unexpected risks and nasty surprises.

The young lieutenant was anguished about the upcoming assault. Though SEALs were highly trained, Kerrey's fears about combat had been building since he left California. "On the way over, all I was thinking about was somebody's gonna kill me up close and personal," he said. "The idea that I was gonna go out there at that point in time and actually do what I'd been trained to do was a pretty terrifying thought." Connolly was not sympathetic. "He kept delaying," Connolly recalled years later. He finally flew down to the junk base to confront Kerrey. In a heated exchange he chastised Kerrey for his foot-dragging and upbraided him by saying the SEALs' "John Wayne" bravado was nothing more then hollow bluster. Kerrey had demanded assault helicopters or fixed-wing aircraft to be on call if things went bad, otherwise he wasn't going. Connolly said he found the request for air support unrealistic. But he did arrange for Kerrey and a naval intelligence officer to fly over the village in search of a safe entry route (they had already entered twice in similar locations and needed an alternative spot). "I remember that flight," Kerrey said, "because I was puking on the damn thing at the end of it."

From the air, Kerrey said he didn't see any of the peasants the SEALs had previously interrogated in the village. As best he could tell, the place was empty. That was odd. The inhabitants could have been sleeping or working in the rice paddies of a neighboring hamlet, a common practice. Perhaps they had been removed for the meeting of enemy leaders that was supposed to take place on the evening of the twenty-fifth.

Whatever the reason, Kerrey would be ready. His Raiders were going in.

Chapter Eight

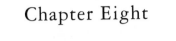

"*OUR FATHER, WHO ART in heaven, hallowed be thy name . . .*"

Lieutenant Kerrey, dressed in battle gear, was quietly reciting his favorite prayer as the team came closer to its insertion point. Huddled near his men, M-16 at the ready, Kerrey was nervous. It was just before midnight on February 25 and Kerrey and his SEALs were on Lieutenant Garlow's Swift boat as it quietly motored up the Song Co Chien River toward Thanh Phong.

The young squad leader had taken to saying the Lord's Prayer on his missions. He didn't think it would stop a bullet; "it was just, you know, it's time to do the Lord's Prayer, and the Lord's Prayer can be very comforting." Kerrey had put "Christian" on his military dog tags. He was dipped in the baptismal waters as a boy in front of his congregation at Bethany Christian Church. When he prayed and listened hard enough, he said he could hear the voice of God telling him what to do.

The spirit ebbed and flowed as he grew older. The Saturday matinee at the Stuart Theater eventually became as sacramental as Sunday morning church. For twenty-five cents and a milk carton, he could shut out his sleepy town and pass the day thinking he was John Wayne or Gary Cooper. "I grew up with Cooper," Kerrey said. "Wayne was big. These are great heroes." Despite his parents' devout faith, the movies were far preferable to reading scripture. As a grown man, his thoughts often returned to Bethany and how his family went to church for an hour then to Bible study. He recalled reading his Bible in Sunday school class, particularly the commandment "Thou shall not kill."

Now, as he approached the target, the prayerful Kerrey was about to violate God's order not to kill. *"Forgive us our trespasses . . . deliver us from evil . . ."*

Garlow was running his boat under radio silence. The only radio chatter the yeoman back at Cook's headquarters was picking up was from the Swift boats ferrying the one hundred other troops into combat. "Ball game in progress," he jotted in his log book, the coded phrase for the opening of the search-and-destroy salvo. As the ground offensive unfolded and the Vietnamese troops razed the village, the yeoman wrote in large letters, "An Nhon—burn." Ten structures and a "VC school" were "destroyed," one hundred rounds of ammunition for an AK-47 assault rifle were confiscated (about enough for one rifle), and ten unidentified suspects—likely just peasants—were captured. The yeoman recorded one Vietcong killed in action.

An Nhon was about the deployment of raw, overt power. The SEALs were on a mission of stealth.

Garlow cut back the power to the boat's engines and glided his warship close to the beach. One by one, over the side they went—Ambrose at the point; Klann carrying a Stoner machine-gun behind him; Kerrey, Peterson, Knepper, and Schrier following. Tucker came last to provide rear security. They slipped into the thick brush of the mangrove trees that grew along the beach. There they sat, waiting, listening, steeling themselves for the task that lay ahead. The moon was a little more than half full—too much light for the Raiders to be comfortable. But there was a haze off the water that aided their concealment. The mangroves were tall, maybe fifteen feet, but certainly not jungle-tall as in other parts of Vietnam, where a triple canopy of evergreens shielded out all light. The trees were dense, though, and for the time being a safe place to find cover. Still, for all the Raiders knew, some native Vietcong who had grown up in these woods could have been watching, gathering enough information to set up an ambush. After a while, the SEALs moved out, ever so slowly.

In a few minutes, the squad came to a small clearing. In the dim light they could make out the edges of a hooch on a tiny patch of land cut out of thick tropical foliage. Sitting out front was an elderly man, the soft red glow of a cigarette between his lips. With each puff, the glow lit up Bui Van Vat's face. According to their intelligence charts, this man and this hooch were not supposed to be here. Yet here he was—the first big screwup of the night.

The veterans, Mike Ambrose and Gerhard Klann, knew what to do with the old man—either kill him or quietly slip away to come back and fight another day. As point man, Ambrose said he had the authority to take matters into his own hands. Even so, he deferred to Kerrey. He crept back and told him there were four people inside the hooch. Ambrose remembers them being both males and females. Years later, it would all be a blur to Kerrey. He said he remembered Ambrose saying, "We've got some men here, we have to take care of them."

Kerrey didn't hesitate. The mission was a "go," he said. Klann remembers Kerrey's exact words as: "Kill 'em." Kerrey saw the people in the first hooch as forward sentries and, as such, hostile. Restraining them was not an option. "It does not work to merely bind and gag people, because they're going to get away," Kerrey said.

Nobody spoke, and each SEAL watched for the hand signals they had memorized. Two fingers pointed one way meant for two men to go right; a closed fist meant to hold; and so forth. Ambrose flashed Klann the signal that meant he should take out the old man. The rest of the team, who were just feet away and trying to remain silent, would then pounce on the others.

The killing had to be quick and quiet, accomplished with knives, lest they betray their presence. A military-issue KA-BAR knife across the throat was not the most reliable means with which to kill, as some victims would survive. And it was messy. "Blood would get on your hands, between your fingers; it would be sticky and smell a certain way," said Roy Boehm, one of the SEALs' most revered teachers, who spent many months in Vietnam. "You couldn't wipe it off easily. Some men could handle it; others couldn't. It would cause them a lot of problems. Sometimes they would never get over it, and they would fall apart. Other times they would do the opposite and become even worse killers."

The preferred technique was to stick the knife in above the kidney and twist, severing a major artery. If it was done properly, an unsuspecting victim would be dead within seconds. "Put your hand over their mouth and stab 'em up in," Gerhard Klann said, "underneath the ribs and twist the knife and then hold 'em. They'll shake a little bit, and then they die."

Either way, using a knife was not always easy on a man's conscience in this type of combat. "You're right up close," Kerrey said. "You're trained to kill somebody with a knife, to kill somebody in tight. It does require a behavior that provokes more revulsion and provokes more moral outrage."

If Klann did it right, the way he was trained to, Bui Van Vat would not know who or what had overcome him. Gerhard did not carry a military issue KA-BAR knife. Instead, he grasped a hunting knife with an eight-inch blade, the one his brother gave him before departing for Vietnam. "Here take this," his brother told him, "you may need it."

It took him only seconds to grab the old man. But like most things in war, the killing did not go according to plan.

"I had a little trouble with my guy," Klann said. "He put up a fight." He wrestled Bui Van Vat away from his family members so they couldn't see what he was about to do. Then Klann thrust the steel blade through the old man's flesh and deep into his back, just above his kidney. As he jammed it in, Klann twisted the blade. "What you do is you usually cut one of the major vessels up there and he bleeds to death in a very short time," Klann said. "A lot from trauma also." But he missed the mark. Bui Van Vat squirmed to face his attacker and grabbed Klann's forearm, the one with the knife. He tried to push the blade away. "He wouldn't die," Klann said. "He kept moving, fighting back." Klann stuck him again in the back and then signaled for assistance. Another SEAL came over and together they finally overpowered him. The others in the hooch met a similar fate.

The killings worried Ambrose. "There was plenty of noise," he said. Somebody had let out a faint scream, and Klann's victim had struggled violently. "I felt compromised," Ambrose said. In his mind, the mission had already been blown—these were not the people they had come for. For a few minutes, the men argued about what to do, whether to abort or go on. It was only one kilometer to the next target, Ambrose said, "but in my mind it was one hundred yards." He recommended turning back, but the others wanted to leave the bodies where they fell and push deeper into the village. They wanted to get the right man.

They doubled back toward the river, crossing over some small dykes to a canal. Thanh Phong was like the majority of the other villages that grew rice in the Mekong Delta. Water from the rice paddies drained into a series of canals which in turn flowed into rivers. The irrigation system made walking through a hamlet difficult, especially at night. One redeeming feature was the thick tropical vegetation and elephant grass that grew on the canals and offered good cover for the

SEALs. They spread out along the canal, "not close enough to see one another," said Kerrey, but still near enough to regroup in a hurry if they ran into trouble.

After about fifteen minutes, Kerrey saw the faint yellow light of a lantern and four or five hooches more than one hundred yards in the distance. Slowly, in the searing heat and humidity, their clammy hands gripping rifles, they crept forward watching and listening for the enemy. The element of surprise would have been with them. But Kerrey recalls the nighttime silence was shattered by a *pop*. Then another. It sounded to Kerrey like gunfire. Had somebody fired on them from one hundred yards away? How could that be? From such a distance, it would be nearly impossible to see seven men in camouflage uniforms who could not even see each other. "I don't know if it's noise. In fact, there is some dispute. I think we were shot at, but who the hell knows," Kerrey said. "I was thinking there were a thousand guys over there. What do I know? The first thing I do is direct Knepper to return fire with a LAW," a disposable launcher designed to shoot rockets. Kerrey then gave the order to fire, and the rest of the team let loose with a fusillade, Kerrey said, as if "every Communist in Vietnam was inside those hooches."

They then saw people trying to flee, about seven of them, Unarmed, they were no match for the SEALs, who quickly gunned them down. "We used everything we had that evening. I think we could have used a lesser amount of fire, especially given the suspicion there might be civilians in the area," Kerrey said.

When they reached the hooches Kerrey's world crumbled. More than a dozen bodies were clumped together in a group. Not hardened Vietcong but women and children, the relatives of Bui Thi Luom, the young girl who had been sleeping in the large bunker with her mother and fifteen aunts and cousins. There was not a man among them and no weapons anywhere. "The thing I will remember until the day I die is walking in and finding, I don't know, fourteen or so, I don't even know what the number was, women and children who were dead," Kerrey said. He said he "was expecting to find Vietcong soldiers with weapons."

By now, there was little to discuss. The mission had been completely compromised and they had to leave quickly. The SEALs were running now, away from the hooches. They had given up on finding the Vietcong leader they had come to get. Tucker turned to Kerrey on the way out, upset at what had just happened. "I don't like that kind of stuff," he said.

"I don't like it either," Kerrey replied.

They radioed for Garlow to come and extract them at a preplanned rendezvous site. A few minutes later, they reached the river and climbed aboard the Swift boat.

After Garlow pulled far enough away from the area, the SEALs sent a communiqué to Connolly.

Received fire from hooches. Returned fire and patrolled to hooches. Observed several personnel running from hooches. Took under fire. Patrolled and extracted by PCF. Met {Coast Guard cutter} Pt. Comfort and she claimed she had 48 hour clearance to fire into area we were in. Expended: 1200 RDS {rounds} M-16/12 RDS M-79/2 WP grenades/2 66MM Law. No friendly casualties this unit. 21 VC KIA (BC).

There was no mention of the first hooch, where they killed Bui Van Vat and his family. Other critical details were left out, but it contained enough to titillate the brass: "21 VC KIA." The death toll of Vietcong killed in action was higher than normal for a small unit of SEALs, which might have raised eyebrows, had the sender not included the letters "BC." Whoever read the message—logged at various Army and Navy commands from Saigon to Cam Ranh Bay—would assume that the SEALs indeed had seen heavy action, that they did not inflate the number of those killed. Headquarters would know that the dead had been tallied by a "body count."

What they wouldn't know, at least not immediately, was that the victims were all unarmed women and children. Kerrey's message described the dead only as "VC," leaving out gender and age. Nor would they know the number was as high as twenty-seven when the family of Bui Van Vat was added and one of the women in the second hooch was found to be pregnant. Their report contained a short reference to the capture of two "chicom carbines," which would support that they acted in self-defense. Thirty years later neither Kerrey nor Klann remember finding any weapons.

Either through haste or intent to cover up the facts, the report was nowhere near to what had happened to the women and children of Thanh Phong that night.

Twenty-one-year-old Tran Van Rung was about 400 yards away from Luom's bunker when he heard gunfire crackle through the stillness. It was from automatic weapons: a succession of quick bursts, quiet, then another series of bursts, then nothing.

Rung, one of eleven guerrillas assigned to guard a group of senior Vietcong who were meeting in Thanh Phong, figured that the Americans were nearby and heavily armed. But Rung also realized from the sounds that he and the other guards had caught a big break. If the Americans were in pursuit of the Vietcong leadership, they were way off. They'd entered into the wrong part of Thanh Phong.

What was not clear to Rung was if someone had fired at them. The guerrillas carried only outdated bolt-action rifles and a few homemade grenades. The weapons had remained at their sides and quiet. Had somebody fired at the Americans? Or had they opened up on their own? Either way, Rung knew it would be crazy to run to the sound of the action, a mistake that could have gotten them all killed. With their antiquated weapons, the Vietcong fighters would have been no match for their well-equipped opponents. They waited, huddled in bunkers until the first light.

When they reached the place where they had heard the shooting, they found Luom's family on the ground in a bloody heap, with body parts strewn around them. They were outside their bunkers, which was odd. Nearly every hooch had a bunker, and at the first sign of trouble civilians instinctively hid in them. Had they been forced out at gunpoint, herded into a group, and murdered? Or had they been caught in the crossfire? There were no weapons, no dead men, no ammunition belts—nothing that would indicate an armed struggle. It was hard to know what happened.

Daylight exposed another grisly scene at the home of Bui Van Vat, the old man who put up such a struggle. In the frenzied multiple attempts to kill him, one of the SEALs had slit Vat's throat, leaving his head barely attached. His wife, Luu Thi Canh, and their three grandchildren, the boy and his two sisters, lay in pools of blood, also stabbed to death.

They soon found Bui Thi Luom, the twelve-year-old girl who had been wounded but had somehow managed to survive the attack. The SEALs didn't realize it, but another woman, Pham Tri Lanh, the wife of a Vietcong fighter, would later claim to have watched them kill the villagers. They both would recount scenes three decades later. The village elders could not understand why they had been so brutally targeted. One vowed to walk the nine miles on the dusty road to Thanh Phu, where he would complain personally to the district chief.

Captain Hoffmann immediately ordered Kerrey's Raiders out of the area, whisking them several hundred miles north to his headquarters in Cam Ranh Bay. Kerrey wasn't sure what this was about—maybe a routine resupply of the team or something else. Because of the brutal killings, he has "blocked out almost everything else, including other things that happened prior to that and afterwards. It's entirely possible Hoffmann ordered our ass out of there."

This was no supply run. Within hours of the raid, Connolly was hearing that some kind of massacre had taken place. He was hectored with a flurry of inquiries from Cook's headquarters. First Cook was told that eight SEALs had been injured. Then he heard that the SEALs had briefly retreated, then returned to Thanh Phong to finish off the village, firing rockets and phosphorous grenades into hooches and bunkers. Soon, the picture became clearer. On February 27, two days after the raid, a message landed on Connolly's desk saying somebody had to "answer charge of violation," in Duc's district. Twenty-five minutes later, another flag: "Koreans are not working in free-fire zone and that charge of killing 25 men and women and children directed against U.S. Navy." (The Korean soldiers, American allies in the war, were notorious for their savagery against the Vietcong.) By then, Connolly was starting to fear the worst. But the next afternoon, the story changed: Now eleven of those killed were Vietcong, clearly suggesting a firefight, not a massacre. "Recommend award for valor for U.S. involved," Connolly was told. "No further info needed." But that evening the picture shifted yet again. "Be advised an old man from Thanh Phong presented himself to district chief headquarters with claims for retribution for alleged atrocities committed the night of 25 February '69. Thus far it appears that twenty-four people were killed, thirteen women, children, and one old man. Eleven were unidentified, assumed to be VC. Navy SEALs operating in area. Investigation continues."

Connolly was beside himself about the Army's threat to investigate his SEALs. "A message flew in from the Army saying that so many of them were women and I just got upset as hell," Connolly said. "He's going to conduct an investigation and I got upset as hell. I asked him who the hell could tell the difference between a Vietnamese man or a woman at two o'clock in the morning when they all wear the same clothing and the women might just as well look like men, no chests or anything like that."

The investigation into the SEALs' operation was a limited one, kicking around for a few days before withering away. On March 3, Duc traveled down to Thanh Phong. His message, more or less, was that the villagers had gotten their just deserts for aiding the Vietcong. "District chief to tell the people why they were shot at," the yeoman in Cook's headquarters wrote in his radio log, "and for them to rally to GVN side. If they do not, they will be shot at in the future."

David Marion, Cook's deputy, wrote in his military journal for March 3: "Duc said, 'An Nohn and Thanh Phong are unfounded and nothing will come of it,'" he said. The higher-ups, Marion said, "probably thought that the only good VC is a dead VC and they were clearly in VC country."

Chapter Nine

———————————◼———————————

ON MARCH 14, ALMOST three weeks after the raid on Thanh Phong, Kerrey's Raiders were bobbing in the South China Sea. Just a few hours earlier, they had been watching a John Wayne movie at an outdoor Navy theater in Cam Ranh Bay, enjoying a few last peaceful moments before beginning another mission. Now it was close to 3 A.M., and they were a little more than 5,000 feet from Hon Tam Island, which sat a few miles off the Vietnam coast in the Bay of Nha Trang. The water, lapping up against and over the gunwale of the small SEAL boat was comfortably warm. The men could feel it trickle on them as they climbed over the sides of the boat and onto the beach. One by one they went: Klann, Peterson, Ambrose, Kerrey, Schrier, Tucker, and Knepper, the whole squad, laden down with their usual assortment of armaments—automatic weapons, hand grenades, knives, communications gear, ammunition, and sundry other equipment needed to carry out and return safely from a secret operation in territory new to them.

Doc Schrier had the additional job of carrying a few medical supplies, morphine, and bandages. These didn't add much to his physical weight, only to his spirit, burdened with having the responsibility of patching up a wounded team member. With them was an eighth man—a *chieu hoi*, as Vietcong defectors were called—who had earlier been captured by U.S. forces on another mission and decided to offer his assistance to the government of Vietnam. He had provided the whereabouts of an enemy camp on the island that the Vietcong used to send sappers—individuals or small units who carried explosive satchels and mines—into nearby Navy harbors to blow up ships or buildings, especially those, if they could find them, that contained sizable amounts of ammunition. There had been a costly raid up the coast at the Navy base in Danang, where guerrillas destroyed ships and an ammo dump, killing nine Americans and wounding thirty-five. Sappers penetrated the supposedly secure Cam Rahn Bay installation as well. The sneak attacks had unnerved Hoffmann, who logged each incursion into his charts and records, but was unable to do much to stop them.

The *chieu hoi* had intelligence that a team of sappers and elements of the Vietcong infrastructure would be on Hon Tam on this night, preparing for a raid into the city of Nha Trang. By sending in the SEALs, Hoffmann hoped they might be able to knock out a few sappers and at least slow down the attacks.

Kerrey established one major objective in planning this mission: He did not want a repeat of what happened in Thanh Phong. The rules of engagement were overly restrictive and put his men at risk. But Kerrey, in his own way, was trying to atone for killing innocent women and children. None of the men had spoken about the raid on Thanh Phong, but several, including Kerrey, were haunted by it. "I made the conscious decision that we were not going to kill anybody," Kerrey said. "We were going to take them out alive."

The easiest route to the island was on the bay side, where the waters were calmer. From this direction, there was a gentle and open ascent to the top of Hon Tam, where eight Vietcong, including one woman, were supposed to be encamped. Kerrey discarded this option precisely because it was so predictable, arguing that it was a sure way of being spotted and killed. He wanted stealth at the expense of ease. That meant coming in from the ocean, where the typically high surf from the South China Sea broke violently onto the rocky beach. Getting safely onto the rough shoreline was not the problem; they had mastered this type of landing during Hell Week. The real challenge was a 350-foot rock cliff that in spots was nearly vertical. Add pitch darkness and the need for total silence, and this was a perilous entry. On the way up, Gerhard Klann could not help but think that if one of the men at the front loaded down with the usual armament and gear stumbled and fell, it was likely they all would plunge to their deaths on the rocks below.

At the base of the cliff, all of them, with the exception of Klann, removed their boots, choosing instead to "go native" and sneak up to their intended targets barefoot. After an hour or so of climbing, the exhausted men reached the top. The Vietcong were sleeping in two camps about fifty to seventy-five yards apart. There were three men and a woman in one camp—supposed Vietcong political leaders—and four enemy males in the other. Under orders from Kerrey to avoid enemy fatalities, Ambrose took Peterson, Tucker, Knepper, and the Vietcong defector and headed to the right, where he planned to circle around the four-man camp and put himself and his teammates into position to attack.

Kerrey, Klann, and Schrier were to follow a path that went to the left and above the camps, then come around so they would be facing Ambrose's group. Once in place, they would signal each other using a flashlight outfitted with a red lens. Splitting the squad in two was a dangerous tactic, not only because it divided their firepower, but also because it increased the chance of a friendly-fire incident. Splitting up was done only when the mission required it. But because of the layout of their targets, they had no choice.

It took Ambrose only a few minutes to reach the perimeter of the first encampment. On the way, however, he got a surprise—the *chieu hoi* broke into a full run in another direction. He didn't want any part of the ambush against his old friends, the Vietcong. There was nothing Ambrose could do, so he let him go. They would have to take their chances that he wouldn't alert any other enemy soldiers who happened to be on the island.

Ambrose waited the agreed upon time that it would take Kerrey and his teammates to get into position, then he took out his flashlight and sent his first signal. Nothing. He tried again and again, but Kerrey never responded. What could have gone wrong in the few minutes since he left Kerrey? There had been no gunfire, so they weren't dead or injured. Had their cover been blown and had they been captured? In the dark, it was impossible for Ambrose to see that he was in a ravine and too far below Kerrey, separated by the hilly terrain. There was no way they could see each other's flashlights.

Ambrose decided not to wait any longer, and with Peterson, Tucker, and Knepper inches behind him, began to edge closer to the enemy camp. Under the triple-layered canopy of trees and foliage that blocked out the stars and moon, it was "one of the darkest places I have ever been in my life," Ambrose said. He could hardly see his hand in front of his face. Unable to use their traditional hand signals, the SEALs had to whisper. In the vast quiet of the night every move was made with determined caution, as if they were operating in slow motion. A broken twig or a rustle of leaves could have fatal consequences. Every step seemed to take minutes rather than seconds. Even their strained breathing could be a giveaway. If the Vietcong could hear their hearts, pounding like drums inside their chests, they would for sure be found out.

They closed in, listening intently as they crept. Then Ambrose's face touched something. It did not feel like a natural part of the environment; it seemed to be man-made. His eyes glanced upward, and to his horror he had brushed up against a hammock occupied by a sleeping Vietcong soldier.

Quietly but with great firmness, Ambrose reached behind

to Knepper, who was just inches away. He grabbed his head hard, "to get my face as far as I could in his ear." Knepper quickly grasped what was happening. It would be impossible to turn around and creep away in silence. Even the slightest sound, particularly metal on metal—a knife on a buckle or a grenade brushing a rifle barrel—would awaken the sleeping guerrillas.

Then there was movement in the hammock. The enemy soldier, likely roused by the casual bump, stood up just inches away from Ambrose, and began slowly to walk away. A man close by in a second hammock woke and followed.

Now the SEALs were in a predicament. Open fire and they put Kerrey in jeopardy; continue to lay low and risk losing sight of two of the four Vietcong. It was more risky to allow armed and dangerous guerrillas to walk away so Ambrose decided to take them out. The team unleashed a barrage of automatic weapons fire, blindly shooting in the darkness and hoping that they had killed the four men. They couldn't be sure.

The familiar popping sound of the M-16 rifles on full automatic fire jolted Kerrey, Schrier, and Klann, who were huddled in the darkness. As they moved into position, Klann said he heard what he thought was Schrier's plastic rifle butt hitting a rock. "This was real rough terrain," he said. "It was pitch black and Schrier tripped. He hit his rifle butt against a rock and goes, 'Oh, shit!'"

The Vietcong, who were less than ten feet away, must have heard it, too. Kerrey, who had been running point, putting him out front and closest to the enemy, drew a bead on the first soldier he saw. "I went into a kind of hurdler's stance with my right foot stuck out over a rock," he recalled, pointing his M-16 at the enemy fighter's head and squeezing off several rounds. The next sound that Klann heard was horrifying: a pin flying from a grenade. The Vietcong had managed to pull the pin before he was shot. Kerrey and Schrier were close enough to take the full blast.

Klann watched as the explosion tossed Kerrey one way and thought he saw his weapon blown in the other direction. Schrier took a piece of shrapnel near his eye and was bleeding heavily. Kerrey was screaming in pain, and it was clear to Klann that his commanding officer was in bad shape. But there was nothing Klann could do at the moment. They were under fire, and Klann was using every scrap of his training and experience to repel the enemy. He was popping up every few seconds to crack off a few rounds from his Stoner machine-gun, a rapid-fire weapon that could shoot hundreds of bullets a minute.

Amidst the fire, Schrier moved over to attend to Kerrey's wounds. His lower calf was a mess, he had large shrapnel cuts and gashes in both legs, and several pieces of shrapnel in his upper chest, arms, hands, and head. The putrid odor of burning flesh wafted up from his wounded leg. His SEAL days were over. No more unimaginable heat, no more fire ants that bit like wasps, no more mosquitoes. "Don't forget the leeches," he said, the little bloodsuckers that attached to a human body while wading through muddy canals. Even so, this was not the way he wanted to go home to Bethany. It wouldn't be in a body bag, which he was thankful for. But life as he knew it had essentially ended. As he lay bloodied and wounded in the dirt among some rocks, Kerrey knew "that I was pretty bad. I knew that there was little chance I was going to be able to walk again."

Tucker, with the other SEAL contingent, could hear Kerrey yelling on his radio, but he wasn't sure if he was giving orders or yelling that he and Schrier had been hit or yelling something else at Schrier.

Kerrey, hanging on to consciousness, was dimly aware of the firefight exploding around him—a brief but brilliant burst of green and red tracer rounds zipping through the darkness. "It was not terribly long, a short firefight," he said. According to Navy reports, Klann had managed to kill the Vietcong and save Kerrey's life.

The initial reports that reached Hoffmann, recorded the SEAL team killing all eight of the Vietcong. It was exactly what Kerrey didn't want to do, but his men had no choice. Any other course would probably have meant their own deaths. Kerrey's insistence on taking everyone alive—clearly borne of the emotional fallout from Thang Phong—may well have cost him his own grave wounds. "It may have been that I went too far in the other direction," Kerrey said, in trying to take his captives alive. Hoffmann had heard such a report, too, and others that came in before the facts could be sorted out. Hoffmann at first believed that the soldier who confronted Kerrey with the grenade was female and that Kerrey waited too long before he pulled the trigger, not wanting to kill another woman. Klann did not remember it that way. He saw a person, whom he was sure was male, intent on killing the SEALs. "Kerrey barely had a chance," Klann said.

When it was over, Kerrey, pumped full of morphine, lay back in Klann's arms smoking a cigarette. Klann held him tightly, gently reassuring him that he would be OK, that he was going to live. The radioman called for a medivac chopper to come in and remove the injured squad leader. The pilot hovered over the thick jungle canopy, looking for a hole in the trees to lower a sling. Kerrey's Raiders loaded their leader, and the chopper swept off, taking him to the 26th Field Hospital at Cam Ranh Bay. He was later sent to Yokuska, Japan, then flown back to the east coast of the United States.

The rest of the men gathered up all of the enemy documents they could find, a bounty of intelligence, the Navy would say, and then at daylight left the island by boat.

Bravo squad had difficulty adjusting to life without Kerrey. They reunited with its sister unit, Alpha, under the command of Lieutenant Tim Wettack, and got a new lieutenant from San Diego who replaced Kerrey. Joseph Quincannon would find it hard going and instinctively knew that the men he was trying to lead never fully accepted him. Despite the adversarial feelings, Quincannon was a professional and did his best to push on.

The full platoon, under the command of Wettack and Quincannon, would spend the last three to four months of its tour operating in and around the Mekong Delta. They would see a lot of combat. Their after-action spot reports were full of encounters in the hamlets and villages they patrolled. Ambrose was constantly carping at Wettack, he said, complaining that the squad leader was taking unwarranted risks. It wasn't until Kerrey was gone that they realized what a buffer he had been. "Bob was protecting us from a lot of crazy operations," said Ambrose.

For Kerrey, a different kind of war was just beginning.

Chapter Ten

———————————————————

LIEUTENANT KERREY HAD NO idea what day it was, but he'd slowly regained enough consciousness to realize he was in the surgical recovery room at the Philadelphia Naval Hospital. Through blurry eyes that were just coming into focus, he could make out two figures sitting on the other side of the room, away from his bed.

Prompted by his stirring, James and Elinor Kerrey moved over to their son's bedside, where he lay with an assortment of tubing, monitors, and other medical devices attached to him. Kerrey wanted to sit up, to take measure of himself, literally, and what the surgeons had done to him. "I couldn't get up far enough to see," he said. He was too weak and immobile from the operation and the medication given to comfort him.

He looked at his mother and asked "an awful question," he said. It was almost unbearable for him to know the answer—and for Elinor to respond honestly.

"How much is left?" he asked.

"Son, there's a lot left," she said, moving close to him. Kerrey knew at once "she was not talking about the leg. She was talking about me. She didn't even look at the leg."

It was the right answer from a mother who was thankful that her son had come home alive, despite his traumatic injury. Elinor no doubt knew something like this could have happened to her boy, but like any mother during a war she knew, too, that such thoughts were best ignored while he was fighting in Vietnam. And her son played along, not wishing to raise her anxiety with accounts of his actions in places like Thanh Phong. His letters home were filled with everything *but* how dangerous his missions were. "Every single letter I wrote back was full of enthusiasm. Enthusiasm is an important device that everyone was reporting out of the war to communicate with friends and loved ones at home. You don't say, 'Jeez, tonight I went out and killed a bunch of people.' You don't go out and say, 'I suffered.' You say, 'Life is good.' You'd think I'm breezing along in a shopping center [from] reading the letters."

Before the Navy flew him back from Vietnam he lay in an overseas hospital bed grappling with how much to tell his parents about his wounds and his abbreviated combat tour. He was determined to deal with his injuries on his own terms. Initially, he instructed the Navy not to inform his family that he'd been maimed, and his superiors complied, sending off a terse message: "Subject does not desire notification of NOK [next of kin]." Eventually, Kerrey wrote home on March 15 and March 18, sending letters on Red Cross stationery from Japan, telling his family that he was fine. "Both letters were full of lies," he said. His next conversation with his parents, a phone call, was upbeat, too, though he told them he wasn't sure the doctors could save his mangled foot. "There's a good chance they'll save it," he said. When it was time to choose between several government hospitals for treatment, he selected Philadelphia, he said, because of its distance from Lincoln.

Kerrey was a changed man when he was admitted to the Philadelphia Navy Hospital on March 24, 1969. The love and patriotism he had once felt for his country were gone; the doubts he had harbored about the war before going to Vietnam had hardened into anger and deep despair. Kerrey was assigned to quarters in SOQ 12, an area of the hospital for sick officers. Instead of the strapping young men he had lived with in the SEAL community, his new bunkmates were the human detritus of war: officers whose arms and legs were blown off or whose eyes and hands were missing.

Suicide was not an uncommon thought in SOQ 12. Depression and despondency often captured patients on even their best days. Some, broken in spirit as well as body, retreated within themselves, resistant to anyone who tried to help them. Amputees with more positive attitudes were determined to master their wooden prostheses from the hospital's limb and brace shop. And there were those, too, who remained defiant and rebellious in their attitude toward the government for turning them into invalids and in some cases freaks who felt they had forever been set apart from the rest of humanity. Gallows humor was in evidence across the ward. Some patients scrawled on the back of their wheelchairs slogans like: "The Marine Corps builds stumps" or "Another project sponsored by your federal tax dollar." Patients threw model airplane gliders, some doused in lighter fluid and set aflame, out of their windows to keep morale up and boredom at bay. Threats of courts-martial under the Uniform Code of Military Justice carried little weight. "What are you going to do, send me to Vietnam?" was the popular retort to administrators.

The mercurial, outspoken Kerrey fit well within the tortured mainstream of military hospital life during his six-month stay. The first time Marine Lieutenant Lewis Puller, Jr., encountered the wounded SEAL he was shouting along to a tape of Aretha Franklin's "Respect," the volume cranked up well above what the rules allowed. While Kerrey sang along with Aretha, he tried to snap pictures of his mangled leg. Handing the camera to Puller, he asked him to photograph his leg so he could send the pictures back to the local American Legion in Lincoln, Nebraska. Puller, who'd just vacated the bed assigned to Kerrey, later wrote that he exchanged glances with his ex-roommate, Jim Crotty, and wondered if the young Nebraskan "was delirious or just marching to the beat of a different drum."

Now living off the ward but returning regularly for physical therapy, Puller knew something about how war ravaged the body and the soul. The son of Lewis "Chesty" Puller, the famous Marine Corps general, he detonated a booby-trapped howitzer shell near the village of Viem Dong. The explosion eviscerated his legs, leaving stumps that barely protruded from his pelvis, removed most of his left hand, and blew off his right thumb and little finger. Nearly a quarter-century later, he would publish a Pulitzer Prize–winning memoir of his struggles, *Fortunate Son: The Healing of a Vietnam Vet.*

Kerrey's pot stirring, encouraged and chronicled by Puller, became notorious. He considered it an invasion of privacy when the medical staff began to check his urine and stools for signs of internal bleeding. Using forceps he lifted from a medical cart, he dropped different-colored jelly beans in his bowel movements. According to Puller, the Navy corpsmen complained that Kerrey was setting a bad example for the enlisted personnel who looked up to the officers as role models. When confronted by the head nurse, Kerrey threatened to replace the jelly beans with his car keys. "I don't know if that was defiant or not," Kerrey recalled. "I mean, I didn't feel defiant."

The over-the-top humor didn't come as easily during his first days as a patient, when doctors began to evaluate the best course of treatment for his ravaged hands and legs. Both hands were heavily wrapped in medical dressings, and both legs had sustained damage, with the right one the worse of the two. Kerrey, initially, refused to take narcotics for his wounds. Other patients, dependent on drugs to blunt their pain, marveled at his high threshold for the throbbing in his limbs. "His stoicism, though unnerving, was a source of amazement to all," Puller wrote of Kerrey. Though Puller knew that Kerrey's wounds were not as severe or as painful as his, he wanted affirmation for his view that morphine was indispensable to recovery. Instead, Kerrey asked for a fungo bat to beat back the phantom pains after his limb had been amputated. The image of a bullet-biting Kerrey refusing to take pain medication became a legend when he was in the Senate. But it wasn't entirely true: His boycott of narcotics was only temporary. "I eventually got quite comfortable taking Demerol to ease the pain," Kerrey said.

Kerrey's wariness of painkillers stemmed from his pharmaceutical training at the University of Nebraska. He knew that narcotics could impair his judgment in critical decisions about his treatment. Philadelphia was the primary amputation center on the East Coast, and patients arrived by the busloads. ("A garbage can where all the ugliness of Vietnam was thrown," Kerrey said of the hospital.) Overworked medical staff had to make spur-of-the-moment decisions about amputations, and there was little time for extended discussion or sentimentality. Kerrey was determined that he would be part of the decision-making process when it came to his own wounds. During one of his first operations, to repair a badly injured hand, Kerrey had insisted on a local anesthetic. It turned out to be a good decision; he had to tell the attending physician that he was prepping the wrong hand for surgery. "Early on I wanted to be as alert as possible to make what was going to be a very important decision [as to] whether to amputate the leg."

The surgeon who had examined Kerrey's right leg had told him he would try and save as much as possible. But when the plaster cast put on in Southeast Asia was removed, it revealed damage that was so extensive there could be only one course of action. "By then it was gangrene in the foot," Kerrey said. "And there were two toes left. Heel was gone. My ankle was gone, and there was just a mass of tissue when they opened up the cast. Wasn't much left." From his discussions with other amputees in the hospital, Lieutenant Kerrey learned that a longer stump was key to a quicker and easier rehabilitation. "Having a stump that was long enough to be able to maneuver would determine how functional I was going to be when I got out," he said. In the end, surgeons removed the lower portion of his right leg to about mid-calf, which put him in better shape than Puller and the other amputees. Even so, it was far from the end of the story. Over the next eight years, Kerrey needed nearly ten operations and prosthetic fittings as part of his physical rehabilitation.

In the days after the military surgeons cut away the flesh and sawed off the bone, Kerrey lapsed into self-pity. He had joined the Navy SEALs, an elite corps that required nearly indomitable physical strength. Now he was a cripple. Emotionally, he had gone from a good kid with strong values to a killer. He was a different man now. Angry. Confused. Weak. Helpless to do little more than protest the morning rounds when doctors tore away bandages to examine the patients' freshly sutured stumps. The bloody process left brave men screaming in pain or hiding from physicians to avoid the daily torture. He came to resent how every day at SOQ 12 seemed to rob him of his independence and pride. "This self-assured boy suddenly could not walk, could not so much as go the bathroom, without asking others for help. It's hard not to be humble," he said, "when they stick a bed pan under you."

SOQ 12's usual visitors were family members and close friends of the wounded. Latch Hoffmann was neither when he walked into Kerrey's hospital room. The Pattonlike captain of Task Force 115 was in civilian clothes, but there was something far more surprising about his look—one of contrition.

Kerrey was astonished at the visit. "It must have been April or May, not long after I was here. He looked completely different. He wanted to talk, he wanted to see how I was doing.

"Something happened. You could see it in his eyes. What I saw when I went over [to Vietnam] was Kurtz," Kerrey said, referring to the officer gone mad in *Apocalypse Now*. "Then I see him when he comes back, there is sadness there. I knew he was very troubled by his command and what had happened. And I knew he took a considerable amount of responsibility. And something . . . happened to him to cause him to wonder about what he was doing. Bottom line is that here is a Navy captain, a four-striper. All of his career he's trained for war at sea. And all of a sudden he's given command in a guerrilla war where the rules are completely different. So you know, he's trying to fight the war the best he can. And he's making good judgments, some of them are bad like we all make, and I have no doubt that he carries the burden of some of those decisions pretty substantially."

Kerrey never learned exactly what had transformed Hoffmann. It may have had something to do with another patient on the floor who served in Task Force 115. Kerrey had become friends with a naval officer who said Hoffmann forced him to take his Swift boat on a risky operation up a narrow canal without air cover. An ambush killed several of his men, and he lost his right leg below the knee to a 50-caliber round. When they met in Philadelphia, he told Kerrey that he planned to kill Captain Hoffmann for his reckless order.

"So when Hoffmann walked into my room I was quite surprised and quite concerned for his health because this guy was just two or three doors down," Kerrey said. "I told him [his friend], 'You're not going to believe who just walked into my room.' My friend broke down. It was a very moving moment."

Years later, Hoffmann spoke bitterly about Kerrey and denied he'd undergone any sea change. "I never went back on the war like he did," he said, with a tone of anger in his voice that grew harsher when he recalled Kerrey openly opposing U.S. involvement in Vietnam at antiwar rallies.

At the time of his visit, Hoffmann was in on an open secret

about young Lieutenant Kerrey. The Navy was in the process of upgrading an award for heroism that Kerrey's teammates, Gerhard Klann and Mike Ambrose, had submitted their commander for. In SEAL training Kerrey told his men that he did not like medals and "would prefer you give everybody a Purple Heart before they get over [to Vietnam]. When they get shot take it away from them. I'm just pretty negative toward the whole medal system to begin with."

Kerrey was originally set to receive a Bronze Star, a medal handed out with some frequency in Vietnam. While Ambrose felt that their foray up the cliff and into an enemy camp "was not an Audie Murphy mission," he thought that his old SEAL roommate still merited a higher decoration. Despite things going poorly, Kerrey was the officer in charge, and he had led a raid that wiped out a small sapper team and members of the Vietcong infrastructure. He wanted to give Kerrey a Silver Star. Klann, who like Kerrey felt a considerable feat of bravery was required for the highest awards, insisted on a Bronze Star. Some naval officer in Saigon changed the paperwork, and Kerrey got a Silver Star. Schrier was to get a Silver Star, too, for taking care of Kerrey while under fire. Ambrose was slated to receive a Bronze Star, and the rest of the team, including Klann, were put in for Navy Commendation Medals.

From there, the peculiar politics of service medals went into motion. The commander in chief of the Pacific Fleet sent a message on April 4, 1969, to the secretary of the Navy and the chief of naval operations: "Recommend approval of Navy Cross vice Silver Star medal to Lt. jg. Joseph R. Kerrey." Back in Washington, Admiral Elmo Zumwalt, who left his job as commander of naval forces Vietnam and was now the chief of naval operations, had decided that Kerrey's Navy Cross, the highest decoration in the naval service, should be upgraded once again. American involvement in the war was close to over, and none of the SEALs, who had been operating for several years in Vietnam, had yet to receive the Medal of Honor.

The naval hierarchy felt that the SEALs needed to be recognized for their bravery and that Kerrey should be the first to win the Medal of Honor. (Before U.S. forces pulled out of Vietnam entirely, two more SEALs would be selected for the award.) Kerrey would learn about the Navy's decision in the summer of 1969, while he was still recuperating in the hospital.

Unarguably, it was a great honor. That's how most saw it, including Kerrey's pals on SOQ 12, who were overjoyed that one of their own would soon receive such a tribute. Their glee was not only for Kerrey, but for themselves, too. "I sat in the hospital with a wounded guy who lost one leg above the knee and the other was mangled," he said. The wounded man had stepped on a land mine trying to save a comrade. "He got nothing. But he was proud to know me. It helped him that someone he liked got the medal." Kerrey's new stature as a hero allowed him to escalate his war against what he believed was an overbearing medical staff, according to Puller. And his fellow patients, only half in jest, taunted their caregivers to watch out or they would sick Lieutenant Kerrey on them.

But the medal also triggered a deep soul searching. Kerrey despaired over his actions on Hon Tam and wondered if they were worthy of such recognition. A good number of veterans selected for the Medal of Honor had the same experience: feelings of inadequacy and shame for being singled out when the men who had fought at their side were just as brave.

Kerrey had the additional burden of his role in the slaughter of as many as twenty-seven innocent women and children. That dark memory made an award for valor seem especially out of place. Even more troubling, was the Navy awarding him a Bronze Star and Combat V (for valor) for the raid into Thanh Phong. The brief inquiry by Cook's headquarters into the massacre was pushed aside and never completed.

Kerrey was angry, confused, and not sure whether to accept the Medal of Honor. It was not easy for him to leave the hospital, and he did so only on rare occasions. But he felt he had to journey back to Coronado, California, to talk with friends and mentors at SEAL headquarters about his initial impulse to turn Nixon down cold and reject the award. One way or the other, his decision would have an impact on the entire SEAL community; for the first time, one of their own was up for the nation's highest military honor, yet he was contemplating rejecting it, an act akin to throwing it back in the president's face. If he went through with his protest, the resulting black mark would taint the Navy's special operations community for years to come. It was only appropriate to consult those likely to be affected.

His last trip off hospital grounds had been a nightmare. In May 1969, before he went to San Diego, Kerrey ventured out to the first annual Martin Luther King track meet in Philadelphia. Though not wearing a uniform, his youthful looks, short hair, and empty pant leg gave him away as a veteran, and he was accosted by antiwar activists. "I was pushed down and called a killer," said Kerrey. "They're some of the most violently hateful people towards people like myself. They believe I murdered their children. They say that in letters and in speeches."

A month later, Kerrey went home for the first time after being wounded. For his trip he wore his uniform though only to get a reduced airfare. The smell of lilacs in the warm early summer air on the drive home from the airport in Lincoln reminded him of his boyhood. And while he wasn't accosted, the visit was another lonely, frightening experience. He stayed in his old room downstairs, but sleep did not come easily. When he closed his eyes, he was haunted by the screams of his Vietnamese victims. When he finally fell asleep, the first bout of nightmares began. He said nothing to his family about them during mealtimes. Kerrey went out on Saturday night to a bar with an old friend and skipped church on Sunday. Later that day he flew back to Philadelphia, relieved to be returning to the safety of SOQ 12.

In his fall trip across country to Coronado, there was one SEAL in particular Kerrey wanted to consult with, Barry Enoch, a devout Christian who had been a SEAL instructor Kerrey admired and trusted. "I valued his opinion," he said. "I am probably not the only man who should give Barry credit for acquiring the skills needed to survive. He was a teacher, a leader who would follow orders, and a follower who knew how to save the rear end of many a green officer . . . and do so to everyone's benefit."

Little had changed in the two years since Kerrey had flown off to Saigon. "The Grinder" was still packed with Tadpoles struggling under the merciless glare of the noncoms. Young men vying for a spot on a SEAL team still ran the beaches with telephone poles and still staggered through Hell Week. Enoch had changed little since the last time Kerrey had seen him: hair high and tight, and, though remarkably fit, he still sported a small paunch around his middle. Even his tours in Vietnam, the last with several students from Kerrey's Class 42 on his squad, had done little to reduce his spare tire.

Enoch was lecturing a group of tanned, muscular students seated at his feet, listening to the words of the old master. Kerrey had once been in the same spot, a young Tadpole who had overcome the physical rigors of SEAL training and then shipped out to Vietnam, where most of these men would be going. Out of the corner of his eye, Enoch caught a glimpse of Kerrey. "He was standing on crutches over to the side, away from us. I could tell he wanted to talk. We walked off to talk and he said he didn't think he deserved the Medal of Honor," Enoch recalled. "I could tell he was hurting about it."

If Kerrey had come seeking a way to accept the medal without compromising his feelings, he found it in Enoch's response. "Barry advised me to accept the Medal of Honor for everyone whose actions weren't seen, reported, or perhaps even recorded. 'Take it for all of us,' he said. And I did."

But Kerrey was not let off the hook so easily by others in the SEAL community. "I would have given him a Purple Heart and kicked his one-legged ass across base for blowing a mission," said Roy Boehm, one of the original SEALs, who years later examined the Hon Tam operation. Kerrey's Raiders didn't back away from their commander's heroism, but a few rolled their eyes at the hype generated by the White House and Navy press machines. The Navy press release, drafted with typically brassy language, was even more melodramatic, and in some cases untrue, not intentionally so, but written in a way to convey the image that Kerrey was a true American hero. The Navy had Kerrey "bleeding profusely" and "barely conscious" but amazingly still in "superlative control." To the best of the team's recollection, and according to after-action reports, no prisoners were taken, yet the "confused enemy quit and surrendered."

The citations of "courageous and inspiring leadership, valiant fighting spirit and tenacious devotion to duty" left some of Fire Team Bravo with mixed feelings that would linger for years. Some SEALs believed Klann should have received the Medal of Honor, or at least the Navy Cross, for his bravery on Hon Tam. "I think he's a great individual, a very aggressive officer, [and a] very good, very good leader," said Klann. But "when I read this award citation it was enough to make me throw up." He was disheartened at the Navy for what he and other SEALs believed was politicizing the Medal of Honor. "We were all upset about that at first," Klann said, "but throughout the years, we said, 'Hey, he's the one that's got to live with it.' He's always had misgivings about accepting that medal. He always has. He told me that on a couple of occasions."

Several months after the May 1970 White House ceremony, Klann and a few members of Delta Platoon were in

New Orleans, and after several hours of drinking they telephoned Kerrey from a bar in the French Quarter. "Get your butt down here," Klann told him. Kerrey obliged, and caught a flight to New Orleans. He was picked up by Mike Ambrose, Dwight Daigle, a member of the other squad in Delta Platoon, and Daigle's sister, in a Tempest convertible. On the drive back, with the convertible top down, somebody threw a lit cigarette into the well the Tempest's top dropped into. A small fire started, so Daigle's sister, who was driving, pulled the car off to the side of the road. The men then urinated on the flames to douse the fire, laughing the entire time.

Later, after another night of drinking, talk turned to the Medal of Honor. The discussion grew ugly as Klann remembers it. "We gave him a pretty hard time," he said. Ambrose recalls the barbs as a bit edgy, but not too bad. And Daigle described it as nothing out of the ordinary when a bunch of SEALs get together. But for Kerrey, it was not a comfortable setting, and he became defensive, reminding his former teammates that he didn't put in for the medal and almost turned it down. He acquiesced because Enoch urged him to take it for the teams—for everybody.

In the end, the medal brought Kerrey more grief than was fair. His bravery was not an issue. Until he was knocked out of the action in the Hon Tam operation, he stood and fought and was wounded in the process. When the firefight was over, he was lucid enough, despite his serious wounds and injections of morphine, to order his team to set up a defensive perimeter. It was the naval bureaucracy that distorted the incident to turn Kerrey into a public hero.

Though he had enough of a conscience to be troubled about accepting the honor, his antagonists in the SEAL community felt he should have refused, regardless of the political pressure from above or assurance from Enoch. "He should not have been given the award or accepted it," said Roy Boehm, whose own combat record was legendary. Kerrey did his best to endure the criticism, but he clearly resented it. Some SEALs "believed that the Medal of Honor operation was all trumped up. So fine. I don't give a shit. I don't care," said Kerrey. "I didn't want the goddamn medal, almost didn't accept it."

Kerrey found a more friendly reception from Puller, his wife Toddy, and Jim Crotty, who shared a room with both men on SOQ 12. Shortly after the White House ceremony, the trio threw a party in Kerrey's honor at the Pullers' Philadelphia apartment. Patients from the hospital were invited, and the place was decorated in red, white, and blue for the occasion. The Pullers brought in food and spirits for their guests. In his memoir, Puller wrote how Kerrey regaled the group with stories about Nixon's bad breath and Secretary of Defense Melvin Laird's diminutive size. And he recounted a debate between Kerrey and a career Marine in which the freshly minted hero defended the antiwar movement's right to carry out peaceful, nonviolent demonstrations. Kerrey astonished Puller when he recounted how he told the enraged Marine that he sympathized with those employing illegal means to protest illegal or immoral policies. "I had never heard him make such a radical statement," Puller noted in *Fortunate Son.* "His thoughts about the political process had obviously gone beyond mine."

What Puller didn't know was the shame and anguish that lay under the surface of Kerrey's words. Kerrey had never confided in him about Thanh Phong, a wartime atrocity the protestors would no doubt label as illegal and immoral. Though Puller and Kerrey grew very close, each grappled with demons of war and memory in his own way. Kerrey found a way to survive but Puller did not. The son of the famous Marine Corps general committed suicide with a gun in May 1994, three years after his memoir was published. Kerrey wrote a moving poem to his friend, with each line written in different colors—reds, greens, yellows, and blues—which he framed and hung in his Senate office. Though troubled by the death, Kerrey told me that Puller had freed his wife from an unbearable burden of having to care for an emotional and physical cripple.

At the party, something else about Kerrey caught Puller's notice. Kerrey "did not allow the medal and its silk-lined box out of his sight for the entire night." As ambivalent as he was, he knew the medal held a magical power. Public recognition as a war hero had its benefits, which Kerrey would come to realize when he began to rebuild his life at home.

Chapter Eleven

─────────■─────────

IN OCTOBER 1969, A GAUNT Bob Kerrey put on his dress blue uniform and caught a military flight to Offutt Air Force base near Omaha. From there, he hitchhiked home to Bethany, slipping back into town with little notice, just another wounded Vietnam veteran returning from the war. There were no cheering crowds or politicians waving welcome-home proclamations, but there was the security offered by his father and the unconditional love of Elinor, which Bob Kerrey desperately needed. "He and my mother probably kept me alive," Kerrey said.

He was only twenty-six, but he looked much older now. The youthful ease he radiated when he entered Officer Candidate School in Rhode Island was gone. So was the taste for mischief and pranks. His face was drawn, and his once muscular body, hardened by the rigorous SEAL training, was frail and diminished. He weighed only 140 pounds, including his new wooden leg. And his blue eyes, framed by dark sockets, carried the look of fear and uncertainty. There was no escape from what happened in Thanh Phong. "It sneaks up on you," Kerrey said. "I'd try to run away from it, but you don't run away from it. It's like running away from your shadow. You can't do it."

Losing the security and camaraderie of SOQ 12 only heightened Kerrey's sense of terror. "I was safe in the hospital," he said. It was a place where he could brood in the company of those who understood what the brutality of war did to a man's soul. At home, outside the walls of the ward, he feared going to sleep because his nightmares were full of screams and the rotting faces of the women and children killed in Thanh Phong. Each one asked him "Why?"

"I couldn't shut my eyes. It was just violent, horrible things happening to me and to others. That's what hell is. You know, when you think about hell and you imagine what hell is, you imagine horrible things happening. You're upside down in ice for a millennium. People boiling in oil and terrible things happening to 'em. Well, hell's not an imaginary thing. It's a real place and you can experience it on earth. I experienced it on that night. I've been there."

Family and friends feared for him and started to wonder whether he would adjust. "We were a little nervous," said his sister Nancy. "No one knew what he wanted to do." To old fraternity buddy John Gottschalk he appeared devoured by grief and in need of comradeship. "The call went out," according to Gottschalk, "that Kerrey was in bad shape, not so much physically as mentally." Kerrey started to wonder if his life was worth living, not to the point of planning specific ways to kill himself, but contemplating suicide nonetheless. "I was afraid that an active effort to remember would cause me to lose the will to live." He carried tremendous guilt, he said, and "guilt gets you to do bad things to yourself."

He decided it was time to tell somebody about Thanh Phong, hoping that it would, at the very least, ease some of the misery that was overwhelming him. The safest person to confide in was Elinor. But almost immediately after sharing his memory with his mother, he realized it was a mistake, that he had inflicted too much pain on her. "Oh, it was a horrible thing to say to her," Kerrey said. "I mean, it was something she didn't need to hear. All she could do was cry and hold me and say, 'It's gonna be all right.' I don't know what I was thinking. After I walked away, I said, 'Jesus, what did I do that for?' I felt like I was just hurting her. I mean, she gave me what I needed. And what she gave me was some love and some self-respect and told me, 'Everything is gonna be all right.'"

His second attempt at catharsis, with his minister at Bethany Christian Church, was less excruciating but no more fruitful. "I was trying to get him to help me," Kerrey recalled. "I used to sit in church—I felt like I was a special person in God's eyes. And I didn't anymore." He approached the pastor, seeking forgiveness. "Reverend, can I ever be forgiven for this?" Kerrey asked. "What do you do with this? Is there anything I can do?" The churchman responded that "forgiveness is possible in all things." But asking Jesus to absolve him and expecting it to happen with a few words of repentance was too simple for Kerrey. It didn't require any suffering, any penance. "I didn't believe him," Kerrey said.

Unable to achieve any sense of peace privately, Kerrey made his first public expiation of his sins. In December 1969, shortly after his formal retirement from the Navy, he gave an extraordinary interview to Gwen Drake, a reporter for his hometown newspaper, the *Lincoln Evening Journal*. "I can tell you this, if I had to go into the military now, feeling the way I do, I would go to jail first." The paper buried the article about the despondent young combat veteran inside on page forty and ran it on Christmas in 1969 with a photograph of Kerrey changing records on a phonograph.

Kerrey complained to Drake that the public was repulsed by the sight of disfigured amputees like himself. "They don't give a damn that I lost a leg over there," he told the reporter. His tone throughout the short piece was full of anger and dark hints about Thanh Phong. "After fighting over there, and doing things you don't want to talk about, you cannot live with yourself unless you believe you did what you did for a reason," he said.

Kerrey even spoke to the massacre at My Lai, exposed a month earlier by the investigative journalist Seymour Hersh. Kerrey's comments were unguarded and telling. He was against any form of personal censure for those involved at My Lai regardless of the brutalities that occurred. Kerrey believed the Army soldiers who committed the atrocities against hundreds of innocent villagers, most of whom were women and children, did so because of intensive military training. "The military establishment in this country trains men to be animals, to kill without thinking about it, and that's what you become over there, an animal." There is little doubt he was referring to himself without the specifics of what he did, subtle expressions reinforced by telling Drake, "I doubt My Lai is an isolated incident."

Kerrey was a bit mortified when the piece ran, not because he had qualms about being described as a "slightly angry young man who appears alienated," but because of his concern that he was accusing family and friends in Lincoln of coldheartedness to veterans. In a letter to the editor of the *Evening Journal*, he claimed that his time at Philadelphia Naval Hospital had made him "extremely pacific and cautious."

As he began giving voice to his pain, Kerrey was also taking his first tentative steps into the antiwar movement. In late 1969 Nebraskans For Peace was gaining notoriety, a difficult task in the conservative heartland. The group had evolved from an ad hoc collection of farmers, mostly Quakers and Mennonites, and antiwar activists at the university in Lincoln. While not as influential as other protest movements around the nation, "it was big for here. It felt kind of dangerous," said Dan Ladely, an organizer who befriended Kerrey.

Kerrey's experience with Nebraskans For Peace was, like his relationship with the military, complicated and laced with ambivalence. His latter-day image as an antiwar firebrand did not reflect the reality. (Nebraska Republicans circulated a rumor, for example, that he tossed his Medal of Honor into a makeshift wooden coffin during a peace demonstration. Kerrey said it never happened.)

"He went to a handful of antiwar rallies, but he wasn't a major player. He wasn't involved in the planning of demonstrations," said Ladely, who helped to seize the University of Nebraska's Military Sciences Building, where Bob Kerrey had done his ROTC training. The takeover occurred just after the May 4, 1970, killings at Kent State, which galvanized the protest movement across the country. To protest the Ohio National Guard's shooting of students, Kerrey chose to attend a large antiwar rally downtown instead of the University of Nebraska sit-in.

Kerrey was uncomfortable with the anti-American, and anti-veteran, character of the peace movement. Unlike many of his fellow demonstrators, he hated only the war, not the grunts in the field who were only following orders and trying to get home alive. He loathed Nixon, not the government. "Kerrey had a genuine interest in keeping more people from dying," said Paul Olson, one of the early founders, with his wife, Betsy, of Nebraskans For Peace.

But the movement and the Medal of Honor–winner needed and used each other. "We thought of him as a carnation we wore on our lapel," said Olson, acutely aware of the marquee value of having a war hero in his camp. As for Kerrey, antiwar activism became therapy by other means, an outlet for the roiling emotions inside. Speaking out gave him the opportunity to lay blame on others, particularly the Nixon White House, for the war and, by extension, for his own hidden deeds. "He was going through some sort of a spiritual search," Olson recalled. "He was a very troubled guy at that point, a man who was suffering psychologically. I'm not sure he knew what he wanted."

Crowds who listened to Kerrey had no reason to suspect his commitment to the cause. Even some of the leaders of Nebraskans For Peace were taken by this young maverick who, to them, had finally seen the light and the folly of Nixon's war. "People around him *wanted* him to be antiwar," said Marilyn McNabb, a statewide coordinator for the group. So much so, she said, that they saw a devotion in Kerrey that wasn't entirely there. "[We] valued him but knew his limitations," Olson said. He was, in fact, a double-edged sword. In one speech in front of the post office in Lincoln, Kerrey mesmerized the antiwar crowds. For Lincoln, the protest was remarkable. Some seventy-year-old women who were hippies got up and spoke. Protestors who were stoned from smoking marijuana went to the stage and addressed the crowd. "Bob Kerrey got up," said Olson. "Wow!"

Olson's euphoria did not last long. Afterward, Kerrey left the horde of antiwar protestors and went to an American Legion post where he delivered a much more toned-down speech to the prowar members.

June Levine, a professor of literature at the university, was intrigued by Kerrey and did not pass judgment on him for his fickleness. He had first approached Levine by asking if he could "do an independent study with me, like a tutorial," she said. His story, what little Levine knew of it, was compelling, and she encouraged him to write about his personal experiences in the war. She could see that "he was in a period of great confusion and anger," and she thought writing would help him work through the inner demons he carried with him. "I had assumed he would want to write about the war. The war was a big thing on Bob's mind," she said. Kerrey had tried, he said, but couldn't make his prose readable.

Levine was sympathetic and became a mentor and lifelong friend to him. At the debut of the antiwar movie *Coming Home*, Levine and a friend saw Kerrey entering the theater alone and asked if he'd like to sit with them. "We were quite shaken by the movie," she recalled, "so we went for a cup of coffee to talk about it. I asked Bob if he felt the movie was accurate." Kerrey replied, "Not really, it was much worse."

Levine was struck by his tone. "He said it in such a way, that I knew [his coming home] had been a deep nightmare."

Kerrey was wandering in an emotional wilderness, searching for some thread of meaning, as the fall of 1970 began. He telephoned Levine from San Francisco and told her he planned to enroll in a writing program at San Francisco State. In a few days, he called again, saying he had switched plans; it was now a masters in business administration from Stanford. But a few days before classes were to start, he withdrew and headed for the University of California at Berkeley.

Kerrey let his hair grow long and then grew a moustache, as befit a wandering spirit who was drawn to existential stories about suffering. Berkeley was at opposite ends on the political spectrum from Nebraska, but Kerrey relished the atmosphere, the free thinking, the openness, and the pleasures of personal exploration. And in writing poetry—about love and laughter, relationships, politics, and his grief over Vietnam—he found another form of therapy that would become a life-long pursuit.

Kerrey enrolled in a course at the University of California at Berkeley called "The Quest for Authentic Self in Modern Literature," and was immediately struck by the professor, Oscar Pemantle, and his reading list: D. H. Lawrence's *Lady Chatterley's Lover*, Herman Hesse's *Demian*, and Franz Kafka's *Metamorphosis*. Pemantle was looking for emotional depth in his students, and used the Socratic teaching method to draw them out and explain their feelings about the books. "I did notice Bob Kerrey right away, from the first minutes of the class," Pemantle recalled. "He had a slightly intense look on his face. Very serious. He caught everything." Fourteen years later Governor Kerrey was still thinking about the professor's class. It had "the most profound impact on the way I read, listen and think," he wrote in a letter to Pemantle. He then brought him to Nebraska to help improve the state's education programs.

Kerrey was in a period of transformation, hungry for West Coast counterculture, but still nourished by his Nebraskan roots. He returned home from California in the spring of 1971 a more confident man but still not fully certain what his future would be. That summer his father's business partner, Larry Price, offered a guiding but firm hand in bringing the young Kerrey back into the mainstream of Lincoln's business community. Price was chairman of the Easter Seals in Nebraska and asked Kerrey to become developmental director for a new camp, a job that required raising money for the $750,000 facility. "It didn't take much convincing," Kerrey told Lincoln's local newspaper, since he'd been interested in helping handicapped children before Price's request. He said he planned to crisscross Nebraska, "living in communities wherever I'm invited." The highlight of his Easter Seals involvement, he recalled years later, came during the camp's opening ceremonies when one of the children "vomited on the governor."

Kerrey was searching for some personal stability, something that would give him direction. But as much as he tried to find and lay down an acceptable structure in his life, the specter of Vietnam kept getting in the way. This time he was drawn back into antiwar politics by Allard Lowenstein, a charismatic campus agitator who had organized the "Dump Johnson" movement to drive LBJ out of the presidency. A one-time acolyte of Robert Kennedy, Lowenstein was now registering eighteen-year-olds, reminding them that they were of draft age and headed for the war in Vietnam if they didn't vote Richard Nixon out of office in 1972. The idea of trying to end the war by actively enfranchising young men appealed to Kerrey. It allowed him to dabble in politics—on a stage larger than the one offered by Nebraskans For Peace. As he made plans to travel to New York to meet Lowenstein, Kerrey, still a registered Republican, stated publicly, "President Nixon should not be reelected." As bland as the remark was, coming from a Medal of Honor winner it made news in Lincoln and was picked up by the national wire services.

At the same time, working with Lowenstein enabled him to pursue a cause he felt strongly about. "I hated the draft. It was so unfairly selective. I grew to despise it," Kerrey said. "It provides a privilege based upon income and based upon class that I think is wrong." The modest wealth of his own family had enabled him to attend college and avoid the draft for four years. Kerrey's devotion to poor, less fortunate families whose sons were forced by the lottery into military service in Vietnam was genuine. It was a cause he refused to abandon and a topic he would debate anywhere.

At a gathering of Medal of Honor recipients in the late 1970s, Kerrey and fellow medal winner Bobbie Howard "got drunk one night" and exchanged strong words about military service. "Draft them when they are thirty," Kerrey told Howard, "then we'll find out if your cause is worth a damn."

Howard was not persuaded and replied that "would never work because of this simple truth: You give me a man between the ages of eighteen and twenty-five, and you give me the power to control when they eat and when they sleep, and I can get any swinging dick in America to do anything that I want for me. But when they get to be twenty-six, twenty-seven, twenty-eight, especially thirty, all they do is ask questions and they aren't worth a damn."

Well into their cups, the two warriors began talking about their dreams. Howard described one of duty and honor that left Kerrey with tears in his eyes. "Bobby said, 'My dream is to be at the top of the hill with the battalion of men that have been fighting with me for two weeks. We're nursing our wounds and digging in our positions. We spend the night on that hill and the next morning as the mist is burning off the ground, before the sun comes up, that wonderful time, such a perfect time to attack because it's very hard to see human beings moving in it because the colors aren't quite there.'

And he says, 'I see something moving and I realize that all the Communists in the world are coming up the hill after us. And I wait right to the last minute and I turn to my men at the last minute and I say, 'Fix bayonets.' "

Kerrey came away still opposed to selective service, but believing Howard's point about age and persuasion was right. "I love warriors," he said. "I love what they do. I'm [a] self-confessed patriot who loves and respects what men and women do when they volunteer their service in the military forces." His only caveat was one of caution for the armed forces. "We should talk about the moral consequences of our action." The recruiters and generals, Kerrey said, who say, " 'Listen, if you talk about this kind of thing, we'll never be able to get them to do what it is you have to do in war,' they're deceiving themselves, kidding themselves. We have to be honest. We don't want to field a battalion of tough guys who have no idea what it is that they're doing. You want a group of people who say, 'I don't like killing, but it's necessary in order for me to accomplish my objective.' "

For Kerrey, joining the Lowenstein cause "was a safer alternative," Marilyn McNabb said, "to the long-haired veterans" who had begun Vietnam Veterans Against the War. The VVAW was formed in January 1971, attracting those who were unsure about protesting against their government, despite their belief that the war was wrong. The timidity did not last long, said Tim Butz, one of the organizers. The initial membership of 500 veterans surged to 10,000 within a year, due mostly to the support of Jane Fonda and an ad in *Playboy* magazine proclaiming that the Vietnam veterans were organizing against American military adventurism in Indochina. With Fonda's personal interest and money, the VVAW became perhaps the leading antiwar effort in the country, attracting a broad spectrum of outspoken heroes like John Kerry, a Silver Star winner who later became a United

States senator from Massachusetts and a close friend of Bob Kerrey's.

By all rights, Kerrey should have been a player in VVAW, but the ghosts of Thanh Phong likely kept him away. That is because one of the organization's goals was to set up a non-disciplinary war crimes tribunal in the United States. My Lai had just become public, and the activists were certain that American policies in Vietnam had spurred additional atrocities that had gone unreported.

In January 1970, the VVAW and several other peace groups established the Citizens Commission of Inquiry into U.S. War Crimes in Indochina. Within a year, that panel evolved into the Winter Soldier Investigation, a 1971 gathering of veterans in Detroit prepared to disclose their own involvement in war crimes or to recount other atrocities they had witnessed. Tod Ensign set up hearings in thirteen cities prior to the Winter Soldier event in Detroit, showcasing traumatized vets and their stories of wartime abuses. The intent was to avoid condemnation and to provide combat soldiers a safe environment for lifting the guilt that plagued many of them, like Bob Kerrey. As diligent as organizers were in screening the participants, years later it turned out that a small number of those who spoke in Detroit either had not been present in Vietnam when they said they had or had invented or embellished their recollection of events.

The Detroit gathering would have provided the platform Bob Kerrey needed for his own catharsis. But confiding to his mother and a minister was one thing. Public disclosure of the slaughter of innocent women and children in Thanh Phong by a Medal of Honor winner was quite another. According to Tod Ensign and another organizer, Tim Butz, Kerrey made no overtures to the Vietnam Veterans Against the War, and the group in turn never sought him out. "I don't think anybody knew to ask him," said Butz. And he wasn't sure that Kerrey would have testified anyway. "I don't know that Bob Kerrey was ready to talk about anything."

Well before the Vietnam quagmire ended, Kerrey had lost interest in the peace movement and protesting the war and began to follow in his father's footsteps as an entrepreneur. Under the name of Robert Development Co., Kerrey set about establishing himself in the early to middle 1970s as a prominent businessman in Lincoln and Omaha. By 1983, he was a millionaire founder (along with his brother-in-law) of a restaurant chain (Grandmother's) and owner of a bowling alley, a racquetball club, and a large fitness center. His convictions about Vietnam began to change, too, taking a more pro-military bent. At Lincoln's Veterans Administration hospital he placed a plaque at the foot of a tree in honor of Nebraska's Medal of Honor winners. The following year, he was the grand marshal in a Veterans Day parade. The national Veterans of Foreign Wars then appointed him aide-de-camp, and he was commander of a Vietnam veterans post he helped start in Lincoln. The old outspokenness, though, was still there. When the Veterans of Foreign Wars asked his post to protest an antiwar documentary, he declined. In a letter to the national headquarters, Kerrey wrote that "those who feel it mocks Vietnam veterans are the big losers: they mock themselves."

War stories still fascinated him. Kerrey got to know a soldier who had fought in World War I, an old man who lived in Lincoln. Kerrey romanticized the toughness of the Great War's combat veterans. "I'm drawn to that era, and I'm drawn to the strength of the characters in it," he said. "It was a more superstitious time, it was uglier in lots of ways, and brutish in some ways, as well. But there were giants and a strength that comes from having to do things that today other people do for you."

The man lived in poverty in a small Lincoln apartment that smelled like urine. But his vivid oral history captivated Kerrey. He talked about the savage fighting of Belleau Wood, and what it was like living and fighting a trench war where 45,000 soldiers and marines took the brunt of the German attack. He recounted the horrendous artillery fire, taking shell after shell all night long while hunkered down in muddy ditches or in the dark woods where bayonets became a favorite weapon. "My eyes got big. Holy cow, all of a sudden my little experience in war got really small," Kerrey said. As he sat with the man, Kerrey remembers thinking, *What the hell am I complaining about?*

In 1976 the local *Lincoln Star* ran a short item with the headline "What Ever Happened To Joseph R. (Bob) Kerrey?" By this time, the tormented Medal of Honor winner and angry war protestor was on the way to becoming "much more whole," said June Levine. His fear and grief would occasionally surface in public remarks about Vietnam, like his comments in 1977: "What you've got are hundreds of thousands of guys aged twenty-five to thirty-five who are carrying guilt feelings deep down inside of them that they did something horrible, which they can't even talk about."

Though still holding back, he was not as haunted, and his pain had been eased by happier times in his life. In 1974, he married Beverly Defnall, a local girl who was an aspiring actress, and in November their first child, Benjamin, was born. Two years later, in August, their second child, Lindsey, arrived. Parenthood was a life-changing event for Kerrey. For the first time in years, the veil of grief that had hung over him lifted, and the beauty of life that he now saw in his two infants "made me want to live again."

But the bliss would not last. The couple separated in April 1978, nine days after their fourth wedding anniversary.

Claiming his marriage was "irretrievably broken," Robert Kerrey's petition for divorce was granted and filed on July 27, 1978. What drove the couple apart was his workaholic devotion to his restaurants. It was all-consuming and took the place of most everything in his life, including his family.

Though his children had liberated him, he yielded custody to Beverly. She remarried in 1980 and briefly moved to Texas, taking Ben and Lindsey with her. But Kerrey made a determined effort to see his children, flying them to Lincoln during the summer months.

Out of his broken family life, Kerrey looked to politics as a possible new career. As an antiwar protestor, he'd experienced the adulation of the crowds, the chance to make a difference. "I thought I might enjoy it, thought I might be good at it."

Still, it surprised everybody but Kerrey and his friends when he announced his campaign to be governor of Nebraska.

Chapter Twelve

———————■———————

"UH-OH, WE GOT A battle here."

Charles Thone, the governor of Nebraska, was getting his first televised glimpse of the war hero who wanted to unseat him in the 1982 election. He saw right off that the thirty-nine-year-old upstart was going to be trouble. "Kerrey came on just like a Hollywood personality," Thone said. "Didn't know an ear of corn from a ukulele, but he came across on television as if he really knew exactly what he was doing and what he would do as governor."

By contrast, Thone was strictly white bread and free of surprise. He was a workmanlike Reagan-Republican in a state where the GOP outnumbered Democrats by 54,000, and a farmer in a state where agriculture drove the economy. Until Kerrey came along, he was hoping to ride the president's popularity to reelection (Reagan won the state with sixty-six percent in 1980). Kerrey was something new, an unknown, an exciting outsider who came off as a person Nebraskans didn't see too often—a natural. Before he even won a single vote, some were comparing him to the state's two most storied politicians—William Jennings Bryan, the prairie populist, and George Norris, the "gentle knight of progressive ideas." Kerrey was handsome, photogenic, and did well on television, which appealed to Nebraska's young voters, especially females, who found the bachelor sexy and alluring.

Kerrey was a novice candidate who made one rookie mistake after another. But like a Kennedy, his mystique acted as a protective shield. Part of it was being a war hero—a Navy commando in Vietnam. "The Rambo glamour," said Ed Howard, the Associated Press reporter who covered Kerrey and Nebraska politics for twenty-four years. "That SEAL business has always been part of the Kerrey mystique." When a group of rakish-looking SEALs came to town to campaign for Kerrey, one friend cracked that it was time to lock up their daughters. "He stood in sharp contrast with the guy he ran against," recalled Howard. "Folks just liked Kerrey from the get-go. He was refreshing."

Even so, it was Thone's race to lose. Kerrey's early polling found that he enjoyed the same level of public recognition as the name of a fictitious person included in the survey. In other words, no one knew who he was. Tom Fogarty, the political writer for Lincoln's afternoon paper, who knew only that Kerrey owned a bowling alley, was reduced to quizzing the reporter on the bowling beat. "Yeah, he runs a good bowling alley," his colleague answered. If political common sense had prevailed, "he should never have run for governor," said Kandra Hahn, who joined the Kerrey campaign early as a strategist. Nobody, she said, "ever believed he could win."

It wasn't long before the ghosts of Thanh Phong were haunting the candidate. The campaign, which knew nothing of the raid, wanted to position him as a war hero, Hahn said, but he resisted. Asked for a photo showing him with his Medal of Honor, Kerrey said, "he couldn't find it." And he was furious when the campaign staff located a picture of him as a SEAL, with a bandoleer draped over his shoulder. Perhaps Kerrey feared it might have led to further questions about his past. Had the revelations of Thanh Phong become public in 1982, it would certainly have been a major political crisis. In the end, it mattered little whether Kerrey's campaign exploited his warrior image; the media did it for them.

It's not surprising that Kerrey's aides pushed him to emphasize his military career. That's because he had almost

nothing substantive to say about the issues. His early campaign speeches were filled with feel-good generalities, like his
vow "to help Nebraskans find a sense of place and a sense of
time." In announcing his candidacy he said: "I shall never forget that while I am warm, there are people who are cold. That
while I am working, there are people who are not. That while
I am comfortable, there are people who are suffering." Even
less than a month before the election, Kerrey was alarmingly
uninformed on the issues. He told the *Washington Post*'s David
Hoffman that high interest rates were "killing Nebraska" and
that Thone's do-nothing approach of waiting until the national
economy recovered was "nonsense." Later he acknowledged to
Hoffman, "The governor can't bring down interest rates."
Said Ed Howard: "Kerrey was the least understanding and
experienced person to run for governor than anybody in the
republic with the possible exception of Ronald Reagan."
Most of the time Kerrey lagged behind Thone in the polls by
at least twenty-five points. The governor had more money
and had the advantage of name recognition from his career as
a four-term congressman and as the incumbent. Kerrey's
fund-raising efforts took in three quarters of a million dollars,
but his selling point was his charisma and the fact that
Nebraska's severe recession was Thone's albatross.

So far, Kerrey's experience in politics consisted of successfully running a friend's state legislative campaign and sitting
on the Lincoln Human Rights Commission, which by and
large supported gay rights. In a state where the favorite book
is the Bible (which castigates homosexuality as a sin), that
experience was more a political liability then a benefit. Privately, Kerrey called homosexuality abnormal. Publicly, he
thought gay bashing was abhorrent and defended homosexu-
als against needless discrimination, which was risky politically for a thirty-nine-year-old single male. "The Republicans
made a whispering campaign that he was gay," said June
Levine, his professorial mentor. The GOP tried out the rumor

on the AP's Howard, who balked. "It reflects how pathetic," he said, "the Republican party of Nebraska had become."

Kerrey handed the opposition other more legitimate opportunities to damage him. As the campaign progressed, it was clear that valor on the battlefield came more easily to the ex-SEAL than sticking to his political guns with interest groups. In a secret meeting with labor leaders, Kerrey pledged, if elected, to sign legislation repealing Nebraska's right-to-work law. When his promise became public, he backed off. He had similar problems on abortion. "I know in his heart he was pro-choice," said Levine, who watched Kerrey waffle and occasionally dissemble on the issue. During a debate with Thone, sponsored by the Associated Press, Kerrey abandoned his earlier position and stated he was pro-life, which fit with the state's conservative traditions.

Thone had tried to seize points by pinning Kerrey down on his true position on abortion. Was he or was he not a pro-life candidate, the governor pressed. Howard clearly remembers how a crafty Kerrey found wiggle room in his answer, saying he got better information as time went on. "I didn't flip-flop; I changed my mind. Only two types of people don't change their minds. Dead men and fools." Afterward he telephoned Levine to apologize. "Come over for a cup of coffee," he pleaded. "I went over there steaming," Levine recalled. "Bob, why did you do this?" she demanded. "I went whoring after votes," Kerrey responded. Levine quickly retorted, "That's what I wanted to say."

Sensing opportunity in Kerrey's capriciousness, the Thone camp ran a series of television commercials accusing him of flip-flopping on abortion, right-to-work legislation and the death penalty. The attack ads had a core of truth to them but didn't work, probably because the Republicans overreached. Radio spots went beyond the issues and described Kerrey as an ultraliberal and "cute like California Governor Edmund G. Brown," widely known as "Governor Moonbeam." While the comparisons to Brown proved in time to be not entirely off the mark (they both dated celebrities in office) Kerrey's stature as a war hero made that kind of ridicule ineffective.

Kerrey was closing in on Thone. Weeks before the election, polls showed that the race had become too close to call. The Republicans had one last card to play: his involvement in the antiwar movement. Of special interest to the GOP was an unconfirmed story that Kerrey tossed his Medal of Honor into a fake wooden coffin during a May 1971 demonstration at the capitol in Lincoln. Kerrey walked among clench-fisted protestors who chanted "Peace now" and who carried placards with the words "Stop the Murdering." The medal story, if true, would be a political bonanza for Thone and a disaster for Kerrey. The governor carefully fanned the rumor, staying a couple of stages removed, but told the press that he had it on good authority, from an eyewitness, that the war hero had thrown away his medal. A top man on Thone's campaign even sought out a television cameraman who covered the rally, looking for incriminating footage. "Dirt," cameraman Don Wright said.

But the Republicans never got the goods. Kerrey's supporters say that a dead-ringer for their man, a friend named Leroy Shuster, pitched his Bronze Star and other citations into the casket, which contained a flag and the names of nearly four hundred Nebraskans killed in combat. Other veterans in attendance discarded their ribbons and medals as well. But neither Shuster nor Wright remember seeing Kerrey drop his medal into the coffin. Still, the story stayed alive, fueled in part by Kerrey's inability to produce the medal and by the conflicting explanations he offered. At first, he said he lost it in the mid-1970s during a move. But then he told Tom Fogarty: "A crazy aunt took it." As conflicted as Kerrey was in 1969 about receiving the medal, he accepted a replacement from the Navy.

Kerrey's role at the demonstration in question proved to be

minor. His jaw was wired shut from oral surgery, so he didn't speak. Instead, he released a written statement which sparked another set of wildly improbable stories that he defended the Vietcong as "angelic" and trashed "ruthless" American GIs. "God, that's got to be terribly out of context," candidate Kerrey later told reporters. He was constantly having to bat down innuendos. He told David Hoffman of the *Washington Post*, "You still have people who say, 'I know you once burned a flag.'"

In the end, Kerrey easily rebutted the principal message behind the Thone campaign's smear: that he was unpatriotic. "I was one month out of Vietnam, sixty days into my artificial limb, and twenty-five years old," he told the *Omaha World Herald* when he first started speaking out against the war. True, but not the whole story. At the time of the May rally he was no naive, hurting kid: almost twenty-eight and home from Vietnam for twenty-seven months, he was at the height of his antiwar involvement. But Kerrey also told voters before the election that protesting against the war had been unnecessary and mismanaged. His antiwar rhetoric, never absolute, had now been clearly abandoned. Within days of the election, Kerrey pulled even with Thone. By the time the polls closed, he squeaked out a victory by a slim 7,233 votes.

Charles Thone was right about one thing—Kerrey admittedly didn't know the first thing about running a government bureaucracy. "God, was I dumb," Kerrey acknowledged years later. "I mean, jeez, I just didn't know the issues. I didn't know what was going on."

But Kerrey wasn't elected for his expertise. He won because a majority of Nebraskans for once had the fantasy candidate they could vote for. And Governor Kerrey did not disappoint. At his inaugural address, a dozen or so Navy SEALs crammed into the far reaches of the balcony overlooking the packed legislative chamber in the capitol—the section the political reporters called deep center field. At the end of Kerrey's speech, the legislative chamber heard something for the first time. A lusty "hoohya!," the warriors' chant of approval, reverberated through a historic room unaccustomed to anything but the most proper decorum. "It was a rousing, prideful, partly bloodcurdling 'hooyha,'" said Howard. "That was an ass-kicker." June Levine later watched the SEALs land in the governor's helicopter on the lawn of the mansion, conjuring up images of wartime machismo. These were his true friends, Levine realized.

It was not a good time to be governor of an agricultural state. The nation was in a recession and low farm prices had hit Nebraska hard, leaving it with a sizable deficit. Kerrey vowed he would not raise taxes to close the gap but had to anyway. Governing like a businessman, he went through the budget "like buckshot through a duck," said Howard, cutting enough to turn a $24 million state deficit into a $50 million surplus. By the end of his first year, Kerrey's fiscal conservatism won him extremely high marks from an unlikely corner—a group of ultraconservative lawmakers known as "Thone's clones," for their allegiance to the former governor. "Part of his strength is his willingness to see the interests of people he doesn't know," said Bill Hoppner, his first chief of staff.

But the more liberal Nebraskans whom Kerrey did know, and who played a considerable role in his victory—women, educators, gays, peace activists, and minorities—were not pleased with their new governor. "He was a middling governor," said Paul Olson of Nebraskans For Peace.

The Left learned the hard way that Kerrey's liberalism was limited and idiosyncratic. He was a fiscal conservative growing increasingly hawkish on military issues. On social matters he was more in touch with liberals, but still often unreliable. "He packaged himself as a maverick and operated in the gray area between Republican and Democratic politics," said Tim Rinne, a longtime liberal activist. One initiative that liberals found especially upsetting was Kerrey's unsuccessful attempt to eliminate three state-affiliated commissions that were advocates for American Indians, African-Americans, and Hispanics. Kandra Hahn said Kerrey had "a profound skepticism" that the commissions were beneficial. Hoppner acknowledged that trying to cut the commissions "was a mistake in judgment." Added Olson: "He had a proclivity for bashing the very groups that gave him credence and power."

Not even avid campaign supporters were immune from the Kerrey treatment. Professors at the University of Nebraska believed Kerrey would be their sustainer. He did sign a bill to help teachers, said Paul Olson, "but not an iota of the bill was ever funded." (Hoppner said it was funded, but not to the maximum that the legislation allowed.) Even so, Kerrey was anything but a sustainer. As part of his effort to reduce the deficit, he went after the university, trying to cut programs, freeze salaries, and eliminate entire departments—even his old school of pharmacy. June Levine, his close friend, had raised money for Kerrey and felt hurt. Still, she was more forgiving than some of her colleagues who turned against him and held grudges for nearly two decades. His war on the university—largely unsuccessful—also cost him the resignation of aide Steve Fowler, a key election operative who became frustrated with Kerrey's leadership.

Kerrey's executive style remained an enigma to those who worked with him. The fecklessness he demonstrated as a candidate became an ongoing joke. While discussing an issue with Kerrey, Kandra Hahn asked him, "When did you change your position?" Kerrey quipped, "Which position?"

The governor didn't seem intentionally duplicitous. On most occasions, he simply made decisions too quickly. "Thinks quick and fast on his feet," said Attorney General

Paul Douglas, who had a friendly working relationship with the governor.

But in his haste, his first conclusions were sometimes wrong or left him vulnerable. So he would simply change his mind regardless of the consequences. "He's unpredictable by any standard," Kandra Hahn said. "It's foolish to look at him through any conventional lens." He could be witty and playful one minute and intolerant the next. "If I was somber," said Hahn, "he'd say, 'Lighten up, let's go get some ice cream.'" In the next instance, if Hahn had come into his office too jovial, Kerrey would snap at her, "Be serious."

With reporters, Kerrey could be especially difficult and easily provoked. During press conferences he would repeatedly throw a reporter's question back at him. "That's not the question, the question is this," he would say. "I stopped him," Howard said. "Governor, wait a minute. If you get to specify the question and specify the answers, why am I here?" Kerrey shot back, "That's not a question for me to answer, that's a question for you to answer." Howard was flummoxed. "Trying to nail Bob Kerrey," he said, "was like trying to nail Jell-O to the wall."

The press eventually accepted this behavior as Kerrey just being Kerrey. One time Howard heard that the governor was going to call a special session of the legislature to break an impasse over an education bill. He confirmed it for Howard but warned, "For god's sake, don't use me as your source." The story made news when it hit the wire and sent reporters scrambling to match it. Fogarty, who wrote for Lincoln's afternoon paper, was with Howard when they bumped into Kerrey at lunchtime. He asked if the governor was indeed going to call the legislature back into session.

"Yes," Kerrey said.

"Can I attribute that to you?" Fogarty asked. Howard watched in amazement as Kerrey, who had just sworn him to secrecy, quickly agreed.

Fogarty filed his dispatch, the second story of the day reporting Kerrey's plans for a special session. But at a press conference later in the day, Kerrey ignored any mention of his decision. As it neared conclusion, Howard recalls somebody yelling, "Governor, are you going to call a special session of the legislature?" "He looked up," Howard remembered, "and said, 'No.'"

He later explained to Howard, "I changed my mind." Minutes before meeting with reporters, he was interviewing a job applicant and asked him if it was a good idea to call the legislature back. The man replied no.

"Kerrey knew him ten minutes, and he takes his advice," Howard said, and "didn't even give him the job."

Despite the erratic and eccentric behavior, the capital press generally swooned over Kerrey. Don Walton, who wrote some of the earliest profiles on him for the *Lincoln Star*, said, "I'm a little embarrassed by the rather rhapsodic view of a Medal of Honor winner written by a young reporter." Walton's pieces were prescient, though, in figuring out that Kerrey was someone to watch. Kerrey liked reporters as long as he felt he could trust them. If not, they were banished. As the AP's man in Nebraska, Ed Howard had extra clout and was almost always welcome inside the governor's inner circle. The two men drank beer, shot pool, and shared what at times was an earthy, locker-room humor.

Kerrey's second chief of staff, W. Don Nelson, remembers Howard storming into the governor's office asking to see Kerrey's "woody." Kerrey had recently been in California, Nelson said, and "had fallen in love with an old-fashioned, 1940s-something, wood-paneled station wagon." Word had it that the governor had bought it, and Howard wanted to see it. When Howard entered and asked about the car, Kerrey instead lifted his trousers and showed Howard his prosthesis.

But after a year in office, Kerrey became restless. He had little interest in the hands-on details that were the heart of governance. "He figured out in a hurry," said Ed Howard, "that governing was boring." Though chief executive of the state, his hands were sometimes tied by the bureaucracy, a lack of money, or the unusual one-house legislature. He was more drawn to the big picture—big ideas and big visions. "'Hopes and dreams,' that's a phrase that went with Bob," said Howard. Some of his starstruck ideas and his almost childish enthusiasm, however, were privately panned by the media. "There were a lot of hopes-and-dreams jokes about him," said Howard.

"He was disappointed in the job," said Paul Douglas. "I don't think he got things done when he wanted to."

Even so, the public gave Governor Kerrey high marks. His secret was simple, said Dick Herman, a senior editorial writer at the *Lincoln Journal.* He was candid and approachable, and people were not intimidated by him. He raised taxes only sparingly and never lost the glow of stardom.

One day while riding his bike, Herman saw Kerrey jogging "by himself, no troopers," and the governor invited him in for chocolate-chip cookies. "He had a passion for chocolate-chip cookies," Herman said. Kerrey appointed Herman's wife to a landscape architect board and called the editorial writer often—not in an attempt to influence him, Herman insisted, but to discuss the issues. When author Francis Fitzgerald was coming to Nebraska on a tour for her new book about the Vietnam War, Kerrey offered Herman a ride on his personal jet if he would come along. Herman could not refuse and enjoyed the trip and the conversation immensely.

Kerrey also had a flair for the dramatic. Inquiring about dinner plans one evening, he called his favorite Nebraska poet, Ted Kooser. "Since he often ran late, I didn't expect him for awhile," Kooser said. "In about twenty minutes, I heard the whup-whup-whup of an approaching helicopter. It was the governor himself, having the pilot set down in the pasture. He got out with a big grin. The wind from the rotors blew our chickens all over the yard." When a friend's father died, he offered theater tickets to *Cats*. "As we were getting ready to go to Omaha that day, the doorbell rang," said Rod Bates. "It was a chauffeur with a limo in our driveway." There was champagne in the back and a dinner reservation for two at a French café. "There's Bob Kerrey for you," said Bates, "compassionate, generous, pretty spectacular."

Chapter Thirteen

WHILE ENTERTAINING BOB KERREY one night in his kitchen, Bill Hoppner revealed his plan to run for the Democratic nomination for the U.S. Senate. His opponent would be Ben Nelson, a popular Nebraskan and friend of both men. Recognizing how awkward it might be for Kerrey to take sides in such a race, his former chief of staff asked him to abstain from any endorsement and remain neutral. Kerrey agreed.

But Hoppner felt crushed and betrayed when he read the next day's newspaper. There was his good friend Bob Kerrey, quoted as calling Nelson the better candidate. Years later, Hoppner said that on reflection, "Kerrey was right." He regarded the governor's sense of loyalty as so strong that he wanted to protect Hoppner from the painful realization that he couldn't win.

But for many others who knew Kerrey well, the story affirmed exactly the opposite: that he had no sense of personal loyalty whatsoever. "There were people who thought Bob Kerrey would fall on his sword for them," said Ed Howard. While he could be exceedingly gracious and generous in his personal dealings, when it came to tough political decisions he typically ran right over friends and allies. In the process, according to Howard, Kerrey would say, in effect, "I'm sorry, was that your ass in the way?"

Added Kandra Hahn: "There is nobody in his world but him."

Kerrey never hesitated in cutting loose anyone who became

a political liability. When State Attorney General Paul Douglas, whom Kerrey called one of his best friends in government, faced impeachment proceedings in the legislature after being accused of improper business dealings and, ultimately, perjury, Kerrey volunteered to testify against him. Douglas, who resigned even though the perjury charge was dropped, said he understood the political realities Kerrey faced, but saw him nevertheless as cold and uncaring. "You never really saw him having a lot of compassion," Douglas said.

Associates sometimes found his lack of fealty and candor bewildering, and his explanations lame. As chairman of the Nebraska delegation to the 1984 Democratic National Convention, Kerrey supported Gary Hart. When it came time to vote for a platform plank offered by Hart or one from rival Jessie Jackson, all but one of the Nebraskans went with Hart. The lone turncoat was a secret until Tom Fogarty of the *Lincoln Star* wheedled it out of a source who counted the ballots. When confronted, Kerrey tried to talk his way out of it. "Oh, I cast the vote," he sheepishly told Fogarty, "but I misunderstood the issue."

Kerrey also demonstrated a penchant for playing fast and loose with relatively unimportant facts about his life. In a speech in Alaska, he declared: "I became a Democrat because of John F. Kennedy, and I stayed one because of Richard Nixon." But Kerrey, who registered as a Republican in October 1964, didn't become a Democrat until October 1978. When questioned about this at a press conference, he said, "I consider other things to be more important than what political party I'm part of."

Other "Kerrey moments" raised more disturbing questions about his ethics and honesty. In November 1983, the state's banking commission shut down Commonwealth Savings Company. With its deposits insured by neither the state nor federal government, the investors in Nebraska's largest thrift company lost more than $65 million.

Commonwealth's owners were the Copples, a venerable and politically influential Nebraska family with real estate and other business interests throughout Lincoln. When Fogarty asked whether the governor and the Copples had ever done any business, Kerrey answered with an unequivocal "no." Fogarty, not comfortable with Kerrey's denial, went to the secretary of state's office and pulled the incorporation records of his companies. It turned out that Copple money, to the tune of $24,000, had made its way into Kerrey's bowling alley. "He was not forthcoming. There was no reason not to be," Fogarty said, because Kerrey's role with Copple had "no bearing on the collapse of the bank." His lack of honesty was not surprising. "I was always catching him in that stuff," he said.

The Nebraska press sniffed around for possible Kerrey connections to the S&L scandal but never came up with anything incriminating. But when Kerrey was running for president in 1992, Washington reporter Morton Kondracke roughed him up in a piece for *The New Republic*: "Corruption may be too strong a word, since no one has proved any wrongdoing—let alone illegality. But there is a pattern—dating back to college and extending up to the present . . ." Kondracke began by recounting how Kerrey had pocketed advertising revenues from the University of Nebraska student council.

He zeroed in on Kerrey's relationship with William L. Wright, a longtime friend and business associate who was knee-deep in the state's S&L crisis. Early in his gubernatorial term, Kerrey had pushed successfully for legislation that combined the existing state bonding authorities into a single new agency, with added power to underwrite commercial ventures. Soon after Kerrey appointed Wright to the board of the newly reconstituted Nebraska Investment Finance Authority, the agency approved a $2.5 million below-prime loan to the Prairie Life Center in Lincoln, a financially troubled fitness club that Kerrey owned.

Wright's law firm also advised state banking regulators

even though Wright was a major owner of State Security Savings Company, another shaky, undercapitalized financial institution. After the state shut down Commonwealth and seized its assets, officials were planning to do the same to State Security. Wright quickly filed for bankruptcy and was able to protect his holdings, then moved to California.

In 1987, the banking committee of the Nebraska legislature investigated and found both institutions were "milked and drained" of funds by their owners. The committee noted that the diversion of funds at Wright's bank had been "more sophisticated and skillful" than at Commonwealth, but state and local authorities declined to prosecute.

Kerrey had a personal financial relationship with State Security, but the panel found nothing improper in his dealings, despite a $2.4 million loan to American Investment Group, a Kerrey-Wright enterprise that bought a small mall called Shoppers Fair. "Previous owners of the mall charged that they were forced to sell at cut rate, or Wright would foreclose on other mortgages they held," Kondracke wrote. "Another group of Nebraska legislators indicated it believed Wright may have acted illegally in diverting a $200,000 fee connected with the AIG purchase to a holding company he controlled. But Kerrey's administration didn't prosecute."

Though he did admit to mistakes in the savings and loan collapse, such as poor judgment and not recognizing conflicts of interest, Kerrey was never charged with any wrongdoing by the various law enforcement and regulatory agencies that conducted investigations. "Kerrey weathered everything," said Paul Douglas. "I'm telling you, that guy has lived a charmed life." The AP's Ed Howard said Wright and Kerrey "made a lot of money together," but Howard believed the governor was clean. "Bob trusted people. Wright came to him: 'There is an investment here, it's a good thing.' Bob said, 'OK.' Bob is not a detail guy."

The public wasn't often exposed to the less admirable sides

of Kerrey's mercurial personality. They saw a dynamic young governor who would walk off the grounds of the executive mansion and stop to play a pickup game of basketball with some youngsters, who would throw Halloween parties, run marathons, and drink Blue Ribbon beer at the Zoo Bar, a blues joint in Lincoln. "The man authentically had star quality," said Tim Rinne, a liberal activist in Nebraska.

Even his detractors had to admit that they were swept along for a ride when Debra Winger came to town.

"Can you keep your mouth shut about something?" he asked Ed Howard one day in the governor's mansion. "He looked at his watch," the reporter said, and a "couple of minutes later Winger came bouncing into the room. She was living in the mansion, which was pretty much a secret at the time."

Winger arrived in Lincoln to film the movie *Terms of Endearment*. At a press conference to welcome the production to the state's capital, Kerrey jokingly inducted Winger into the landlocked "Nebraska Navy," and cracked that he was "a naval officer myself and sometime gentleman." Afterward, Kerrey noted to an aide that she wasn't wearing a bra. He sent the high-spirited actress a note that Winger called "quite romantic." The governor affectionately began to call her "Wing," but the press used the nickname that Winger's costar, Jack Nicholson, gave her, "Buck." "It was just love," Kerrey said. "I mean, we fell head over heels in love."

The national press also fell hard for the war hero and his Hollywood flame. "A Tornado Named Debra Winger Has a Whirl with Nebraska's Governor Rockin' Bob Kerrey," was the headline in *People*. Soon after, United Press International selected him as one of the country's most eligible bachelors, edging out Tom Selleck, who played a fictitious Navy SEAL on the television series *Magnum P.I.*

The local folks were excited about the celebrity sightings of the youthful couple, who popped up everywhere from Washington, D.C., to London to New York, where they were seen sitting in the audience of *Saturday Night Live*. But at home Nebraskans gave them their space. The couple moved around Lincoln easily, enjoying intimate dinners, holding hands in public, jogging together, or going to one of Kerrey's favorite blues clubs. Most people were simply curious, down to a few of the groundskeepers at the governor's mansion, who hid in the trees to watch Winger sunbathing. (She kept her clothes on.) Even on the occasions when Winger thought she was in Hollywood Hills and not Lincoln—she was ticketed for speeding in an official state car and driving with an expired license—it was a one-day news story.

"I've never been in love with a governor before, and I haven't learned all the rules," she explained on a local radio show.

Opinion polls were positive, finding that few Nebraskans were troubled by the divorced Kerrey living with a single woman in the governor's mansion. Many were swept up in the storybook quality of the relationship, even those not favorably disposed to the governor. While riding in a parade in southeast Nebraska, Kerrey was surprised to see Winger waiting for him near the end of the procession. He had left her in the governor's mansion, and now she was teasingly yelling to him, "Hi governor, hi, Bob." Kerrey told the driver to stop, exited the car, and walked over to Winger. "He grabs her under her arms, picks her up, spins her around, and gives her a kiss," said Howard. "The crowd loved it." One die-hard Republican woman looking on was taken with the spontaneous romantic display: "Awwh, he kissed her," she said.

There were critics, of course, most notably the Reverend Everett Sileven, a fundamentalist preacher who mixed scorn with partisan politics. "I think it's [a] very bad example for our governor to have a mistress in his house," the churchman scolded in one breath, while in another taunted that he'd run for Kerrey's job. Few took him seriously.

But living in a fish bowl—even one in Lincoln, Nebraska—

produced tensions. In 1985, after two years and serious discussions of marriage, she decided to break off their romance. It has never been clear how much, if at all, Winger broke Kerrey's heart. But that didn't stop the guessing. After the breakup, Ernie Chambers, a Democratic state senator, wrote a teasing song called "The Ballad of Bob and Debra":

> *"Stung by rejection,*
> *awash in despair,*
> *foul grew his temper,*
> *baleful his stare.*
> *Anger engulfed him*
> *in great swelling tide,*
> *he went to bed Jekyll,*
> *awoke Mr. Hyde."*

With Winger out of his life, the last year of his governor's term was a time of uncertainty, a time of exploring old thoughts but in new ways. Vietnam was on his radar screen once again. "Never forget I'm a SEAL," he told Ed Howard over a game of pool. Kerrey never could forget, nor could he put out of his mind what happened in Thanh Phong. For four years he had lived in relative peace, with love helping to keep his demons in check. But there had never been a moment, he said, when Vietnam wasn't there, in some way, waiting to suck him back into a world of pain and suffering.

With his approval ratings above seventy percent, Kerrey was politically bullet proof, and it was a given that he would walk into a second term as governor. But he astonished Nebraskans by deciding to complete his term in 1986 and quit politics. His characteristically cryptic reason: the "need to find a little danger."

When he found the danger he was looking for, it was in an unexpected place—a classroom at the University of California in Santa Barbara.

Chapter Fourteen

———————■———————

WAITING FOR ROBERT KERREY when he arrived in Santa Barbara in 1987 was Walter Capps, a large man at 6'4", with a generous and forgiving heart. Professor Capps was a man of peace who sought to teach healing and reconciliation in his religion and ethics courses. His classroom was open to all and was a favorite among students. Capps presented mostly Vietnam veterans as guest lecturers who used their personal experiences to illustrate that war was not something to be glorified. Originally from Nebraska, Capps was friendly with Kerrey and had invited the ex-governor to coteach one of his Vietnam courses. "It was the first time that I had gone back and really examined the history of the war and the politics of it," Kerrey said, "the causative events and all that sort of thing."

Kerrey joined a long list of prominent lecturers and writers who had contributed their time and work to Capps. He compiled their words and their writings in *The Vietnam Reader*, a thoughtful book about the war. Kerrey contributed an essay titled "On Remembering the Vietnam War," a searing piece and his closest pass yet at a public confession to what happened at Thang Phong:

> Around the farm, there is an activity that no one likes to do. Yet it is sometimes necessary. When a cat gives birth to kittens that aren't needed, the kittens must be destroyed. And there is a moment

when you are holding the kitten under the water when you know that if you bring that kitten back above the water it will live, and if you don't bring it back above in that instant the kitten will be dead. This, for me, is a perfect metaphor for those dreadful moments in war when you do not quite do what you previously thought you would do. I do not choose to recount such moments here now, because I find myself unable and unwilling. However, this is an experience that is not mine alone, but is faced by everyone, whether in war or in peace time: one has a moment in which one makes a decision, and afterwards one feels as if one has fallen from grace. One receives not only one's own judgment, but the judgment of other human beings, and, in the end, the judgment of Almighty God.

Kerrey's last words were almost confessional: "I come away feeling fortunate to have survived, painfully aware that dead men tell no tales."

His time with Capps was yet another form of postwar therapy. Eighteen years after he left Vietnam, he still had a pent-up rage inside of him. He knew he had to address it. "You don't get better through hatred. You get worse," he said. "The object of your hate doesn't suffer at all. The man I hated the most on earth," Kerrey said, "was Richard Nixon." By listening to Capps preach about forgiveness, Kerrey learned in California that it was all right to let go of his anger. "All of a sudden I started feeling sympathy for the man. I forgave Richard Nixon. Now, I'm sure he didn't notice, but I did. I felt like something had been lifted from inside me. I mean, I felt a great burden lifting from me."

Nixon became more of a human being to Kerrey. When he got his first glimpse at government documents concerning American soldiers still missing in Vietnam, he understood the burden placed on the president. "I just saw a human being who made terrible mistakes."

In Santa Barbara, Kerrey spoke eloquently to the students in Capps's class of how the war was a colossal mistake, how the government had led the nation down a path of lies. But he never talked about his own short time in Vietnam, nor how he lost the lower portion of his right leg. In class one day, a student finally chided him for holding back. Kerrey looked down at his plastic foot and started singing.

> *Then a big Turkey shell knocked me ass over head*
> *And when I awoke in my hospital bed*
> *I saw what it had done*
> *And I wished I was dead.*
> *Never knew there were worse things than dyin'.*
> *No more waltzing Mathilda for me.*

When he finished "And the Band Played Waltzing Mathilda," a World War I Australian ballad about the slaughter at Gallipoli, the classroom was silent. The students started to applaud, louder and louder as tears streamed down their cheeks.

The next time Kerrey sang "Waltzing Mathilda" was on the night he was elected to the United States Senate in 1988. The response from the crowd was the same; there were few dry eyes in the crowd. The local television correspondent was so overcome that she could hardly describe the scene for viewers.

Kerrey stayed only a few months in Santa Barbara; he left early after receiving a telephone call from Jim Exon, Nebraska's senior senator, urging him to run for the Senate. The state's other senator, Ed Zorninsky, had died, leaving the seat open to challenge in November 1988. "You've got to quit being so damn selfish," Exon told him. "We need you here. You can do some good."

Nebraskans welcomed their glamorous, if eccentric, prodigal son back with great enthusiasm. Kerrey commissioned a series of patriotic, Reagan-style, morning in America–type of commercials and stuck to positive themes. He won easily. In short order, the man who used to speed around town in a '48 Ford "Woody" with a "I'd Rather Be Surfing" sticker on the bumper, was a member of one of the world's most exclusive clubs.

Kerrey was strictly a fringe player early in his Senate career. In an institution where camaraderie and personal rapport are essential to success, Kerrey was a loner. And while his war record was widely admired, "Cosmic Bob," a nickname he loathed, began to take hold. "I came much more with an executive mind-set thinking more like a governor or a business person," he said, "than somebody who has to get a consensus."

He worked hard, however, spending considerable time mastering wonkish issues like health care, intelligence, and tax reform. Kerrey also made a genuine effort to learn the tradecraft of politics at the senatorial level. His mentor was another fiery iconoclast, Pat Moynihan of New York. Like Moynihan, Kerrey was capable of rich oration. His performance defending the right to burn the Stars and Stripes, during a testy debate on a Constitutional amendment restricting such protest, was riveting.

One Senate vote Kerrey deeply regretted was his decision to oppose the use of force in the Persian Gulf in early 1991. "That was one of the dumbest fucking things I ever did," he said bluntly. He now believes that an invasion of Iraq—not merely the ejection of Saddam Hussein from Kuwait—would have been the right decision. "Had people like myself gone to President Bush in 1991 and said, 'OK, God bless you. You've drawn a line in the sand. You're protecting an oil interest over there, an important economic interest for us. But I will support your effort if you'll change the objective from just simply liberating Kuwait to liberating Iraq,' I think we might've had a different political situation."

Buzz about White House aspirations followed Kerrey from the moment he was elected governor in 1982, and only intensified when he came to Washington. It seemed like the next logical step. He had mastered everything he'd tried in business and politics. Running for president, in his estimation, would be no different. In mid-1991, Kerrey had barely completed the first half of his first senatorial term, but when he looked at the field for the 1992 Democratic nomination, it seemed eminently beatable: Bill Clinton, a governor with big personal problems from a small southern state; Senator Tom Harkin, a bombastic liberal from Iowa; Paul Tsongas of Massachusetts, a former senator and cancer survivor; former California Governor Jerry Brown, the original cosmic candidate; and former Virginia Governor Douglas Wilder.

The 1992 campaign started with promise and excitement. Many Democratic pollsters and operatives thought that the party had, after so many lean years, finally found another Kennedy. Kerrey seemed to be the whole package: handsome, intelligent, witty, and a war hero with a dash of Hollywood added. *The New Republic*'s Sidney Blumenthal, writing about the Nebraska rally where Kerrey announced his candidacy in the fall of 1991, said the scene "appeared golden, as if it were an illustration in a storybook. With the great plains of Nebraska stretching out in the distance, the native son stood in the brilliant September sunlight before the dome of the statehouse." His campaign theme song, Bruce Springsteen's muscular "Born to Run," blared and Kerrey rallied the crowd. "I want to lead America's fearless, restless voyage of generational progress." Elegant and a bit high-flown, the speech was all Kerrey—the dreamer, the man of vision and big ideas.

Under the flash and glitter, however, some significant weaknesses lurked. Kerrey was starting a national campaign with no real political base. He was a household name only in Nebraska, an overwhelmingly Republican state almost certain to go with President George Bush again in the general election. Nationally, he was probably better known as Debra Winger's ex-boyfriend than for anything he'd done in the Senate. And the press sometimes confused him with Massachusetts Senator John Kerry, another decorated Vietnam veteran with presidential aspirations. Nonetheless, he was confident that he would beat the long odds, just as he had done against Charlie Thone.

But other problems caught up with him. One involved health care, which Kerrey had hoped to make a signature issue based on his experiences in a military hospital. Kerrey supported universal health insurance, but some of the restaurant chains he and his brother-in-law owned were nonunion, and provided coverage to only a small minority of their 780 employees—an inequity that gave his message a hollow ring. And Kerrey was fined $64,000 by the U.S. Department of Labor, which charged his chain of restaurants and health clubs with 106 child labor law violations, mainly for overworking fifteen-year-olds. Kerrey explained the fines away by pointing out that he was not involved in running his businesses. His in-law kept the books, he said, did the hiring and firing, and was generally responsible for the bottom line. Kerrey's main role was to read a regular report about the company's operations that his brother-in-law provided. The alibi may have gotten him off the hook technically, but in passing the buck Kerrey looked like anything but a potential president.

Kerrey was also exposed by Nebraska's *Midland Business Journal* for speculating at least seventeen times in cattle futures while a member of the Senate Agricultural Committee. This was considered a breach of Senate protocol, if not ethics rules. There was no evidence that he used inside information to enrich himself, but the apparent conflict of interest was just one more signal that Kerrey had, at the very least, used poor judgment and, at the worst, seemed to believe that the rules didn't apply to him.

Finally, there was the campaign's biggest weakness—the candidate himself. Kerrey was never able to formulate a coherent explanation as to why he wanted to be president. It seemed as if he believed charisma alone would carry him through. His speeches were often rambling and listless, and once again he was deeply ambivalent about his military record. Some days he would scarcely mention that he served; on others it was all he would talk about. Aides found him indifferent to the rigors and challenges of presidential campaigning, once even preferring to watch a movie on the VCR in his van than focus on the day's events.

As prospects eroded, his staff was plagued by backbiting and confusion. Shortly before the New Hampshire primary, Kerrey's pollster, Harrison Hickman, faxed an anonymous memo to *The Boston Globe* about Clinton's draft record. After finishing a weak third in that state (behind Clinton and Tsongas), Kerrey himself attacked Clinton, warning that come November he was "unelectable" and was "going to get opened up like a soft peanut" by Republicans exploiting his character weaknesses. ("Boy, was I wrong about that," he would say years later.) Kerrey won an essentially meaningless primary in South Dakota, and by early March he was out of money and out of the race.

While his 1992 presidential campaign was a conspicuous failure, it did little to tarnish his luster in Washington. The same qualities that won over Nebraskans worked in the nation's Capitol as well. As a U.S. Senator, Kerrey remained the power-besotted city's perhaps most eligible and sought-after bachelor. He was rich, handsome, a winner of the Medal of Honor, and still a politician on the rise.

Kerrey enjoyed the Washington press, especially the women.

One in particular was Martha Sherrill, a leggy, attractive reporter and highly regarded writer for the *Washington Post* and other publications. In a piece for the January 1996 *Esquire*, she came closer than any journalist to getting inside of Kerrey's complicated and manipulative personality. In descriptions of late-night telephone calls and other encounters, she painted a portrait of Kerrey smitten.

He was quite embarrassed by Sherrill's recounting of his reaction to a short story by Flannery O'Connor, one of his favorite authors. In "Good Country People," a woman named Hulga is seduced by a traveling Bible salesman who then steals her wooden leg. After reading it, Kerrey left a telephone message for Sherrill. "He was talking in a deep southern accent," Sherrill wrote. " 'This is Hulga Hopewell's Bible salesman friend, and I've got something in my suitcase for you.' Then his voice turned senatorial: 'Ah, it's Bob Kerrey at about five after nine P.M.' Then, he became Bob: 'That was the strangest story you gave me. And I don't remember why you did that. But it's very unsettling and I enjoyed it. Bye.' "

Kerrey said he opened up to Sherrill "more than I should have. I may have been close, but I was closer than I should have been. She would call my telephone and leave a voice mail message. I would call her back, and she would put my voice mail messages in her story. She was using all kinds of statements that were . . ." Kerrey said, his voice trailing off in a halfhearted acknowledgment that he had been complicit in his unmasking.

The most telling moment in Sherrill's piece was not about Kerrey the flirt, but Kerrey the soldier. Once again, in his own tortured way, he crept to the edge of confession to the sins of Vietnam. During one visit to his Senate office, Sherrill noticed an artist's drawing board in a corner. Kerrey used it to cut photographs out of newspapers and paste them into a collage. The pictures were often bleak images of people deep in grief, like Jordan's King Hussein, wiping away tears at the funeral of Yitzhak Rabin, the assassinated Israeli prime minister. Around the picture, Kerrey had written some of the words spoken by Rabin's granddaughter: "We are so cold and so sad. . . . My pain and feelings of loss are so large, too large."

Also in his office was a watercolor he'd painted. With a black marker Kerrey had written the words to an Emily Dickinson poem in the center.

> *Remorse is memory awake,*
> *Her parties all astir—*
> *A presence of departed acts*
> *At window and at door.*
>
> *It's past set down before the soul,*
> *And lighted with a match,*
> *Perusal to facilitate*
> *And help belief to stretch,*
>
> *Remorse is cureless,—the disease*
> *Not even God can heal;*
> *For 'tis His institution,—*
> *The Adequate of Hell.*

When he finished reading it to Sherrill, he spoke softly. "That's me," he said. "That's all you need to know."

Chapter Fifteen

———— ■ ————

WHILE ROBERT KERREY WAS making his first million dollars as a Nebraska businessman, his old SEAL teammate Gerhard Klann was risking his life on a dangerous covert operation inside Iran.

Klann had volunteered for the job, and there were moments, as he dodged checkpoints manned by the Revolutionary Guard, when he wondered if he was going to make it out alive. Desert One—the April 1980 rescue mission to free hostages held in the American embassy in Tehran—was a catastrophic failure. Klann was part of the next effort, dubbed Operation Snowbird and Honey Badger, that began immediately after Desert One. The Iranians were on a heightened state of alert when Klann surreptitiously slipped across the border to assess defenses erected since the last botched rescue and to locate where the Americans were being held. Lacking any real assets in the country, the CIA turned to the Pentagon's secret warriors—men like Klann. He belonged to a small, ad hoc, clandestine counterterrorism unit known to only a handful of U.S. government officials. It was code-named Mob-Six.

CIA officials, trying to assess Klann's fitness for the mission, interviewed him several times to determine his "mental state, background, feelings and beliefs." During one session in a safe house, a German-speaking agent queried Klann on how he would carry out a border crossing into East Berlin. What would Klann do if he was stopped and accused of being a spy? "As I was trying to talk my way out of it, the [CIA] guy pulled a gun and stuck it in my face to monitor my reaction," Klann said. Klann shot back in German. "I called him an asshole . . . told him I was a German citizen and he had no right to treat me like this."

At CIA headquarters in Langley, Virginia, Klann was briefed on the dangers of the mission: "The chances of coming out alive were zero to none," Klann could see. Nobody would say it outright, but everyone Klann talked to hinted that it was a suicide mission. Without the shield of diplomatic immunity, the United States could easily disown Klann and deny the mission if it went bad. Had he been caught during this stormy time of the Iranian Revolution, Klann would have been showcased in a public trial, then promptly sentenced to death for espionage. If he was lucky, he'd be left to rot in a jail for years. One of the CIA men recruiting for the operation told Klann, "I'll leave you for a short while, while you think this over and let it all sink in."

Klann didn't hesitate. "I told him I would undertake this mission impossible," he said. He didn't have much time. The operation was to begin in two weeks. Klann was introduced to a CIA operative named Hans who had an import-export company that did business in Iran. Klann was to be Hans's Austrian assistant and assume the name of Karl Dieter. His travel documents included a forged Austrian passport, a worker's visa for West Germany, and other personal items to verify his name, date of birth, and job status. He was to carry no communications gear or weapons.

The two men traveled overland in an old Volkswagen bus from Austria to Yugoslavia, through Bulgaria and Turkey, and into Iran. Their first stop was in Tabriz, Iran, where Klann tried to make contact with a CIA case officer. They arrived around 10 P.M. during a dust storm, "making it almost impossible to find out where we were going," Klann recalled. The streets were crawling with "ragged-looking" Iranian Revolutionary Guards and roadblocks that randomly halted traffic. "They all had weapons and were not too friendly," Klann said after twice being stopped and questioned. The next day, after being forced from their van and held at gunpoint for fifteen minutes while the vehicle was searched, Klann said to Hans, "Let's get out of here."

In Tehran, Klann checked into the Hotel Elizabeth, six blocks from the besieged American embassy. His assignment was to case the city, collecting intelligence on the whereabouts of the Americans, and to prepare a "target assessment"—an "eyes-on" evaluation of building defenses, guard routines, routes in and out of Tehran, traffic patterns, and other physical requirements for the planned rescue. With a car and Armenian driver provided by Hans, Klann went to work. He checked out the telephone exchange that would have to be taken down by the U.S. troops, went to the big prison that had housed American businessmen rescued in an operation funded by Ross Perot, and drove out to the airport to get an update on antiaircraft missile and radar stations. "We found what we were looking for," Klann said. "The place was heavily fortified." Finally, he looked over a large soccer stadium that was to be "used for a landing site to disembark added troops for [the] second assault."

He spent the next several days on foot, evading roadblocks and Iranian Revolutionary Guards. At the American embassy, where the hostages were still being kept, Klann counted bunkers with armed men, different types of communication lines, and discovered a "heavily-fortified secondary entrance" protected by armored vehicles. After six days of spying, he rendezvoused with Hans and headed to the airport for a flight to Athens.

Air traffic out of Tehran was sporadic, and Klann's flight was delayed for six hours. He nervously sat in a lounge patrolled by guards and bought some Iranian souvenirs. Then he hunkered down, doing his best to avoid the eyes of anyone who might mark him as an enemy of the state.

Klann met his CIA case officer in Athens then flew back to the United States, where he debriefed officials at the spy agency and at the Pentagon. The plans for a second rescue never had to be put into action. Shortly after Ronald Reagan was sworn in as president, Iran released the Americans.

After the Iran debacle, the Navy disbanded Mob-Six and created SEAL Team Six, a permanent supersecret group of elite commandos who would be called on to fight terrorism anywhere in the world on a moment's notice. Klann was among the first of seventy men to be chosen for the new Navy team.

Klann retired from the Navy in January 1990 and went home to Butler, Pennsylvania, an old blue-collar community of German, Italian, and Irish families about thirty miles from Pittsburgh. He returned to school for a degree in computer-aided design and held down a steady job with a steel processing plant, the town's largest employer.

Klann was the classic quiet man. Few if any of his coworkers or neighbors knew that the boy with twelve brothers and sisters who immigrated from Germany at age six was a real-life James Bond who had secretly operated in Iran, Latin America, and the Middle East, among other hot spots. Klann preferred it that way, deflecting praise even from Dan Rather who hailed him in a *60 Minutes II* interview as a silent hero, a man who has "seen a lot of hell for our country."

"No," he told Rather, "it was just something that had to be done."

He was not a boaster, and those who were, especially phony ones, irritated him. While drinking a beer at a veterans hall, Klann overheard a patron crowing about his days as a Navy SEAL. "What class were you in?" Klann asked him. The man stammered, not sure what to say. "Any SEAL would know

After graduating from the University of Nebraska, Kerrey had no interest in joining the military or in Vietnam until he was drafted. He went to Officer Candidate School to become a naval aviator but ended up in Underwater Demolition Team training and the SEALs, where he struggled to make the cut. "He used to come in last in the swims," his younger brother, Bill, said. "But he kept at it."

U.S. Navy

During training in Coronado, California, prospective SEALs spent hours in mud that had the smell and feel of raw sewage. They carried telephone polls in it, did push-ups and sit-ups in it, dove into it, and ate their lunches in it.

Kerrey (left, standing) with Gerhard Klann (right, sitting). Kerrey had his own fears and doubts about the war. "I remember sitting in the audience and listening to Joan Baez say, 'Say yes to the boys who say no.' That's a terrifying thought, that I was gonna get excluded here somehow." Years later, a media-savvy Kerrey relished his commando role: "I was ready to go at Hanoi with a knife in my teeth."

Kerrey handpicked Tucker, Klann, and Ambrose for his team. Tucker, a pro-baseball prospect before Vietnam, called Ambrose "The Mouth" for his cocki-ness. "I had a lot of ego at that time," Ambrose said. Tucker wore rose-colored glasses and blasted "Purple Haze" during training. Leaving Thanh Phong, he told Kerrey, "I don't like this stuff." Kerrey replied, "I don't like it either." Ambrose said, "People were killed for senseless reasons. I cried pretty hard."

Tucker and Klann shared duties carrying the Stoner machine gun. The most experienced of the Raiders, Klann was later handpicked for SEAL Team Six, a super-secret counterterrorism unit. In 1980, he surreptitiously slipped across the border into Iran to assess defenses for a second planned mission to free American hostages. His team leader, Ted Macklin, (back row, second from left, and next to Klann) put him in for the Medal of Honor.

Captain Roy "Latch" Hoffmann (center), Kerrey's swaggering commanding officer in Cam Ranh Bay, was all-Navy and no-nonsense. He carried his own M-16 into the field, along with a silver-handled revolver. "I damn well expect action," he intoned. If no enemy were captured or killed, he said: "You'd hear from me." Kerrey said he was out of *Apocalypse Now*. "He was the classic body-count guy," he said.

Lieutenant William Garlow's Swift boat, PCF 102, (third from left) transported Kerrey's Raiders to Thanh Phong. After the raid, crewman William O'Mara sensed something went terribly wrong. "I knew something was up. They were really quiet. It was eerie."

Thanh Phong was located in the Mekong Delta about seventy-five miles south of Saigon. Remote and desperately poor, the tiny hamlet was, for the most part, untouched by either war or progress. About fifteen kilometers from the county seat of Thanh Phu, there were no school and no young men of fighting age, only older men, women, and children. The SEALs walked on paths by the canals that led to the village.

Kerrey's Raiders came ashore here, on the outskirts of Thanh Phong. It was their first big operation.

A Vietnamese man points to the site where he says the Navy SEALs massacred his relatives around midnight on February 25, 1969.

Pham Tri Lanh was thirty and the wife of a Vietcong fighter when, she says, she witnessed the killings of unarmed women and children. At one site, Lanh said, "After they cut the throat of the old man, they went out and stabbed the three children." At the next site, Lanh said, "They lined them up and shot all of them." Approximately twenty-five women and children were killed that night.

The two large tombs are marked with the names of Bui Van Vat and his wife, Luu Thi Canh. Beside them lay three small, unmarked mounds of cement painted white. They are the apparent resting place for three small children: a boy not yet nine; his sister, about a year older; and the eldest girl, who was approaching thirteen—the grandchildren, Klann said, who were killed in the first hooch. Two other graveyards contain the remains of victims whom villagers say died at the hands of the SEALs.

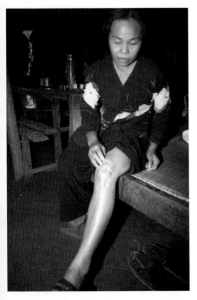

Kerrey's Medal of Honor mission took place on Hon Tam Island, which sat off the mainland coast in the Bay of Nha Trang. His Raiders were after a team of Vietcong sappers encamped there. To maintain surprise, the SEALs scaled a 350-foot rock cliff in pitch darkness and total silence. If one of the men at the top had fallen, it's likely they all would have plunged to their deaths.

Bui Thi Luom was twelve when she barely escaped the massacre that killed at least fifteen of her relatives at Thanh Phong. Showing her wound to foreign correspondents, she said, "If I could get revenge, I would." Her story substantiated accounts given by eyewitnesses and Gerhard Klann.

The mission was a catastrophe. Kerrey, Klann, and Lloyd "Doc" Schrier unexpectedly encountered four Vietcong. An exploding grenade injured Kerrey and Schrier. According to documents, Klann, using a Stoner machine gun, "was instrumental in keeping the sappers from overrunning his element's position and in quickly suppressing the hostile fire." In layman's words, he saved his two teammates' lives.

Richard Nixon was the man Kerrey "hated most on earth." Kerrey contemplated using the Medal of Honor ceremony to take a public stand against the war: "I didn't want the damn medal." Privately, he adored it. At a celebration party, his friend Lewis Puller noticed Kerrey "did not allow the medal and its silk-lined box out of his sight for the entire night."

Plagued by nightmares, Kerrey would rise early and run to the Vietnam Memorial. "You have to be steely-eyed," he said of his visits there, "if you really want to avoid sobbing like a baby." On one trip, he stenciled the name of James Gore, a member of Kerrey's sister squad, Fire Team Alpha, who died in a helicopter crash in Vietnam on June 23, 1970.

A smitten Governor Kerrey sent Hollywood film star Debra Winger a "quite affectionate" note when she came to Nebraska to film *Terms of Endearment*. Kerrey nicknamed her "Wing." Opinion polls were positive: Few Nebraskans cared that the divorced Kerrey was living with a single woman in the governor's mansion. "We fell head over heels in love." Kerrey said.

Bill Clinton and Bob Kerrey shared a complicated relationship, a combustible mixture of rivalry, mutual respect, envy, mistrust, and loathing. The two dynamic baby-boomer politicians had known each other since their days as governors but had never become close. Kerrey called Clinton an "unusually good liar" but said "it would have been difficult not to say yes" when Clinton was considering him for vice president. Kerrey believed that Hillary nixed the idea.

Kerrey carried his secret through three decades of what was, by all appearances, a storybook existence: war hero, self-made millionaire businessman, governor, and a United States senator. His final conquest was a run for the 1992 Democratic nomination for president. He started with promise and excitement, but after a few months, he looked like anything but a potential president. He was deeply ambivalent about his military record. Some days he would scarcely mention that he served, on others it was all he would talk about. He won South Dakota but floundered elsewhere, eventually dropping out early.

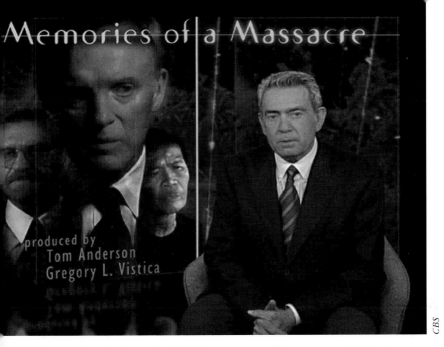

Memories of a Massacre

produced by
Tom Anderson
Gregory L. Vistica

CBS

After leaving the Senate in 2002, Kerrey agreed to interviews with *The New York Times* and *60 Minutes II* for a joint reporting project on the Thanh Phong raid. Dan Rather was determined that the *60 Minutes II* segment would be fair and show Kerrey every courtesy. "The truth of the matter is I came to this interview saying it's the stupidest thing I ever did in my life," Kerrey said.

Veteran newsman and *60 Minutes II* producer Tom Anderson interviewed Pham Tri Lanh. Her story matched up with Klann's in critical details. When told about Lanh, Kerrey became visibly shaken and later accused both media organizations of collaborating with the Communist Vietnamese government.

After his first interview with Rather, Kerrey came back a second time to rebut Pham Tri Lanh's story. In doing so, he acknowledged committing an "atrocity." Kerrey leaked his version of the story four days before the *New York Times* article was to be published. He wanted to undermine the *Times* and CBS.

what class they graduated from," Klann said. "I said to him, 'You can either get up and walk out of here in one piece or I'm going to throw you through that plate-glass window.' The guy got up, didn't even finish his beer, and left."

Soldiering was a noble tradition to Klann, who came from a long line of German military men. His father and uncle had fought against the Americans in World War II; his grandfather had been in the German Army during World War I. Four of Gerhard's brothers joined the U.S. military. One became an Army Green Beret. His best friends were retired military or ex-SEALs, and he kept in touch with most of Kerrey's Raiders. The Raiders' closeness didn't make Thanh Phong an easy subject. Some of them occasionally flirted with it in brief conversations and pledged to one day hash out their memories. But the attempts always faltered. Klann said some of the Raiders intended to air their feelings when a recuperating Bob Kerrey came to New Orleans in early 1971. "We thought we'd sit down and discuss this," he said. "It never came out. It's like everybody has it blocked out." Instead, they ended up razzing Kerrey about his medal.

Nearly thirty years later, memories of that night were still an impassable frontier. In the summer of 2000, six of the seven Raiders came to Washington on the thirtieth anniversary of Kerrey's receiving the Medal of Honor. Only Tucker did not attend. The others planted a tree on the grounds of the Capitol in Kerrey's name. They spent two days together, visiting the Vietnam Memorial but never addressing the incident at Thanh Phong. "I've talked about it to my wife," Kerrey said. "I've talked about it to ministers. I've talked about it to maybe one or two other people. But I have never had a conversation with my men."

Still doing research on Kerrey, I attended the tree-planting ceremony. Each of the SEALs knew that I had uncovered most of their secret (I caught Peterson pointing me out to Knepper during the ceremony), but they still lacked the will to revisit that night with any forcefulness. "They feel the same way I do," Klann said. "They're all sick. And still they live with the haunting memories of that night just like I do. If you could take it back, sure I'd take it back. Everybody would. But it's one of those things that happened, and I think we all paid for it," he said. "None of us could come up with an answer why it happened, how it happened, how we let it happen."

Klann never had the destructive feelings of rage or went through the tormented soul-searching that drove Bob Kerrey to thoughts of suicide. Instead, he carried his guilt quietly, going about his daily business and confining his memories to a small circle. He unburdened himself to doctors at a veterans' medical center and quietly shared what had happened in Thanh Phong with SEALs he trusted, including one of his commanders. "This goes against my whole moral fiber," he told one of his superiors.

A man as guarded as Klann does not open up easily—especially to a journalist.

I first tried to persuade him in a March 1997 letter to talk about what he and Kerrey had endured in Vietnam. The letter went unanswered. I telephoned his house, leaving messages on his answering machine. He never telephoned back. I caught him once by phone, but he was hesitant. "I've been told that Kerrey killed a bunch of women and children," I said. "We all did it," Klann said. He hung up promising to think about going further. He'd call back, he said. But he never did.

It was time to confront him in person. I drove from D.C. to Butler, crossed my fingers, and knocked on his front door. No answer. I left a note with my number at the Pittsburgh Hilton asking him to please call. By ten that evening I had given up hope. Maybe Kerrey was right. SEALs really didn't talk. Then the phone rang, and in a nasally voice he agreed to meet after work the next day in the bar of a Days Inn. Klann had decided to "cleanse [his] soul."

I arrived early and took a seat near the entrance to the bar. We were both at a disadvantage in that neither knew what the other looked like. But there was no mistaking the large man who bounced through the door around five o'clock. Gerhard Klann was about 6'2" and weighed at least 220 pounds. The lean waist and wiry build of his Vietnam photos was gone. (When he volunteered for the SEALs, his brother said, "You're too skinny; you'll never make it. They'll kill you in there.") Now he was thick, powerfully built like a bruising fullback, but he walked with the grace and agility of a dancer. He was wearing a T-shirt, jean shorts cut at the knee, and running shoes. His hair was sandy, and there was a touch of gray in his neatly trimmed beard. Large glasses perched on a long nose in a broad face.

Except for the bartender, we were alone in the tacky lounge. We sidled up to the bar, ordered a couple of light beers, and exchanged small talk, tiptoeing around Vietnam. Klann had an easy confidence to him and didn't put on airs. He had come from an honest working-class family in a blue-collar town. He went to college on a basketball scholarship but ignored his academics. That meant only one thing in the sixties. "If you didn't have a certain [grade] point average, then stand by for the draft, boy." His oldest brother had just been discharged from the Navy so Klann decided to follow his lead. Then he heard about the SEALs and found his calling.

Even when Vietnam came up, it still seemed indelicate to raise Thanh Phong outright. So we started on the margins, discussing his teammates and what he remembered about them. He laughed easily, remembering how Doc Schrier "turned green" after they drank some cheap booze. Kerrey "was a good leader, who joked a lot," Klann said. Tucker was "crazy" in an OK way, and Ambrose was "a good operator." Peterson and Knepper were his friends.

The closest he came to Thanh Phong that first day at the

Days Inn was to say, "I've regretted it ever since the day it happened, and I'll take it to my grave, which by all rights I should, for what happened then." Even that brief confession produced a sense of relief that he was finally "getting this off my chest," as he put it. We would meet several more times and exchange numerous telephone calls, and Klann would sit with Dan Rather for an hour-long special on *60 Minutes II*. Always his words came the same way—guarded at first, then slowly pouring out. There was no rant, no self-pity, only fastidious attention to detail, shrouded in great regret and remorse.

"You coming up?"

It was Gerhard calling several months after we first met. He seemed eager to recount the story in more detail. "There are some things I haven't told you yet that you should know," he said.

We met around 4:30 P.M. in a bar not far from Three Rivers Stadium in Pittsburgh. The place could have been used for a scene in *The Deer Hunter*. Again it began with light beer and small talk. But he cut short the conversation and offered to take me to the private German club he belonged to. We climbed into his large pickup truck with a camper and sped off.

It was as if we had stepped into a Haufbrau House in Munich. Men and woman, mostly seniors, were in traditional dress and speaking the language of their homeland. Dark beer flowed and accordion music wafted through the room. Klann was proud of his heritage and felt at home. And it was here where he felt safe enough to really open up. "It's just one of those things that never goes away," he began. "I can block it out from my mind, but it only stays gone for a little while. There's a number of things that bring me right back to that day as if it happened last night."

He appeared almost trancelike, as if he were visualizing every move, every small detail, every terrible moment of his actions in Thanh Phong. There was no equivocation, no intentional fuzziness in his recall, no attempts to dissemble or avoid. He stiffened himself with light beer and an occasional shot of Jagermeister. Klann was, after all, confessing to what, by his own description, was a horrendous war crime.

He didn't want to attack or place blame on his friends, he said, but Kerrey's Raiders had indeed made a terrible mistake. The killings, he said, just happened. Somehow their training had broken down, and they ended up murdering innocent civilians. "We're not killers inside. We are just SEALs and our training makes us different, more intense," he said. "We do not have that cold heart to go out and [just] kill somebody." But in a war, Klann knew that elite SEALs could, if the circumstances required it, be stone-cold killers. "It was never set out in any class or in any written book or in any class lesson that says that's what you're gonna be," he said. "It just came with the program. It was a thing that was never said outright."

He started with the story of Duc, the district chief, who told the SEALs about the two grade-school children blown away by a grenade near his headquarters. " 'I want to even the score,' " Klann remembered Duc saying. "He didn't want anybody not loyal to the government left alive. That was his absolute wish, that anybody we came across in there we had his permission to eliminate."

The American-trained Duc may have wished for revenge, but Kerrey had another objective that night, taking out the village secretary. Their orders were clear: "Bring back anybody if you think they're gonna be of any intelligence worth," Klann said, "or eliminate them." This was their immediate task at hand, and they considered it dangerous enough. Though Klann says they talked about Duc's desire to avenge the schoolchildren, it was not their intention to slaughter the innocent inhabitants of a peasant village. "We never, ever thought that that's what we would do," said Klann.

In Klann's account, the operation went wrong almost from the beginning. First there was the hooch that didn't appear on their supposedly flawless maps of the village. It was Ambrose, the point man, who first realized their mistake, that they had stumbled onto old Bui Van Vat, his wife, and their grandchildren. Though it was around midnight, he was sitting out front, smoking a cigarette, Klann recalled. "We were right beside the hooch and we were virtually standing inside the door before they even knew that we were there. And a few of them were in a bunker." Moving swiftly but not yet violently, the invaders secured the four remaining family members.

"What happened then?" I asked. It was obvious they had screwed up. Kerrey's Raiders now had a frightened family of possible Vietcong sympathizers who were unlikely to be cooperative with the Americans. In tours past, Klann had faced similar dilemmas. In each instance, the villagers they held were questioned then freed. But this was a new team, facing combat for the first time.

There was no question the raid had been compromised by the noncombatants. Only one issue—an enormous one—was on the table: abort or push on. If they retreated, their first major sortie to take out a target would be remembered as a flop. It was Kerrey's call. He didn't like the idea of tying the captives up; someone could get loose and alert the Vietcong. The team stood ready to follow the orders of their command-ing officer. "We were in a war zone. And that's not the time to question orders," Klann said. "You got one leader there, and that's his job. He leads. The rest of us were there. We are in the chain of command. He gave the order and we obeyed."

Without flinching, Klann said the order was to kill them. "We were gonna continue on with the op and head toward the main village." Klann recalled how difficult it had been to kill Bui Van Vat. He had wrestled Bui Van Vat away from the children so they couldn't see as he stabbed the old man twice. "But he wouldn't die. He kept moving . . . fighting back. He was so strong for somebody who was dying. I couldn't believe it. It was a terrible thing. I'll never forget his eyes."

As Klann struggled with him, he got help from a fellow SEAL. "Kerrey came over," Klann said. "I said, 'Hold this guy down,' and he put his knee on his chest after I knocked the guy down. I grabbed the guy by the hair and pulled his head back and cut his throat." The old woman and the children met a similar fate at about the same time, he said. It took them "a very short time," Klann said, to dispatch with the family. "We never looked at them as a family. We looked at them as the enemy. They were not an initial target," Klann said. "This little place just happened to be there. Wrong place, wrong spot."

They sheathed their bloody knives and quietly turned in the direction of what they believed was the heart of Thanh Phong, where they would find the village secretary's meeting. It was slow going, Klann said. Their path took them through thick brush on the canal that ran near Thanh Phong's rice paddies. In the darkness, they could barely make out the hooches, "three or four main ones, a couple of bunkers, a couple of big bunkers, and then there were some small outer hooches," Klann said. "I think there may have been a few little places outside of that. But the main village, I'd say, couldn't have been more than about four or five hooches."

But they safely made their way to what they thought was the meeting site. "No shots were fired," Klann said. "We more or less went in and took everybody by surprise. We gathered everybody up, searched the place, searched everything." Using the Vietnamese interpreter they brought with them, the SEALs started questioning the villagers. But it was a dead end. "We didn't get nothing," said Klann.

Now deep into Thanh Phong they realized the operation

was totally botched. The target of the mission, the Vietcong village secretary, was not among the some twenty-one people now cowering before the SEALs. "It was very tense, and we were in a bad situation. We dug a hole for ourselves," said Klann. Once again, they faced a stark choice. "It wasn't a long discussion," he said. "I mean we didn't have time to carry on a great debate about this. Our chances of survival would have gone down the longer we stayed in there."

Letting the prisoners go put the Raiders in danger. Once freed, the villagers would almost certainly trigger an alarm and some kind of ambush before the SEALs reached the Swift boat, or so they thought. Tying them up was out of the question. There were too many people, and all it would take was one wriggling free to cost them their lives. "It was brought up: 'Let's look at what we got here. If we try to leave now, we're never gonna get outta here. We're gonna have to fight our way outta here tooth and nail, and we're not equipped to do that.' Everybody was pretty much of the same mind," Klann said. " 'We got twenty-one people here now. What are we gonna do with them?' "

About six feet separated the frightened villagers from the men who came to be known as "the devils with green faces." There were women and children, even a baby, huddled together. "I would say, from what I saw, there was probably a couple of small babies. Out of the group, probably the majority of them were kids. And some women."

Again, the decision belonged to Kerrey. "I don't remember his exact words, but he was the officer in charge. The call was his."

The situation was made more complex by the killings in the first hooch. "We already compromised ourselves by killing the other group," he said. "Everybody knew the SEALs were in the area."

"Everybody" was the American military who could easily place the Raiders in the vicinity. The second killings could be explained away as a firefight. The first could not, which was perhaps the reason for deleting it from the after-action report.

The order, as Klann remembered it, was straightforward. "We're gonna kill 'em and then we're getting out of here."

"We lined up, and we opened fire. Thirty seconds. Sporadically for a minute. There were still some people alive. We found out who was still alive and shot them. Everybody opened up. Yeah. Raked them." They stopped for a "little bit," Klann said. "It was quiet. It was dead quiet. Then you could just hear certain people, hear their moaning. So we would just fire into that area till it was silent there. And that was it, until we were sure everybody was dead. I remember one baby crying. That baby was probably the last one alive. Shot like the rest of them. I can see it. I relive it often enough. It was just carnage. We just virtually slaughtered those people. I mean, there was blood flying up, bits and pieces of flesh hitting us." Klann was carrying the Stoner, the rapid-fire machine-gun, and he remembers shooting 750 rounds. "I shot up about three-quarters of my ammo that I was carrying. So that takes it right about [to] seven hundred fifty. Everybody else was firing. I would say, with everybody's ammo load, [we shot] eleven hundred to twelve hundred rounds."

A body count revealed at least fourteen dead. It was now time to get out quickly. Where a few minutes earlier they worried that an escaped prisoner could alert the Vietcong, they could now be sure that the automatic weapons fire had just woken up the entire village. What they didn't know at the time was that the massacre hadn't been necessary to gain safe passage from Thanh Phong. Hunkered down fewer than 400 yards away, eleven Vietcong guerrillas were guarding a meeting of VC leaders. The guerrillas, who carried outdated weapons, made the decision, according to one of them, Tran Van Rung, to keep silent and not to engage.

The SEALs radioed to Garlow's Swift boat with the message "Start heading in, we're coming out," Klann said. They took an alternate route back to the river, using a mixture of walking and running. "A little bit of both," Klann said. "We didn't run to the point of being careless. We moved out smartly." Once aboard the warship, their departure was delayed by a fishing net tangled up in the propellers. Several SEALs dove into the water and cleared the tangled netting.

Kerrey's Raiders were quiet on the trip back to Cam Ranh Bay. When they got back to their base and began to clean their weapons, it was obvious to Klann that everybody had fired their guns at the unarmed villagers. "The realization of what did occur that night didn't hit me until we were back at our base. I don't think I slept for three days. I just could not get that out of my mind. Even to this day, I still can't get it out of my mind," Klann said. "It breaks my heart every time I think about it. I try not to dwell on it."

It was close to eleven o'clock when Klann finally finished talking and put down his last Jagermeister. He wasn't drunk, but he was punchy, depleted emotionally. "Somehow things just changed that night. Looking back on it, I don't know where the turning point was, what brought it on. It was just a turn of events. As they unfolded, they started to get worse."

One of the last things Klann said that night was in defense of Kerrey. "He's done great things, and he's a great individual," Klann said. "He's dedicated a lot of time and effort for causes, good causes. And no matter how they view this, or how they look on him now, they should never forget what he's done in the meantime."

It was an amazing story. But was it true? In a court of law, Klann's confession would be called "an admission against interest." A court usually gave more weight to the testimony of a person who admitted guilt than to one who denied committing a crime. It would be human nature to deny such a grisly deed. But was Klann mixing up different operations?

Had alcohol impaired his memory as some would later charge? Was it faulty? After interviewing Klann, I spoke to William O'Mara, a crewman on the Swift boat that carried the Raiders to Thanh Phong. Without being prompted, O'Mara recalled the boat's propellers becoming entwined in a fishing net while trying to depart. Klann had recalled that same story as well, which made me feel more comfortable about his memory of that night. Could it be that Klann had a vendetta against Kerrey? And most important of all, what would Bob Kerrey say about all this?

Mike Walker, the archivist at the Navy's historical center, always wore a cheap white medical coat that hung to his knees. It was soiled black around the pockets, stained from hours in the stacks each day handling the documents that composed the storied history of the United States Navy. His expertise was Vietnam, but his real interest was SEAL operations. He knew SEAL history as well, if not better, than anybody. During the war Walker had been a "lerp," a soldier who went out on a small team to conduct long-range reconnaissance patrols deep into enemy territory. It was dangerous work.

For months, I had been plowing through SEAL spot reports that Walker had been pulling from the stacks. I didn't tell him about Kerrey, only that I was researching an article on a particular SEAL squad. To help Walker narrow down the search, I gave him dates and locations provided by Klann, but nothing more. The archive was often crawling with journalists, academics, and authors who would relish a scoop on a Medal of Honor winner who allegedly had committed a war crime. Had the Navy known what I was after, my investigation would have become more difficult. Word of my findings would rocket up the chain of command to the Navy's legisla-

tive affairs office on Capitol Hill, which would inform the
senator. Then Kerrey, who already suspected that I was on to
what had happened in Thanh Phong, would know for sure.

Yet, so far, the thousands of pages I had reviewed contained not a scrap about Kerrey's team. Mike Walker
explained that the SEALs were terrible record keepers; at
command headquarters in Coronado a few years ago, thousands of Vietnam-era reports were destroyed before they made
their way to the archives. It was not done out of malice,
Walker said, just convenience.

Eventually Walker was able to steer me to a large volume
of boxed-up material labeled "Market Time," the name of
Latch Hoffmann's command. It hadn't been declassified, prin-
cipally because nobody had the time to review the records
until I requested it under the Freedom of Information Act.
A Navy petty officer at the archives promptly examined the
boxes of material I wanted and stamped the records as
releasable. I had spent most of the summer of 1998 in the
archives without much excitement. Now I had a glimmer of
hope when Walker told me about these files, but so far they'd
revealed nothing. I was about to give up when I found a February 28, 1969, "attaboy" from the commander of the Special
Warfare Group in the Pacific sent to Roy Hoffmann at Cam
Ranh Bay.

**Market Time SEALs have gained a well deserved
spotlight as a result of their successful and highly
productive operations in the Vietcong infested
Than Phu Secret Zone. These special operations
resulting in 21 VC KIA, destruction of 2 structures
and capture of 2 chicom carbines establishes Delta
Platoon as an important fighting unit of TF 115.
The Kerrey Raiders of Market Time ably assisted by
PCF 102 not only surprised the enemy in his own**

sanctuary but struck him a severe and fatal blow.
Well Done.

The date of the message (Feb. 28) was close to the date of
the raid (Feb. 25). The location fit, and the numbers of dead it
described were roughly the same. But the document in itself
proved nothing. In fact, it did not entirely support the version Klann told me. It only reported that the SEALs killed a
lot of people in an engagement their superiors were proud of.

In another box was a February 14, 1969, after-action
report to Commander Connolly in Cat Lo describing the
"searching of hooches and bunkers" and how Kerrey's team
"interrogated fourteen women and small children." It contained dates, times, and insertion and extraction coordinates.
I checked the coordinates on a military map against a grid
and the location. Not surprisingly, they matched up for the
village of Thanh Phong. This message appeared to substanti-
ate that the Raiders had gone into Thanh Phong on at least
one previous mission and rounded up only women and children and no men.

Then I located the February 25 spot report that the Raiders
had sent just after their bloody incursion. It described the
action as the "abduction of the Thanh Phong village secretary." "Received fire from hooches," it said, and reported that
the SEALs returned fire, shooting 1,200 rounds, then killing
"personnel running from hooches." The number of dead was
twenty-one, which was about what Klann remembered and
what was reported on the "attaboy" message. But the report
contradicted Klann. He said they had not been shot at. This
report clearly stated they were apparently firing in self-defense.

So far, the documents revealed that Kerrey and his team
had been involved in a horrible mess and that a lot of women
and children perished as a result of the raid. If the records
were an accurate reflection of the events in Thanh Phong, the

deaths of noncombatants were a mistake, a terrible accident of war. On February 14 the noncombatants were described as women and children. Yet the message recounting the killings on February 25 described the victims only as "VC." It appeared the report was shading the truth, if not attempting to cover up the most pertinent facts of the raid—that they had killed the wrong people.

A third message was even more suspicious.

> **District chief advised that area is total free-fire zone. He said that if people weren't GVN [Government of Vietnam] he didn't want them alive.**

Klann had used almost the same words to me in describing Duc's wish for vengeance. Duc delivered a similar ultimatum to villagers in Thanh Phong and An Nohn during his rush south in response to the grenade attack. And now, according to the Navy message, the SEALs were apparently being authorized by Duc to enforce his edict.

The message went from the SEALs to Captain Hoffmann, who promptly forwarded it to Admiral Zumwalt, the Navy's top commander in Vietnam, on February 27, 1969. By this time, Cook's Army headquarters in the Thanh Phu District had sent several disturbing messages to Connolly, one of which said "atrocities" had been committed in Thanh Phong by a squad of Navy SEALs. It appeared from Hoffmann's message that Zumwalt either wanted to know what had happened or that Hoffmann was breaking the news to his old friend. The message included a reference to the SEALs taking fire and responding, which would establish, if correct, that they acted in self-defense.

Had Kerrey's team not filed the February 14 report about their interrogation of women and children—a report that included the exact coordinates of the village of Thanh Phong—it is possible that nobody would have been able to document Klann's claims. The later after-action reports only described the dead as "VC." Those dispatches standing alone would probably not have been questioned.

I found other documents that supplied pieces of the story: records of the Swift boats that transported Kerrey to Thanh Phong and around the Mekong Delta, spot reports from his squad's combat sorties after he was wounded and sent home, and dozens of pages filed by Kerrey's sister unit, under the command of Tim Wettack. But the biggest piece remained missing.

It was now time to call the senator.

Late in 1998, Kerrey was keeping a frantic pace of political activity when I telephoned his office seeking a time and date for an interview. He clearly had his eye on another presidential run in 2000, with appearances in New Hampshire and Iowa, fund-raisers for other candidates, and dozens of speeches. Making time to rehash his short military career in Vietnam was not a high priority for the senator. Although Kerrey had ostensibly made himself available—at the *Newsweek* lunch in June, he said "when you're ready . . . just give me a call"—he also said "SEALs don't talk." Now, in November, after talking with every Raider and spending months at the naval archives, I was ready to do what journalists call the "confrontation interview."

His scheduler could squeeze me in on December 7, but the meeting could only take place in Nebraska, not Washington. The Nebraska part was fine, but the December date was disquieting—the day Pearl Harbor was attacked. I was not sure if the man who wanted to be president would survive the bomb I was about to drop.

Chapter Sixteen

BOB KERREY'S APPROACH TO the 2000 presidential campaign was everything that his run-up to 1992 was not: focused, thoughtful, tireless. Just as in 1992, Kerrey saw an opening. While the Democratic nomination had once been considered Vice President Al Gore's to lose, Bill Clinton's scandal-drenched second term scrambled those assumptions. Monica Lewinsky, as well as Gore's own fund-raising excesses in 1996, had made him politically vulnerable.

This time, Kerrey moved decisively. He had already established political networks in Iowa and New Hampshire, the two states that drove his party's nominating process. In 1998, he spent as much time as his Senate schedule allowed in each state, taking a combined twelve trips.

He also became newly serious about money, something he'd sniffed at in the past. He accepted the chairmanship of the Democratic Senatorial Campaign Committee and turned it into a money-making boot camp for the party. Tom Daschle, then the Senate's minority leader, told *Time* magazine that Kerrey would bray "like a drill sergeant, knocking out orders for the amount of fund-raising he expected." The nearly $90 million he raised for fellow Democrats were also political IOUs that Kerrey could cash in for another run at the White House. He sprinkled donations strategically, with special attention to states that would be important in a primary battle with Gore, including New York, Florida, California, and Washington.

Kerrey disliked the dominant role money played in American politics, but he was a natural fund-raiser. His after-dinner speeches weaved stories about his military career with patriotic themes, and a video of his singing "Waltzing Mathilda" on the night of his election to the Senate in 1988 delighted campaign contributors. His own political action committee, created to advance education policy, one of his major issues, easily collected $1.3 million in less than five months. He gave nearly half of it to Democratic candidates up for election in November 1998.

Although they were both Vietnam veterans and one-time Senate colleagues, Kerrey and Gore never had much of a relationship, personal or professional. One exception was a strange episode at the height of the 1996 campaign. Kerrey, then vice-chairman of the Senate Intelligence Committee, learned that Gore had instructed CIA director John Deutch to not notify Congress that the agency was covertly helping to protect Gore's two daughters during lengthy stays in Spain. The agency is required by law to provide Congressional notification on all covert operations. It ultimately did so, telling the Democrats first, then waiting months to tell the Republicans. "That's a bad thing to do," Kerrey said of Gore. "He must have assumed something was wrong. It's one of those gray areas."

The CIA had taught the girls classified techniques on how to live under an alias. Karenna Gore, who was going to work as a reporter at *El País* in Madrid, would use the nom de guerre Karenna Aitcheson—her mother's maiden name. She was given a false passport and was provided a phony driver's license from the state of Tennessee. And she was given a special telephone number to call—one that would bounce through several different telephone switching stations before it arrived at the vice president's phone. The same arrangements were made for Karenna's sister, who planned a shorter trip.

Jeff Smith, then the CIA's general counsel, advised Deutch that the agency had the legal authority to carry out the assignment but said it was "exceedingly ill advised." Despite Deutch's approval of the operation, the CIA's top management recommended against helping the Gores. If something went wrong, if the girls were hurt or abducted, the agency would take the blame for doing too little or not doing enough. "There were risks in this operation," said Smith. He insisted that Congress be told. "This was clearly within the four corners of the kind of activities that we routinely notified Congress about," Smith said. But Gore balked at the recommendation.

I had uncovered the story for *Newsweek* in October 2000, then went to Kerrey for a comment. Without divulging anything classified, he said the operation was "an inappropriate use of CIA resources. We've never done this before." But he sympathized with the agency's number two official, George Tenet (now CIA director), who had pushed for full disclosure. The story never broke, and when Kerrey became president of the New School, he gave Tenet a standing offer to join his faculty should he wish to leave the CIA.

On December 2, 1998, Kerrey and Gore were scheduled to preview their campaign themes in speeches to the Democratic Leadership Council (DLC), a major organization of party moderates. Kerrey had yet to be openly critical of Gore, but when he saw an advance copy of the vice president's speech he was livid. Entitled "Practical Idealism," it was Gore's attempt to frame a message that appealed to both centrists and liberals. To Kerrey, it simply reflected Gore's timidity and lack of vision. Appearing first, he went straight for the vice president:

"Let us be practical, yes, but let us not dress practicality up in a fancy costume and let it go masquerading as a vision for America's future. Practicality is not America's ideal. Shrinking from a challenge, settling for less than our dreams, taking the easy route away from the tough problems. These are impractical."

Kerrey was still steaming when he got into his car after the speech. He turned to Greg Weiner, his communications director, and picked up where he left off a few minutes earlier with the DLC. "Normandy was not a practical mission," he said. "Putting a man on the moon was not a practical mission. Changing Medicare was not a practical mission."

Kerrey clearly sounded like he was in the hunt. He'd also grown more at home in the Senate since 1992, polishing his legislative skills and putting himself in the middle of the debate over reforming so-called entitlement programs like Social Security and Medicare. He found the business of writing laws to help people exhilarating. "Citizens," he said, "underestimate the good that the law can do."

He also took on the White House, and the man who beat him out for the Democratic nomination, Bill Clinton. The two dynamic baby-boomer politicians shared a complicated relationship, a combustible mixture of rivalry, mutual respect, envy, mistrust, and loathing. They had known each other since their days as governors but had never become close. "I wouldn't go so far as to call him a friend," Kerrey said.

With Clinton in the White House and Kerrey in the Senate, the two men did their best to keep their relationship civil and professional, but the scars from 1992 remained raw. The Clinton camp never forgot Kerrey's devastating "soft peanut" sound bite. And, long after the votes were counted, Kerrey still seethed over losing to someone he clearly viewed as the lesser man.

Clinton's search for a vice-presidential running mate only made matters worse. He had flirted with Kerrey, holding out the prospect of a spot on the ticket. Even with his reservations about Clinton's character, "it would have been difficult not to say yes," Kerrey recalled. But when he flew to Little Rock for his meeting with Clinton, he saw that Hillary was absent from the room. "I sort of smelled the air," he said. "I figured this was a two-person selection process." Stories, probably prompted by a leak from Kerrey, had the First Lady-to-be nixing him.

A year later, Kerrey held the swing vote in the Senate on final passage of Clinton's 1993 economic plan, the early centerpiece of the Clinton presidency. Kerrey believed that the administration had not gone far enough in cutting entitlements, and the two argued bitterly over Kerrey's initial decision to oppose it. "Fuck you!" the president snapped when they spoke over the phone. Clinton believed that his entire presidency rode on the economic package.

At the height of a desperate effort by the White House to change Kerrey's mind, he slipped out to a movie at Union Station near the Capitol. He ultimately came around, and "regretfully" voted for the economic package. But the showdown only deepened the residue of resentment and mistrust between the two. In a later effort at rapprochement, Clinton gave the ex-Navy SEAL a copy of *Blackhawk Down,* and asked him to review the account of the failed Army commando raid in Somalia. Kerrey thought the gesture considerate but meaningless.

As hard as Kerrey worked at his transformation to statesman, the old anger and sarcasm was still there beneath the surface. He never squandered a chance to kick Clinton in the shins, describing the president to an interviewer as "an unusually good liar." (Publicly he tried to take it back, but in private his contempt for Clinton remained undiluted. "Oh, that fucker Clinton, he's the biggest liar . . . he lies better than anyone," Kerrey said after dinner one night in 1999.) Kerrey subtly needled the president during his second inaugural, wearing his Medal of Honor to the parties and dinners that celebrated Clinton's victory. The message was not lost on Washington's cognoscenti, who had never seen Senator Kerrey wear the prestigious medallion with its blue sash. Clinton was the draft dodger who skipped the war. Kerrey was the hero who shed real blood.

Just when supporters were ready to say that he had grown up, old Cosmic Bob floated back into radar range. At one point in the process of exploring a presidential race, Kerrey announced that he would not be an anti-Gore spoiler. "I don't intend to enter a race to cause anybody any difficulty," he told reporters. Friends just threw up their hands.

Still, Kerrey seemed to have changed. The senator who a few years earlier had voted against authorizing the use of force in the Persian Gulf was now more conservative, even hawkish, on military matters. (He still had a dovish streak in him, but one limited to the reduction of nuclear weapons.)

On Vietnam, he had come full circle. The occasional war protestor who once said he'd go to jail instead of into the military, now saw the Vietnam War as a noble but corrupted cause. Kerrey told audiences that his "heart saw what his eyes, blinded by anger, pain and confusion, had overlooked. The courage of hundreds of thousands of Americans who traveled across a strange ocean to a foreign place to lay their lives and bodies and innocence on the battlefield for the freedom of people they did not know."

One of the most dramatic manifestations of Kerrey's conversion came during a debate with Robert McNamara at the University of Nebraska. McNamara, a principal architect of American involvement in southeast Asia, had written a controversial 1995 book (*In Retrospect*) in which he accepted blame for prolonging a war he knew the United States could not win. Now, McNamara was speaking out around the country against America's involvement in future wars. Once asked to state his views in the form of a bumper sticker, McNamara told Nebraskans, "OK. I'll give you a bumper sticker: Reduce Carnage."

Kerrey at first tried to make peace with McNamara. Craning his neck to see him (he was sitting at the far end of another table) Kerrey said, "I harbored hatred toward the men I believed responsible for the failure of Vietnam—Johnson, McNamara, Nixon, and many others. So, Mr. McNamara, for whatever it's worth, I stopped hating you long ago." But Kerrey refused to accept his mea culpa and insisted the United States had done the right thing in fighting the war. "I'm a peace-loving guy, but Al Capone said, 'A smile will get you a long way in life, but a smile and a gun will get you further.'" As his hometown crowd applauded its approval, Kerrey said, "The fight for freedom is the highest value of all." McNamara just sat there, looking pained and confused. If there were lingering questions about Kerrey's past allegiance to the peace movement, he answered them that night on the stage in Lincoln. The "peacenik" had effectively traded places with a man who was once among the most formidable of hawks.

In speeches, Senator Kerrey condemned Vietnam's leaders as evil Communists and embraced his newfound patriotism. He told the story of his "zealous love" and "fierce loyalty" for his nation and how Vietnam had at first robbed him of those youthful feelings. "I will tell you a story of one American," Kerrey would intone to his audiences. "A man who lost faith in his country, whose love became bitter disappointment when he discovered his leaders had lied and betrayed him. Before the betrayal he was patriotic. Afterward he was not. Before, he believed in his country. Afterward he distrusted it. Then, much later, his love came back. His patriotism returned. And his patriotism grew stronger because it was a choice."

When the Clinton administration planned to normalize relations between Washington and Hanoi, Kerrey telephoned his old nemesis the day before the announcement. He warned that he would walk out of the White House ceremony if there was any hint of apology. "The people of Vietnam are grateful," Kerrey said. "They recognize that we cared enough about their freedom to put 58,000 names on a wall. We ought to go in with our heads held high and our chests out and proud for what we did, saying, 'We're the United States of America, and we're here to try to extend freedom in this country.'"

It would be easy to label Kerrey's reversal as simply political repackaging, putting him more in step with the country's growing conservatism. And perhaps it was nothing more than that. But more likely, he was returning to the values he had grown up with on the prairie before departing for Vietnam. Kerrey was no die-hard liberal—he was still a registered Republican at thirty-five. Still, his shift earned him some withering commentary from pundits and other critics, who called him "quicksilver" and "flip-flop Bob."

Kerrey was an all-but-announced presidential candidate when he met me in the conference room of his small Omaha office on the chilly, gray morning of December 7, 1998. The strain of his precampaign mobilization was visible. He coughed from a lingering cold, and his handsome face was drawn, looking much older than his age of fifty-five. His blue eyes were framed in a face lined with stress. Although he had tinted his graying hair to make it appear blonder, it didn't work well. There were noticeable streaks of yellow running through it. Instead of something soothing to drink, he settled on a large cup of black coffee. He didn't touch the cookies laid out by the corps of cheerful, grandmotherly women who staffed his field office.

Kerrey and I both knew this would be a difficult meeting. Other reporters had accepted Kerrey's Vietnam history at face value and routinely wrote positive stories playing up his gallantry. To his credit, Kerrey never liked nor sought the title of hero. In his mind, his wartime actions meant shame, not heroism. But that was his secret, and it remained buried for thirty years. It did not surface when he ran for governor, or during his shoo-in race for the Senate. Nor did it emerge during his first campaign for the presidency. Now, on the eve of a momentous political decision, he faced the prospect of exhuming memories he would just as soon keep buried. It all seemed to leave him edgy and filled with a sense of foreboding.

Joining me in Omaha that day was Evan Thomas, an assistant managing editor at *Newsweek* who specialized in writing smart, revealing pieces about the weaknesses of ambitious men. When I told him that I was digging into Kerrey's role in Thanh Phong, his response was that of any good editor: "Don't spare anything. Do whatever it takes to get the story."

The first moments of the interview were awkward and slow going. I was reluctant to jump right into Klann's allegations. How do you ask a man if he was a murderer? I was also concerned that Kerrey would throw us out or storm from the room. (In the middle of a sentence, he did get up and walk out for a brief moment.) I began the interview by showing him some photographs of Kerrey's Raiders given to me by William Tucker. They were in full warrior mode, gripping their weapons and decked out in jungle fatigues and facial paint, with bandanas or stockings pulled tight over their hair. Still boys, but lean, confident, and proud. There were other snapshots, including a particularly menacing one of Klann sporting a thin goatee and a forlorn Gene Peterson dressed in Vietnamese-style black pajamas.

"How do you think your men saw you?" I asked.

"Hell, I don't know what to say about that," Kerrey answered. "I think they understood that I was in charge."

Slowly we inched the questioning toward the topic of the dead women and children.

Surprisingly, Kerrey first broached the subject indirectly by recalling his relationship with Captain Hoffmann and then saying it was not uncommon for SEALs to carry out assassinations during the war. "It was quite clear what he wanted," Kerrey said of Hoffmann on several occasions. "He wanted hooches destroyed and people killed." What lifted the

tension in the room, for a few minutes, was the story of Hoffmann visiting Lieutenant Kerrey in the hospital, not knowing that a patient just a few feet away in another room wanted
to kill him. Kerrey laughed but then turned serious again and
blurted out that Hoffmann wanted his squad to hit the monks
in the monastery.

"What do you mean hit the monastery," we asked.
"Destroy it, kill the people?"

"That's correct," he said without a trace of emotion, adding
that the mission was not well thought out. The monks were
secondary actors in the Vietnam drama. The SEALs went after
people in the Vietcong infrastructure "as high up the food
chain as we could," he said.

"Were you supposed to capture them or kill them?"

"It depends," said Kerrey. "You were authorized to kill if
you thought it would be better. If you thought it would be
better to bring them out, you were authorized to bring them
out."

The next obvious question was whether they were ordered
to kill the peasant inhabitants in the Thanh Phu Secret Zone
where they were operating. I was not certain how much Kerrey knew of my reporting on the operation. I had timed my
in-person interviews with the rest of his SEAL unit for when
Kerrey was out of the country in South America. I assumed
his platoon would phone him for instructions on how to deal
with my queries, and some did. But Kerrey was not available
to return their calls. It had been only a matter of weeks since
the interviews, and it was possible that he hadn't been fully
informed about what I knew of the raid. But Kerrey was
smart enough to know what I was after. Before I could ask, he
jumped in.

"I have a rough idea of where you're heading," he said, his
voice rising. "You're going to get into this Thanh Phu operation pretty quickly. And you're going to start asking me

questions that I feel like I've got a right to say to you it's none of your damn business."

What followed was a long, angry monologue about war and memory. "One of the things that I'm very much aware of is that this is thirty years ago, and, you know, you've already popped out a couple of memories of Klann and Ambrose that I don't have at all. I tell you to be careful about it. Memories are fair game. Old experiences are fair game. I just disclose to you that I'm alert to that and I don't like it. There's a part of me that wants to say to you all the memories that I've got are my memories and I'm not going to talk about them. Part of the reason is that I've got to deal with them. My men have to deal with them. This is a war where there was never a declaration of war. We thought we were going over there to fight for the American people. We come back, we find out that the American people didn't want us to do it. And ever since that time, we've been poked, prodded, bent, spindled, mutilated, and I don't like it. I don't like to wear those memories around, they're binding."

He was pounding the table with the palm of his hand as he went on. "Part of living with the memory, some of those memories, is to forget them. I think it's a healthy way to deal with some memories you just don't want hanging around."

With some resentment, he spoke about the scrutiny faced by Vietnam veterans who struggled to put the war behind them, while the private lives of the men who liberated the world from tyranny more than fifty years ago were seemingly off-limits to prying reporters. "This is an example of why it's different," he said. "There were rules of engagement in World War II that permitted people to do terrible things. All the way up the Italian peninsula the rule was take no prisoner. There's ugly things under that expression. And the men who carried out those orders felt terrible for the rest of their lives, but it was a great cause and as a consequence you were able to go ahead and do it." Had General Curtis LeMay, the architect of the fire bombings of Japanese cities—which in one night killed an estimated one hundred thousand people—been captured by a victorious Japan, Kerrey said, LeMay "was quite certain he would have been tried and shot as a war criminal."

But World War II was the good war and Vietnam was not. It was the undeclared messy affair that the American public believed was being waged in un-American ways. While it was clear that Kerrey had contemplated his own culpability as a war criminal, he was also determined to keep whatever personal verdict he'd rendered to himself. "I carry memories of what I did, and I survive and live based upon lots of different mechanisms," Kerrey said. "I'm very much aware that there's a lot of permission granted to come in thirty years later and make moral judgments about what people did then. And you know, I may draw the veil up here. I may say, 'Look, I'm not going down that road because I have to live. I've got a son, I've got a daughter, I've got a life to lead, and I'm gonna try and live that life.' "

The room fell silent for what seemed like a long time. I was astonished at his sudden burst of candor. Without being directly confronted, Kerrey had gone a long way toward confirming that his SEAL team had killed innocent women and children.

"We didn't come to draw moral judgments," I told Kerrey. Thomas added, "This is not a gotcha story. We have some documents we want to talk to you about and show you, and there's some memories of your mates that we want to walk you through."

It was time to show Kerrey what I had, but he continued on. "All I'm saying to you is that when a man kills another human being, and that's what I did . . . I mean, I was trained to kill people. I tried to kill them according to the general rules, which were not as specific as they should have been.

And we were given a hell of a lot more latitude than we should have been in my judgment. And our operations were not as coordinated and organized as they should have been. It's the memory of killing that haunts people like myself. I've said it before but I believe it to be true. It's easy to say now that I'm alive, but I thought dying for your country was the worst thing that could happen to you and I don't think it is. I think killing for your country can be a lot worse. Because that's the memory that haunts."

I handed Kerrey a stack of SEAL reports I had found at the naval archives. He pulled a couple of them within inches of his eyes, as if to make sure they were real. His hands trembled slightly, and a look of anger and agony overtook his face as he read intently. He never knew they existed, and he "didn't know who filed them."

He placed the documents on the table in his Senate office. "Understand," he said, "that at some point I may not want to help you. I may be more concerned with the help of myself, and it's got nothing to do with politics. It's got everything to do with how I conduct my life. It's not fear of disclosure, because you've got interviews and you can tell the story anyway you want. But I've got to live, and I may choose at some point to say, 'I won't talk about that.' "

I wanted to ask him why hadn't he come forward if he wasn't fearful of disclosure. He'd had any number of opportunities—from the Winter Soldier investigation to the classroom of Walter Capps—where he could have unburdened himself on his terms, not a journalist's. But I didn't ask. By this time, Kerrey was testy and emotionally charged. I needed him to stay put for a while longer. I pulled out a map that illustrated the dates, times, and locations of his operations in the Thanh Phu Secret Zone and his team's approaches to the hamlet of Thanh Phong. Kerrey looked surprised that his raids had been laid out in such detail.

"Hoffmann did not direct this one. This came from the

NILO," he said, meaning the naval intelligence officer who was stationed in Vung Tau, where Commander Connolly had his headquarters. Kerrey said he was also provided with intelligence from the Australian special forces and local Vietnamese sources. The combination of these reports were used, he said, "to identify this particular area where we were of the opinion that there was going to be problems from the people on this particular night." They had gone into the hamlet on two occasions, he said. On the second visit, the night of the raid, Kerrey had expected the village to be empty of civilians. He had flown over Thanh Phong and assured himself that noncombatants would be gone. "We were told there was going to be a meeting that evening. We found four men who were guarding the area. And we killed these four men," he said, "with knives." These were the occupants of the first hooch, which Klann said was the home of Bui Van Vat, his wife, and their three grandchildren. The SEALs moved toward the village, Kerrey said, "and we took fire and we returned that fire, a substantial amount of fire. And we came in the village and the women and children were dead. And no men in sight."

His memory was similar to the spot reports that his team had filed. But he had gone beyond what his radioman had stated in the old reports, about the killings in the first hooch. Kerrey said they confiscated two weapons there, though later he recalled finding none.

"You saw four men with guns?"

"We found four men with guns," he said.

Kerrey's recollection of the encounter at the first hooch was that of a military action against armed guards; the second action was self-defense. I handed him the message that Hoffmann had sent to Zumwalt, the one that reported Duc's desire to kill anyone who wasn't a supporter of the government of Vietnam.

"Look at the report, at the bottom," I said. "The district chief didn't want anybody alive. To kill everybody."

"I don't remember this," Kerrey replied. "It's certainly consistent with what my understanding of the area was. I don't remember the district chief saying to us that he didn't want them alive."

He said on a number of occasions that his memory of the events of that night was not sharp. It was entirely possible, Kerrey said, that he was psychologically blocking out his recall. What he remembered clearly about the second hooch was how his men "unloaded a tremendous amount of rounds into that area." But then he said something odd, something not mentioned in the after-action spot reports. All of the dead people "were almost entirely in a group."

"Do you tell everybody to open up or does everybody just open up on their own?" I asked him.

"I give the order to open up."

"You say fire?"

"That's correct."

"Was that the first time that you'd ever been shot at?"

"That's correct," Kerrey said. "I think this is the first time."

That the dead women and children were in a group seemed to suggest they had been taken out of their homes and rounded up. Yet it was well known that villagers in the region kept bunkers within or right behind their hooches. At the first sign of trouble they routinely rolled into them, often spending the night. But to hear Bob Kerrey tell it, they did the opposite of what was common practice. His story so far hung on two implausibilities. One was that instead of jumping into their bunkers, villagers ran toward the sound of gunfire. The other was that gunfire from more than 100 yards away, unleashed by a panicked, largely green squad shooting in the darkness, killed every single member of the group. Their return fire certainly would have been directed at the very bright and unmistakable light of a muzzle flash, yet Kerrey never mentioned anything about seeing one.

There was no point in holding back any longer.

"Couple of men have a different version," I said. "One was that . . . there was one old man, one older woman, and children at the first hooch, and that you guys, the rest of the team, knifed the women and children, then you went to another village and—"

"God, who's got that version?" Kerrey injected. He had a look of terror in his eyes and seemed to panic momentarily.

"Went to another village and there were fourteen people there and you lined them up and shot them there. And they heard a baby crying and opened up again. And they then all left and after that went back to the boat. Totally wrong?"

"Different than my recollection of it," Kerrey said. "But you know, I'm not going to make this thing worse by questioning somebody else's memory of it. It would not surprise me if things were going on away from my line of sight that were different than what I was doing. It would not surprise me at all. The operating procedures would have permitted all of this. They permitted this and far worse. We were basically writing the rules as we went."

"You got a Bronze Star for that," I said.

"I got a Bronze Star for that."

"Who put you in for that?"

"I have no idea. Probably Hoffmann."

"Did you tell them you didn't want that, too?"

"No."

I glanced over at the fourth person in the room. Greg Weiner, Kerrey's communications director, was a pro at getting politicians out of tough jams. It looked as if the blood had been drained from his face. He likely never knew about Thanh Phong. Here was his boss, just days away from announcing whether he would seek the presidency, describing events that his opponents were certain to say were war crimes. On top of that, he had accepted an award for valor for the raid, even listing it in his official Senate biography. Kerrey's political enemies would have a field day regardless of whether or not he stayed in the Senate or ran for higher office.

Everyone in the room understood what was at stake. A presidential candidacy and a political career were hanging by a thread. "It's going to be very interesting to see the reactions to the story," Kerrey said. "I mean, because basically you're talking about a man who killed innocent civilians."

Chapter Seventeen

———————————■———————————

I HAD MIXED FEELINGS when I left Kerrey's office. On one level, I was numb. On another, I felt regret. In the parking lot of the restaurant where we'd gone to lunch, I told him: "I'm sorry about this. Please know that it's not personal." Yet I also thought that the interview was exceptionally powerful. Evan Thomas was ecstatic when we reached the airport and called to brief Ann McDaniel, *Newsweek*'s Washington bureau chief. Thomas was hot to get the story into print. Legendary for his speed, he wrote a draft on the plane ride home and gave me a printout the next day.

What I read was surprising and distressing. He had written gracefully of Kerrey's remorse and how he had lived for years with such a terrible secret. But nowhere in the elegant prose was there any mention of Gerhard Klann's more troublesome account, which represented nearly two years of reporting. It was Kerrey's confession and nothing more. The piece, as written, would evoke tremendous sympathy and forgiveness.

Kerrey insisted at our meeting in Omaha that he had decided "months ago" whether or not to run for president, and that he would make an announcement soon. It was difficult to believe that the answer was anything other than a "yes." Kerrey had planned a Nebraska economic summit for later that December, inviting a lengthy roster of prominent academics, businesspeople, and writers. That kind of elaborate event was not the mark of someone opting out of the race. But that was before I had brought Thanh Phong back into his life.

On December 12, 1998, five days after I met with Kerrey, the senator gathered his key Nebraska supporters and advisers to discuss his presidential ambitions. Among the members of his kitchen cabinet was Warren Buffett, the billionaire investment tycoon. The man who grew to be one of the nation's richest men by picking profitable stocks was a long-time Kerrey booster. "If Bob were a Republican, I'd vote for him," Buffett, a Democrat for thirty years, told the local newspaper. The vote of confidence was gratifying, but would a national poll reflect the same mood of support? Kerrey was skeptical.

Kerrey played devil's advocate in the meeting, listing reasons why he should not run. There was Gore's advantage as an incumbent vice president. Money was a big factor. Could he raise the necessary millions? He was up for reelection to the Senate in 2000. Wouldn't he have to give up his seat? His advisers said he could seek both offices, but Kerrey was apprehensive about the ethics of such a plan. He said it was one job or the other. One negative Kerrey did not mention was Thanh Phong.

The next day, Sunday, December 13, Kerrey announced that he would not contest Al Gore and Bill Bradley for the Democratic nomination. "My choice is not whether or not I will try to lead," he said at a news conference. "My choice is how best can I lead. I have made this decision here at home with my family and with my friends. They simply will not allow conceit or selfish hunger for power to seduce me into making a false choice." Again, there was no mention of Vietnam.

In the meantime, Kerrey had a much more historic role to play—as a juror in the Senate impeachment trial of President Bill Clinton. The drama on the Senate floor was a final chapter in the stormy relationship with his old rival. Kerrey had been among the first Senate Democrats to publicly rebuke Clinton for the Monica Lewinsky scandal. On September 3,

1998, a staffer rushed breathlessly into Kerrey's office with the news that Senator Joe Lieberman of Connecticut was on the floor, "talking about the president and Lewinsky." Kerrey, who didn't have a television in his office—not even a floor monitor to keep track of Senate business—got up from his desk and joined a group of aides gathered around a set to watch Lieberman upbraid Clinton. "I'm going to the floor," he said.

Within a few minutes, Kerrey was on television. His tone was scolding, but he kept his criticism of the president genteel. "I do not come to the floor arguing that I have a superior moral authority to comment on the President's behavior," Kerrey said. "But the President's actions were inappropriate. If Clinton didn't go further in explaining himself," Kerrey said, "it would damage the moral fiber of our children upon whom we depend so much."

Kerrey believed in a strong presidency, but not in the man now residing at 1600 Pennsylvania Avenue. If it came down to Kerrey holding the swing vote required to save Clinton's presidency, then the White House was in trouble. "In that case," Kerrey told Erskine Bowles, Clinton's chief of staff, "you can't count on me." But in the end, Kerrey voted to acquit.

So did my editors at *Newsweek*. The magazine decided not to publish a piece on Kerrey's actions in Vietnam. Citing his decision to drop out of the presidential race, Evan Thomas said it would unfairly be piling it on. Kerrey's people had done their best to undermine the story. They telephoned *Newsweek*'s senior editors to say I had gotten Gerhard Klann drunk and promised to make him rich from a book and movie deal. I thought such smears were beneath Kerrey, but, as I learned later, they would be standard practice when it came to Klann's story.

I saw Kerrey several times over the next two years, often over meals at La Brasserie, one of his favorite French restaurants around the corner from his office in the Hart Building on Capitol Hill. The discussions, usually over several glasses of red wine, were for the most part friendly and expansive, with lengthy exchanges on everything from the draft to mothers, children, and parenting.

But as pleasant as our meetings were, the unfinished business of Thanh Phong always hung in the air. And while Kerrey didn't seem to harbor any resentment toward me for taking him to the brink of exposure as a possible war criminal, he must certainly have known that this wasn't behind him. Indeed, I hadn't given up on publishing what I believed was an important story. By staying in touch, Kerrey appeared to be following the maxim of keeping his friends close and his enemies closer.

By the time we met for dinner at La Brasserie in the late fall of 2000, we had both made significant changes in our lives. I had decided to leave *Newsweek*, and Kerrey was retiring from the Senate when his term expired in January 2001.

Even friends were taken by surprise when he announced that he would not seek a third term in the Senate, despite overwhelmingly favorable poll numbers. His actions in Vietnam, he told me, had no bearing on his decision to quit elective politics, presidential or otherwise. He left, he said because he wanted to launch a second career while he was still young, in a field he felt was critically important to the nation's future: education. He accepted the presidency of the New School in Manhattan, a left-wing institution known for its antiwar positions and famous for notable thinkers like Thorstein Veblen and Hannah Arendt.

Kerrey clearly didn't view himself as being through with public life. By entering academia, he was following the pattern of another warrior-politician from the Great Plains, Dwight Eisenhower. Ike served as president of Columbia

University in New York before his successful bid for the White House. The New School is not the Ivy League, but it is still a prestigious place to hang a shingle. And New York, after all, is the media capital of the world, a perfect place for an iconoclast like Kerrey to stay in the public eye.

Still, leaving active politics was no easy thing. He said he wanted to move on, but at the same time he missed the action. In the end, he couldn't stay away from the dogfight in Florida, where he quickly got into a tussle that made headlines. Some Bush supporters had made a disparaging remark, thought to be humorous, about Kerrey's missing leg and had "thrown" mud on him. It turned out that only a few drops had been accidentally kicked on his trousers. But it gave Kerrey enough of an opening to cry foul, enabling Gore and the Democratic leadership to demand that Bush apologize to the Medal of Honor winner. At dinner, Kerrey laughed the whole episode off as nothing more then good-natured political fun. He had, after all, managed to be the center of attention again.

He even took a last dig at Clinton before they both left office. The president waited until the final days of his second term to visit Nebraska and was amazed by the large, exuberant crowds that greeted him in a Republican stronghold. Kerrey, who could see that Clinton was touched, couldn't resist bursting one final bubble. "I leaned over into Clinton's ear," Kerrey recalled, "and told him, 'They're not here for you, they're here for the office of the presidency.' "

After I severed my relationship with *Newsweek,* the *New York Times Magazine* and *60 Minutes II* were both interested in the story of Kerrey's Raiders. Over our dinner in the fall of 2000, I tried to steer the conversation back to Thanh Phong.

And Kerrey, for his part, seemed to think that the best way to steer me away from the story was to offer me a job. He described his plan to create a twenty-four-hour cable news channel at the New School devoted to public affairs reporting.

"What do you think?" he asked. "Are you interested in it?"

He was even more direct the next time, during lunch in New York. I had come to interview him again about Thanh Phong, and Kerrey once again laid out his plans for a cable program but in more detail, focusing on the news of the day, a story in the *New York Times* about the Marine Corps' controversial Osprey aircraft. Kerrey saw his cable operation as something that could provide more detail than the limited account in that morning's *Times*. He again asked if I was interested. Finally, I had to make it clear that I didn't want to go to work for Bob Kerrey.

"I don't want to talk about anything like that until I'm finished with you," I said.

"Until you're finished with me!" he said in an angry, mocking tone. He realized that he had little influence over my desire to pursue the story. He tried yet again, in his campus office, when he put the question to me in front of Tom Anderson, the CBS producer working with me on the Kerrey story. Afterward, Anderson was incredulous. "Do you know what he just did? He tried to offer you a job, to buy you off!"

But Kerrey was beginning to realize that he would have to cooperate with me.

We exchanged e-mails the first week in December of 2000. In mine, I suggested we meet and said, "I want to talk about how we should finally resolve your story."

"Tomorrow night is fine, but my story cannot be finally resolved," he wrote.

At dinner I made my pitch. "Let's do your story," I said. "I've left *Newsweek*; you've left the Senate. I can write it for *The New York Times Magazine*."

Kerrey was not overly enthusiastic about the idea. "You sure have a bone in your throat about that story," he said, and told me he'd think about it and let me know.

I e-mailed him again on December 6, saying I wanted "to get this bone out of my throat. My goal is to get it historically right." I told him I would be fair and warned that if other investigative reporters latched onto this story, he'd likely be branded a war criminal and his reputation ruined. I knew at some point we'd have to confront the question of war crimes, but this wasn't the moment. In addition to the *Times*, I asked him to consider appearing on *60 Minutes II*. Friends at CBS had put me in touch with Jeff Fager, the executive producer of *60 Minutes II*. A hard news journalist, Fager was eager to convince Kerrey to appear on the show. Adam Moss, the editor of the *Times Magazine*, said it would be fine as long as the newspaper went first.

Kerrey responded around 6:30 the next evening, and his answer was characteristically eloquent and evocative. "I am willing to do this, but please understand that my memory of this event is clouded by the fog of the evening, age, and desire. From what you have told me already, my men and I in some cases have completely different stories, almost like we weren't together that night. Also, please know that a day rarely passes without remorse rising into my chest to choke all other feelings. It was the worst thing I ever did in my life. As a young man going into war, I imagined many possibilities, from heroism to cowardice, but never did I imagine this. We should have been trained with this possibility in mind instead of being encouraged to engage if we were threatened. But no should haves will ever be offered by me as a way of shifting blame. I did something terrible once that cannot be undone or forgiven."

About forty-five minutes later, he sent a follow-up message: "One very important point: I am doing this with you because I trust that you will tell the story as best you can, not because I fear someone else getting there first and doing something that will damage/destroy my reputation. The only motivating fear I have is that someday I will face my maker. The opinion of other human beings matters, but the less it motivates me the better. I will talk with you not because a public accounting will help me, but because it just might help someone else. In my search for my father's brother I have had dreams that I met my uncle on the moonlit Philippines beach where he was last seen. In my dream, I am about to leave for Vietnam and he warns me that the greatest danger of war is not losing your life but the taking of others and that human savagery is a very slippery slope. I look forward to talking with you."

Chapter Eighteen

ROBERT KERREY LOOKED DOWN and lowered his voice to almost a whisper. His eyes were dreamy when he raised them again as he began to tell the story about his mother and her deathbed testimonial. We had been talking for an hour or so in his office at The New School, and it was getting close to dusk. It was January of 2001, and the winter sun was fading. What little light was left came through tall slender windows, casting Kerrey in soft gray shadows.

Kerrey dropped his shoulders, slouched forward, and held his clasped hands in his lap. Below the table his ankles were crossed and he looked like a little boy sitting in an oversized chair. I had asked about his relationship with his father, James Kerrey, and to answer me, he first had to tell of his mother, Elinor, and how, on her deathbed, she told her son about his father's own sad life. "She drew me close and in a soft and raspy voice, a loving and beautiful voice, my mother told me about my father's difficult youth," Kerrey said. Soft and raspy, the words rolled out of Kerrey's mouth as he imitated his mother's weakened voice, lowering his tone to a hush as if he was hearing her words again for the first time. She was succumbing to Lou Gehrig's disease, and it had affected her ability to speak. Kerrey's eyes moistened around the eyelashes and he seemed as if he was going to break into tears.

His ability to recall the tender moments in his life with such radiance appeared authentic. Yet, in the next instant, he could abruptly and effortlessly shift his mood. One minute

214 Gregory L. Vistica

he was somberly saying "my best hero's my mom and dad" or slipping into a depressed daze—muttering about his "shame, guilt, and remorse." The next instant he had gone off on an entirely different track about politics with little evidence of grief.

I had seen him shift gears on a number of occasions. During one long interview in his office at the New School, he was sermonizing about crimes of war when a knock on the door interrupted him. His secretary entered with a note. "This will be a fun call," he said with a broad smile, showing me the small slip of paper. Written on it was the name of Senator John Kerry, the Massachusetts Democrat and likely presidential candidate in 2004. "He's calling to see if I'll support him," Kerrey said as he picked up the phone. "John boy," he started, then, half in jest, "this is the closest I'll ever come to being president." Back at the conference table his mood was still cheery.

Two minutes earlier, before the call, Bob Kerrey's disposition had been sulky and mournful. Now he was buoyed. I asked if he planned to run in 2004. "Probably," he replied with his usual ambivalence, before again drifting into a state of melancholy as we switched back to what happened in Thanh Phong.

Kerrey had been gone from national politics only a few months, yet he appeared to be a new man. The ragged, exhausted visage was now gone, and he was much more at ease. His new academic post was already less stressful then being a senator. Even so, Kerrey would miss the political interplay and the inside tales about friends like John McCain. McCain, himself a maverick, at first thought Kerrey was a "flake." Now the former prisoner-of-war stands up out of respect when Kerrey enters a room. In turn, Kerrey found it hard to support Democrats running against McCain. When one Democratic candidate attacked the Arizona Republican in front of Kerrey, Kerrey let loose. "Zinged her?" he said. "I put a flamethrower on her." He was so enthralled with

McCain's maverick streak, he contemplated publicly supporting the Republican senator for president against George W.
Bush. "It would have been hard not to support him," he said.

Kerrey's memory drew from an amalgam of personal experiences and his favorite novels and movies. The stories often
had moral overtones to them—of good guys and villains, of
heroes, cowards, and ordinary people trying to do the right
thing. He often seemed more comfortable in a world of fiction and often escaped into fantasy. As a boy watching action
movies, he imagined himself a leading man. He would pedal
his bicycle out into the cornfields on the outskirts of Bethany
and think of himself like a character in *The Hobbit*, "at the
edge of the end of the universe," he said. As he grew older,
he could at times live vicariously through characters in novels or movies. "I acquired the stories from them," he said.
"You saved the girl, you saved the people, it was a good
thing."

His yearning for the Navy and Officer Candidate School
came after reading Herman Wouk's *The Caine Mutiny*. His
boss in Vietnam, he said, was the real-life Colonel Kurtz in
Apocalypse Now. Other times Kerrey was Whit Wade, the
World War II veteran wounded in action who experienced an
emotional rebirth in *The Foreseeable Future*. Did Bob Kerrey,
with blood on his hands in Vietnam, die and come back to life
like Whit? "It is true—a part of me died but a part of me was
reborn there." On the 1992 presidential campaign trail, he
identified with Pat Conroy's protagonist in *Prince of Tides*, and
when he arrived in the Senate, he urged his colleagues to read
only fiction.

After Vietnam, the horrors of war and burdens of secret
keeping colored much of Kerrey's preference in books and
films. He vividly recalled a scene from *The Fall* by Albert
Camus, about a man walking one night along the Seine in
Paris. "He hears this splash in the water. Somewhere in his
mind, he knows it's a human being. It torments him, con-

stantly torments him," Kerrey said, because the man, who thought he was brave, had failed to rescue a person in need.

He loved *Forrest Gump*, he said, because the war protestors were the villains and the man in uniform a hero. When he saw the film *Gods and Monsters*, Kerrey easily understood Jimmy Whale's inspiration for Frankenstein—how the body of a World War I soldier caught in barbed wire gradually bloated, decayed, and turned into a ghoulish monster. After viewing *Saving Private Ryan*, Kerrey laced his speeches with the message "Freedom is not free." Kerrey had clearly come to view his own life as a Greek tragedy, the hero haunted by his own past. "This is not John Wayne," he said. "I'm not a hero."

But for thirty-two years, he had to act like one.

In some ways, Kerrey was like Ronald Reagan, who made fiction and fantasy such a part of his own story over the years that it became a part of him. In his office at the New School, Kerrey recalled with clarity the day he was arrested for fighting in Bob's Supermarket in Lincoln. "By strange coincidence, the man who arrested me became the attorney general of Nebraska," he said. He was speaking of Paul Douglas, who held the post during part of Kerrey's term as governor. The story, as Kerrey told it, was of a humiliated Douglas forced to resign over the Commonwealth Savings Company fiasco.

But Kerrey's version was too good to be true. Douglas was never a cop. "He should have known better," Douglas said. "I never arrested him." But Kerrey liked the tale enough to retell it to *The New Yorker* magazine in their profile of the president of the New School.

After the many talks I'd had with Kerrey over two-plus years, I came to see that he regarded the truth as fluid—something that could be modified, mixed, or diverted to suit his needs at the moment. He could change his story at the drop of a hat. While he loved to rail against Bill Clinton's lies, truth was sometimes the first casualty in a conversation with Kerrey.

Some of Kerrey's diversions from the truth were subtle, perhaps explained by normal lapses in memory. Others were immediately obvious as attempts to deceive. As we sat in his university office in January of 2001, I asked about the chain of events that had led up to the final night of bloodshed in Thanh Phong three decades earlier. I began with his first visit to the hamlet twelve days prior to the killings, when his SEALs rounded up the women and children and interrogated them.

"I don't have a memory of going into the area before," Kerrey said.

For a moment, there was dead silence. I was too flabbergasted, and Kerrey sat there apparently blind to his backtracking. His answer conflicted in every way with the account he had given in his Omaha office in 1998.

"When you went in the first time," I had asked him then, "you searched hooches and bunkers, interrogated fourteen women and small children?"

"That's correct," Kerrey had said.

"Were you concerned at all, based on having seen women there," I asked him, "that they might be there when you returned on the night of the killings?"

"Yes," Kerrey said. "But it was a subordinate concern to finding people that were armed and dangerous."

"Why go back if you know there's a bunch of women and children. Why go back? Was the mission that critical?"

"We felt, I felt, it was critical."

Now, two years later, with a perfectly expressionless face, Kerrey erased his previous account from his memory. On my next visit, I asked him again the same question about his first visit to the hamlet. I had shown him his spot reports, with his name on them, which placed the SEALs in the village twelve days before the killings. And I reminded him of our initial conversation in Omaha.

"That definitely is not my memory," he said.

"You just don't remember?" I asked him now.

"No."

Had he simply forgotten? Was it a conscious effort to mislead? Were the Navy documents in error? Did something worse happen in Thanh Phong that he was covering up? Or was something else at work, some deeper psychological issue tied to the killings?

"It's entirely possible that I'm blacking a lot of it out," he said.

I needed to know once and for all if Kerrey was dissembling. He maintained that the killings at the first hooch were of four armed men. Gerhard Klann said they were Bui Van Vat, his wife, and three grandchildren. Kerrey said his men were under attack when they fired into the darkness, killing unarmed civilians in the second hooch. If Klann's version was correct, Kerrey ordered the execution of a group of cowering women and children. As the story stood now, it was a "he said, she said" dilemma—Kerrey's word versus Klann's.

It was hard to accept that American fighters could agree to such an act of terror. But it was also true that the rules of land warfare were not always observed in Vietnam. Other special forces operators who worked with the SEALs remembered their reputation for toughness, even brutality. One, a retired Green Beret, told me that "nasty happenings routinely came with the territory." Based on his own operations, it was hard for him to believe Kerrey's version. "Wonder if when he was a twenty-five-year-old fire-breather if he had any remorse. [I] seriously doubt it. Pulling the trigger on those folks," he said, was an easy choice. "Must admit, I would have in a heartbeat."

But had Kerrey done it? Had he intentionally ordered the murder of innocent women and children? Changing his story on this occasion, and in the weeks to come, made him look as if he was trying to hide something. "You can tell my war story, the whole damn thing if you want to," Kerrey said. "But I don't feel like I'm withholding information."

Bob Kerrey was late for his early afternoon taping session with Dan Rather on January 24, 2001. I was convinced that at the last minute he got cold feet and decided to back out. As I suspected, he was giving it some thought. When his black limousine arrived at the CBS studios on West 57th Street in Manhattan, he said he'd been "trying to figure out some way to call ahead and complain of a bad stomach" or some other malady. "The truth of the matter is I came to this interview saying it's the stupidest thing I ever did in my life," Kerrey said.

He made his way upstairs and was ushered into the green room where he could relax for a few minutes before the television cameras began to roll tape. The room had a toy basketball hoop attached to the wall about six feet from the floor. Kerrey, grateful for the diversion, took off his suit coat, picked up a ball not much bigger than a baseball, and arched it for the basket. We shot hoops for about fifteen minutes until Dan Rather walked in to say hello. The two men had met for the first time only a few days earlier. Rather had invited Kerrey to his anchorman's office, overlooking the *CBS Evening News* set, to see if there was any chemistry between them. It was not an easy story for either man. Rather is immensely patriotic and respected Kerrey's sacrifice on behalf of his country. The veteran newsman and war correspondent was determined that the *60 Minutes II* segment would be fair and show Kerrey every courtesy. Their conversation was vague but genial, and Kerrey left, unsure what course the interview would take.

On the way out, he pulled Rather's producer, Tom Anderson, aside. "This isn't going to be a hatchet job, is it?" he asked. "No," a surprised Anderson responded. Then Kerrey wanted advice on how to comport himself on camera. "I can only tell you the same thing I tell everybody else," Anderson said. "If you tell the truth, the camera will be kind to you." Kerrey nodded his head and said, "OK."

Anderson and I had spent the previous week preparing for the taping, drafting questions and pouring over the declassified documents. We both knew the importance of respecting Kerrey's stature as a Medal of Honor recipient and an admired public servant, and we were determined to be thorough in our reporting.

I had deluged Anderson with material on Thanh Phong. Much of it described Kerrey's remorse and search for redemption, and his efforts to make sense of what he claimed was a terrible accident. I mentioned the story told by some of the Raiders, but Tom and I had not fully discussed Klann and the more serious allegations with any specificity.

Raising accusations of a war crime would certainly have spooked Kerrey, perhaps even compelled him to walk off the set. But I had also held back from laying it all out verbally for Anderson because I could not be certain who was telling the truth, Kerrey or Klann. I wanted to give Kerrey the benefit of the doubt that his inconsistent recollections were not calculated but might be tied to psychological strife.

For whatever reason, it was very clear that Kerrey's story had changed significantly. Gerhard Klann had been consistent in recalling what he believed happened in Thanh Phong. The facts he recounted to me were the same he had given to his commanding officer more than a decade earlier. (Neither had spoken to the other for years before I interviewed them independently.) Klann had no apparent reason to hide behind a false story or make up events to suit his purpose. If Kerrey did have a motive, it could have been his aspiration for the White House. At some point, I knew we would have to push him hard on his memory lapses—especially why the villagers were all found dead in a group, as if they had been executed. But now was not the time.

There was an eerie stillness on the *60 Minutes II* set when Kerrey took a seat across from Dan Rather. A sound technician wired the former senator with a small microphone and the cameramen adjusted their lenses. Anderson and I sat off to the side, watching through two television monitors. The image I saw, a slightly nervous Kerrey, was the one that millions of Americans would soon see. Broadcast journalists liked to say that "the camera doesn't lie"—that speaking in front of a camera was like taking a polygraph. The lens absorbed subtle physical gestures like a sponge and magnified their impact. Nervous tics, hand fidgeting, unusual facial movements, looking away from the camera—all conveyed to viewers the possibility that a person they were watching was not being honest. I wondered if Kerrey would pass or fail.

Rather was an old pro at using his Texas charm to calm a jittery guest, while at the same time never straying far afield in his questioning. He moved Kerrey nimbly from topic to topic, touching on Bill Clinton and Kerrey's own presidential ambitions but always steering him back to the subject at hand—what happened in the village of Thanh Phong.

"Was this the worst thing you ever did in your life?" Rather had asked him.

"Oh, there is no second place. If I'd lost both arms and both legs and my sight and my hearing, it wouldn't have been as much as I lost that night," Kerrey said.

"It's easy for me now to look back in lots of ways and replay that whole night because of all the things I've ever done in my life, it's the only one that I really repetitively say, 'My life would have been much better had I not done those things that night.'"

Rather asked him what thoughts went through his mind when he saw the dead women and children. At that, Kerrey gave a nervous chuckle. "I just killed my own family. I just did something really bad. All I know is I carry with me the faces of those women and children in that village. I should have done it differently than I did."

When Kerrey spoke of his "real, dark, painful, traumatizing pain," Rather was genuinely moved. "Surely, you understand, Senator," he said, "that you wear the Congressional Medal of Honor. Nobody sees you in the picture of shame. You're a hero."

"Heroes are a mix," Kerrey said. "Heroes aren't perfect."

Kerrey's four-hour performance was, as they say in the business, great TV.

The well-polished recital of his lifelong suffering was so moving and convincing it left me with a big knot in my stomach. It was the dilemma I had faced all along with Kerrey. His charismatic presence was so compelling it became difficult to remain independent of his charisma and keep focused on the "whodunit." I was falling into the trap that Ed Howard had warned me about: That those who entered Kerrey's orbit started to believe he was a friend. I was violating the number one rule of investigative journalism: Don't get too close to your subject. I had to wonder if my feelings were clouding my judgment.

After the taping session ended and before he departed, Kerrey and I stepped back into the green room for a private conversation. Again, I felt the need to protect him.

"I'm sorry for putting you through that," I said.

"That's OK; I willingly sat down for it," Kerrey said.

Kerrey was now committed to going public. It was finally time, he said, to reveal what he had managed to keep secret for so many years. Several times over the previous few months, he had mentioned his desire to help others come to terms with similar misdeeds in Vietnam and even in other military actions. "Maybe telling the story helps somebody listening to it," he said. But he also knew there was a downside to going public.

"Well, it's risky now," he said. Doc Schrier, Kerrey said of his SEAL team medic, "thinks I'm just a fucking pussy for worrying about what we did."

We both knew it was too late to go back, that Kerrey had finally made his break with the past. He did it on his terms, never mentioning that his Raiders may have committed the crimes that their teammate Gerhard Klann was certain of.

But the story was far from over.

Chapter Nineteen

———————■———————

ANY DOUBTS I HAD about Klann's story regarding Thanh Phong began to disappear when my phone rang in Washington a couple of weeks later. There was urgency in Tom Anderson's voice. "Derek called from Vietnam. I've got some interesting and disturbing information. You'd better get up here."

Anderson had assigned Derek Williams, a veteran cameraman from New Zealand, to shoot footage of Thanh Phong and Hon Tam, the island where Kerrey was wounded on his last mission in Vietnam. Before he left, Williams and I spoke briefly and corresponded by e-mail. I purposely did not tell him that a SEAL unit may have murdered innocent civilians. And Anderson, who was not yet fully engaged in Klann's allegations, kept mum on the subject, too. Williams knew only that we were preparing a segment on a SEAL raid in Thanh Phong led by former Senator Bob Kerrey.

Listening to Anderson's voice, I was certain that Williams had uncovered evidence damaging to Kerrey. I caught the next train to New York. Riding north from Washington, it seemed to me that the answer to who was being more truthful had shifted to Gerhard Klann.

Williams was a good choice for a sensitive assignment. An old Vietnam hand familiar with SEAL missions in the Mekong Delta, he now operated out of Bangkok, where he lived with his Vietnamese wife. He was well versed in Vietnamese culture and traditions and knew enough of the language to get by.

He was perhaps the first Western journalist to visit the remote hamlet of Thanh Phong in years. Clusters of villagers followed him around, curious about his intentions and eager to talk. Throughout the day, Williams kept hearing bits and pieces about a killing spree. He was taken down to the waterfront and told "how the Americans came up the river," he said. Then the villagers brought him to the village's small graveyard. There he saw two large tombs each marked separately with the names of Bui Van Vat and his wife, Luu Thi Canh. Beside them lay three small mounds of cement, painted white. The unmarked graves were the apparent resting place for three small children—the grandchildren Klann said were killed in the first hooch. In a nearby field were other graves. And across the river, still more. All held victims, according to the villagers, of a brutal American attack.

Williams was starting to suspect the worst. But so far, none of the people he and his interpreter interviewed claimed to have actually witnessed any killings. It was all secondhand knowledge, mostly from those who said that relatives or friends were murdered by the Americans. One of the men Williams met said he had been at the meeting of local Vietcong leaders thirty-two years ago, some 400 yards away, when Kerrey's Raiders came ashore. He was just a boy then, a member of the Communist youth league. Shortly after dawn he discovered a massacre. "It made you throw up," he said through an interpreter. "If you saw it today you would faint. The stench of blood filled the air."

When Williams asked if there were any living eyewitnesses, he was told about Pham Tri Lanh, a Communist revolutionary who was married to a Vietcong fighter during the war. A young woman then, she said she had seen the SEALs at the home of Bui Van Vat. Williams went with Lanh to the site where he and his family had been killed. "I was hiding behind the banana tree and I saw them cut the man's neck, first here and then there," she would say on videotape. "His head was still just barely attached at the back. There was an old woman, an old man, two girls, and a boy, and they were all young. They were the grandchildren. The three children were scared and they crawled into a ditch," she said. The Americans grabbed Bui Van Vat, she said, and "dragged him out to the water pump, and that is where they cut his throat. After they cut the throat of the old man, they went out and stabbed the three children." The wife also died the same way, she said.

Lanh recalled watching the SEALs slip away toward the center of the village and then running to her own hooch to be with her children, who were sleeping in a bunker. The Americans went next to a nearby group of hooches where Bui Thi Luom and her fifteen relatives were sleeping. Lanh explained how she crept close enough to see what the SEALs were doing. "They ordered everybody out from the bunker," she said, "and they lined them up and shot all of them."

Williams had stumbled onto something he wasn't prepared for. He had done some preliminary taping to document the story he was hearing from the villagers. But he needed an experienced producer like Anderson to come and grill Lanh and the others for holes in their stories. "I called Tom," Williams recalled, "and said, 'Look, you've got to get your ass down here.'"

In New York, Anderson and I met with the executive producer of *60 Minutes II*, Jeff Fager, and his deputy, Patti Hassler. When Anderson recounted Lanh's story, I was struck by how similar it was to Gerhard Klann's. Just like Lanh, he had described the knifing of an old man, his wife, and three children in the first hooch, which matched with what Lanh was claiming. The details of the killings in the second hooch also matched up remarkably well. It would have been impossible for Lanh and Klann to somehow have coordinated their accounts. Klann had never been back to Vietnam. Nor could the Vietnamese government have told Lanh what to say. On his visa application, Williams wrote down as much as he knew about the assignment: that he was coming to Thanh Phong for a *60 Minutes II* segment on a former United States senator who had been in the war. Government authorities in Hanoi did not know what we were up to, so there was no way they could have coerced any of the villagers to embellish or falsify their accounts.

"That's exactly the same story that Gerhard Klann told me," I blurted out. I took them through my previous interviews and meetings with Klann and said he might be willing to go on the air. We decided to bring him to New York as soon as possible.

In the meantime, Anderson had to get to Vietnam. He needed to investigate what Williams had uncovered, and interview Lanh and anyone else who saw or heard what had happened that night. My task was to figure out a way to reapproach Kerrey. It would not be easy; he no doubt would be wary. Spinning Gerhard Klann's story to blunt its impact might not be a stretch for the press-savvy former senator. But corroborating evidence from an eyewitness would be something else entirely.

On March 20, I zipped off an e-mail to Kerrey at the New School. "There are a couple of holes in the story that need to be filled," I wrote.

"What are the holes?" Kerrey wanted to know. "Based upon what you know about these stories, what kind of response will there be? I don't need details; I need advice."

It was obvious that Kerrey was growing worried about the story. The holes could only mean one thing to him—new and damaging information that he would have to account for. By asking for advice, he was trying to play on the sympathy I'd expressed. This time, I offered little in the way of aid or comfort. With each passing day, Kerrey was again looking less like a friend and more of an investigative target. "The holes concern some things we want to understand better about Thanh Phong," I wrote back. "As for advice? The best advice I can give you is to take an hour with us. It will help us and I believe it will also help you."

Five minutes later, he e-mailed back instructing me to make arrangements with his secretary.

Shortly before 4 P.M. on Wednesday, April 4, Tom Anderson and I took the elevator up to Kerrey's penthouse office at the New School. We were escorted into his office and took seats around the small conference table. Kerrey was in a foul mood, acusing us of acting like prosecutors, cross-examining him and his SEAL teammates. "I don't like it," he said.

"I'm just telling you I do not find myself in a situation where I'm able to tell you with one hundred percent certainty what happened that night," Kerrey said. "For a whole range of reasons. Some of it I didn't see; some of it I don't remember."

The reason for the meeting was to spring Derek Williams's explosive news: There was an eyewitness who contradicted Kerrey's account. Before we got to that point, though, I had a checklist of items to go over. Did Kerrey ever have any training under the Geneva Convention on the treatment of prisoners or noncombatants? "No, absolutely not."

Why didn't he go around the first hooch and avoid the killing there? "That's not what we did."

At the first hooch, did he remember the old man out front? "No, no."

When pressed on Bui Van Vat, Kerrey started to qualify his story on how the old man died and laid the blame on others. Ambrose and Klann had done all of the killing in the first hooch, he said. "We're all near the first hooch, but I'm not killing these people," he said. "I'm one hundred percent positive."

"Ambrose and Klann did all of the killing?" I asked.

"Yeah, yeah," Kerrey said. "My memory includes Klann having difficulty, but I don't see what it was that he was having difficulty with."

"What do you mean, he was having difficulty?" Anderson asked.

"He was having difficulty killing one of the people he was trying to kill."

"So who helped him?" I asked.

"I don't know."

"Klann said it was you. Ambrose said it was either you or Peterson." In 1998, when I first met Ambrose in his Houston office he was certain that it was Kerrey who had come to Klann's aid. He had even drawn a map on a yellow legal notepad of the hooches in Thanh Phong and where old Bui Van Vat had been sitting when he was ambushed. But in recent weeks, Kerrey had called Ambrose and other members of the squad to compare memories. Now Ambrose's recall was not so sharp. "*Maybe* it was Bob," he said.

"I understand you don't want to get into a pissing match with your guys," Anderson said, but there were "huge" differences in the various versions. "Is it possible," he burrowed in, that the women and children "were shot down in cold blood, not from one hundred yards, but from five to fifteen feet away?"

"No, no. I do not believe it's possible that's what happened," Kerrey said. Then he began to qualify his original story. "It's possible that a slight version of that happened, ah, it's possible that some additional firing occurred after the main firing, if you follow what I'm saying."

"Finishing off people who weren't dead already?"

"Yeah, that's possible. But, boy, it's not my memory of it. Let me be clear. I don't think it's easier to live with it either way. We killed. What we got at the end of the operation is dead women and children."

I glanced over at Anderson and gave him a slight nod. We were near the end of our allotted time and Kerrey had to catch a train to Philadelphia. I wanted Anderson to reveal what we had come for. He hesitated for a moment, then told Kerrey about finding Lanh. "What am I supposed to make of that? What am I supposed to do with that," Anderson asked. He said it was important for Kerrey to come back on with Dan Rather and explain "why people might have different memories. We would like to do it if you would like to do it."

Kerrey was visibly shaken. He got up out of his chair and began to pace around the room. As he picked up his briefcase and started to pack things into it, he questioned the veracity of the woman, implying that she was a dupe of the Communist government. She'd say anything, he said. Why, then, did her story so closely match Gerhard Klann's in basic chronology and critical details?

Kerrey, growing more agitated, had no answer. "What honestly is going on now is the real possibility that this is not just a . . . that this is a story that is going to produce a significant alteration in my life and I have to figure out how to deal with it. I mean, I have to figure out what I'm going to do."

Then he started to ramble. "It's not just a question of what am I going to do, am I going to do a follow-up interview, this is a possibility . . . which is a major turning point in my life. I have to figure out what to do."

With that, we followed him from his office out of the room and piled into a crowded elevator. All the way to the lobby, Kerrey and Anderson stared at one another from a distance of less than two feet. Neither man blinked.

Outside, we squeezed into the backseat of his black limousine. Kerrey was in the middle, with Anderson and me as bookends. As the driver took off for Penn Station, Kerrey asked me to ride with him on the train. He was going to talk on Social Security at the Annenberg Institute, and I was heading back to Washington. I hesitated at first, not sure I wanted to be around him after just hitting him with such hard news. But reluctantly I said yes.

The ride to the train station felt like one of the longest drives in my life.

"Fucking Klann," Kerrey muttered angrily. "It's every man for himself now," he said.

We were standing beneath the large black train schedule hanging from the ceiling in Penn Station, and Kerrey was steaming at the sudden turn the story had taken. He said he'd have to tell the New School's board of trustees about Thanh Phong. "I might have to resign," he said. Until now, he'd been careful not to malign Klann. But here, in the middle of the station, he was attacking Klann's reputation and wondering out loud about his motives. "Klann's pissed off at me for not helping him get the Medal of Honor," Kerrey said, for his secret mission in Iran. "I called the CIA, and there wasn't enough material. I tried to help him." Then he said something out of the blue that shouldn't have surprised me, but it did. "My wife is going to have a baby." He had just married Sarah Paley, a New York writer, and now she was pregnant. It was pure Kerrey to drop that little bit of good news amidst all the bad.

On the train, Kerrey took out some paper and started to scribble the main points of the speech he had to deliver in a few hours. "I'm not trying to avoid you," he said. "I have to do this. I sure don't feel up to this." Yet he simply tuned out, successfully finding separate intellectual compartments for the nuances of Social Security reform and allegations that he was a murderer.

After a while, Kerrey calmed down and began to sound

pensive. "I'm thinking about starting a truth commission," he said. Was he serious? "Yes."

Truth commissions in other countries, notably South Africa, had proven to be cathartic. One of the significant stories of the late twentieth century was the movement in nations like Poland, Serbia, Chile, and Rwanda, among others, to confront and reconcile brutal national histories of mass murder and genocide. It was "generally" accepted by all but the revisionists who were trying to rewrite the history of the war that U.S. forces systematically violated the rules of land warfare in Vietnam. Seymour Hersh told me he was convinced there were more incidents like My Lai. Neil Sheehan, the award-winning reporter and author of *A Bright Shining Lie*, recounted how he learned that American bombs and naval gunfire had destroyed fifteen hamlets and killed hundreds of Vietnamese civilians in Quang Ngai. Jonathan Schell, a writer for *The New Yorker* during the war, reported that seventy percent of the estimated 450 hamlets in the Quang Ngai Province had been destroyed by U.S. forces. In his book, *Son Thang, An American War Crime*, Gary Solis, a retired Marine prosecutor who taught war crimes law at West Point, wrote of a Marine "killer team" that executed sixteen women and children. Even Lewis B. Puller, Jr., had written about "grisly" acts, needless death, and mutilation in his biography, *Fortunate Son*. There were 122 convictions of Americans for war crimes in Vietnam, but most involved small-scale murders or rapes, according to experts like Solis, and reflected only a small portion of the overall atrocities believed to have occurred. Still, such acts would account for only a fraction of the 3.8 million Vietnamese who died in the conflict. The Americans and their Vietnamese allies were not the only troops engaging in brutality and terror. The Vietcong were equally as vicious.

While the United States has never attempted to officially

come to terms with wartime abuses, there have been informal attempts by those in power. Former Congressman Ron Dellums and a handful of other liberals held "unofficial" hearings in 1971 that were not sanctioned by the House leadership. And the Winter Soldiers investigation in Detroit tried but failed to bring attention to the subject of war crimes. The country's mainstream political leadership and establishment media by and large ignored both initiatives.

As a Medal of Honor recipient, Kerrey had the credibility to raise public consciousness of the issue. Even so, it was unlikely he could prod his fellow SEALs and other veterans to provide full confessions of any transgressions in Vietnam in exchange for amnesty. For the most part, Kerrey was not well liked in the SEAL community. The generally conservative SEALs don't like Kerrey's politics and view him, however mistakenly, as a die-hard war protestor. Many SEALs were pleased when the name of a training facility in the San Diego area was changed in the early 1990s from Camp Kerrey to Camp Billy Machen. When he returned to San Diego for a SEAL reunion, after being elected governor, few people wanted anything to do with him. "Nobody would sit with him," said Larry Bailey, a retired SEAL captain. "I should have done it but I didn't."

Kerrey was confident that his raid on Thanh Phong was not an aberration. He had heard other stories about abuses, he said, some of which came from his own unit. "I have been over the years called by a number of people both in SEAL team and outside SEAL team," Kerrey said. "They tell me horrible stories and how horrible they feel." Kerrey mentioned a few instances of other SEALs confiding in him about what amounted to war crimes but asked that I not repeat them.

I was also aware of several other questionable actions independent of what I'd learned from Kerrey. One SEAL platoon, headed by a friend of Kerrey's, was on a nighttime patrol inside a hamlet. "Something moved," the squad leader told me, and they opened up with automatic weapons fire. When the shooting stopped, they realized they had killed all but one member of a family, who was wounded. They administered morphine to the dying peasant, then executed him. A SEAL commander recounted how during one mission he told a teammate to "take care of the prisoner," thinking the commando would guard him. "A few minutes later, we heard a gunshot and we all jumped," said the officer.

Another SEAL described how he tortured prisoners whose hands were tied behind their backs. The Vietnamese subject was laid on the ground and a wet towel was placed over his mouth. As water poured down his throat, the victim would begin to drown. After five or six times, his American captors sat him up in the mud and attached electrical wires to his testicles for a series of shocks. When he and a more senior officer were done, he would take the prisoners out and place them in a boat. Primacord, a type of explosive device the SEALs used, would be wrapped around their necks. If one of the weakened prisoners fell, they'd pull the pin believing it would take off their heads. He said the pins needed to detonate the devices had been removed, but the prisoners didn't know that.

When we pulled into Philadelphia, Kerrey got up from his seat by the window. He turned to me and we shook hands. "Don't do anything rash," I said. Kerrey smiled and walked away.

It was the last time we would meet face-to-face.

Two days later Tom Anderson sent me a stunning e-mail. Kerrey's thirty-year patchwork of fantasy, reality, and perhaps self-deception was starting to disintegrate.

"I have just had a fairly extraordinary forty-minute telephone conversation with Bob Kerrey," Anderson wrote. "He called me. This is what he said. 'You have shaken my confidence that I know what the truth is. It may be worse than I remember. I guess it's gonna be worse. It may be different from what I remember. My capacity to tell the truth rather than what I remember is gone. For a long period of time, I was afraid of the truth and the consequences of what would happen to me. I tended to rationalize what happened. As far as what happened at the first hooch, I thought I knew everything that happened before we talked. Now I know I don't. My men told me that night there were four men in the hooch. They have never told me anything different. I do know that Klann was having trouble with his guy. Someone from the unit helped him. It was not me. I am not going to tell you who it was. It was definitely not me. I did not kill anybody or assist in the killing of anybody at the first hooch. I have to be prepared to ask the people who suffered for mercy, even though I understand their need for vengeance. I am prepared to examine the truth for the first time and tolerate the consequences. I would like to talk to Dan again, but I would prefer to do it off-camera first.' "

The next day, Kerrey telephoned Anderson again.

"Gerhard Klann is angry at me," Kerrey said. "He holds grudges. I am happy and have a good life. He does not. He had a glamorous ops life, and now he works at night in a steel mill. He is angry and bitter. He believes he, too, deserved the Medal of Honor for a separate op and I tried to help, but he didn't get it. Don't get me wrong, I love Gerhard Klann. He has always been insubordinate. That's why I like him. I have to talk to Gerhard to reach out to him."

"Klann says you want him to change his story," Anderson said. Kerrey and Ambrose had been calling Klann, and according to Klann, putting pressure on him to back down from his allegations that the SEALs intentionally killed the peasants in Thanh Phong.

"He won't," Anderson told Kerrey. "Now you are saying bad things about Klann. Unfair?"

"Well, then, perhaps it is not appropriate for me to discuss Klann with you in the future," Kerrey said. "I don't want to hurt him and I would not want anything negative I say about him to leak out into the public. I will be criticized by fellow SEALs for saying anything."

Tom Anderson had met Kerrey only once before. He had gone bowling with him in New Hampshire during the primaries. Now, Kerrey couldn't get enough of the *60 Minutes II* producer. Kerrey telephoned again a third time. His voice was firmer, more confident. He was calling Anderson by his last name now, not his first, and referring to himself as Kerrey. But Anderson also was taken aback by Kerrey's lack of focus.

"He was all over the place."

Chapter Twenty

IN OUR THREE YEARS of taped interviews and other informal meetings Bob Kerrey's memory repeatedly failed him when it came to the most critical facts of the deadly raid on Thanh Phong.

He couldn't be certain they had taken fire. Then he was. He didn't know that Klann had trouble killing Bui Van Vat. Then he remembered the struggle. In one interview he clearly recalled being in Thanh Phong prior to the killings; in others he insisted that he was never there. As for Klann's charge that women and children were gunned down in cold blood in the second set of hooches, Kerrey originally said, "I'm not going to make this worse by questioning somebody else's memory of it."

This time in his second session with Dan Rather, he was certain.

"I don't have any doubt about this part. We engaged from a distance," said a tense and standoffish Kerrey. "Now it may be that there were people still alive as we came up close, but we didn't go into a village and round people up and shoot them in cold blood."

"That is exactly Gerhard Klann's story," Rather said.

"That is not what happened that night," Kerrey said. "No doubt about it. It is neither possible nor probable."

Rather asked if Klann held any kind of a "grudge" against him.

"No," Kerrey said. "We haven't been intimate for thirty-one years. On the night I was injured, Gerhard Klann put the morphine in my thigh. Gerhard Klann held me in his arms like a baby while I smoked a cigarette and waited for a medivac helicopter to come and pick me up. I can't presume anything bad about him." All he wanted to do for Klann, Kerrey said, was "to try and help him do what I've been trying to do—live with this horror."

The interview shifted to a sensitive subject.

"All but one of the victims were women and children," Rather said. "There was one man described as an older man. That being the case, why shouldn't it be considered a war crime or an atrocity or [there] be an investigation?"

"To describe it as a war crime, I think, is wrong. Or to describe it as an atrocity, I would say, is pretty close to being right. Because that's how it felt, and that's why I feel guilt and shame for it."

"Are you concerned at all about the consequences of this becoming public?" Rather asked.

"I've got to be able to tolerate any consequence of this. I understand that there are all kinds of potential consequences, up to and including somebody saying this is a war crime and let's investigate and charge him and put him in prison."

Kerrey telephoned me the next day to assess the damage from the Rather interview. He was clearly worried about his use of the word "atrocity" and that Rather had pressed him hard on the question of war crimes. Kerrey was concerned this was the focus of the broadcast. I assured him it wasn't, that the story was broader than that, which was true, and that he would have ample opportunity and time to explain his version of events.

"Did I commit a war crime?" he asked me.

I knew sooner or later this conversation was inevitable, and it was not something I looked forward to. While I believed he was sincere in asking the question, I also suspected he was fishing, trying to figure out what was in my *Times* story and what we planned to air on CBS.

In any event, Kerrey didn't need to ask me. The Army Field Manual is explicit on the subject of war crimes. Although it is an Army instruction, it represents United States policy on the law of armed conflict and is applicable to all branches of the service. Gary Solis, the war crimes expert at West Point, had sent me the appropriate sections of the manual:

> **A commander may not put his prisoners to death because their presence retards his movements or diminishes his power of resistance by necessitating a large guard, or by reason of their consuming supplies, or because it appears certain that they will regain their liberty through impending success of their forces. It is likewise unlawful for a commander to kill his prisoners on grounds of self-preservation, even in the case of airborne or commando operations, although the circumstances of the operation may make necessary rigorous supervision of and restraint upon the movement of the prisoners of war.**

Walter Rockler, who was a prosecutor at Nuremberg, told me international law was equally clear. "The basic rule is that in enemy territory you don't kill civilians, particularly unarmed civilians."

I told him I thought his actions in the first hooch, where the SEALs killed five people, could be considered a war crime, regardless if it was Bui Van Vat and his family or even Vietcong fighters. The situation in the second hooch was not as clear-cut, I said. If his SEAL squad had indeed been fired at, I told him I thought he had every right to defend himself, although there would be questions about whether too much force had been used and if they had killed any of the wounded they had come upon. But if Klann's version was correct, I said, then he had committed a war crime in the second hooch. There was no statute of limitations on crimes of war. He could be prosecuted and, if convicted, sent to jail.

Kerrey asked for the name of the war crimes expert I had been consulting with.

"Why?" I asked.

"I'm going to call and ask if I committed a war crime."

He also asked if I had included Gerhard Klann in my *Times* story and if Dan Rather had interviewed him for the *60 Minutes II* segment. I was hesitant to answer both questions, but I had always been straight with Kerrey throughout the three years of my reporting on this project. Besides, he knew I was aware of Klann's accusations, and he also knew that if my story included him, he would have to face allegations that he was indeed a war criminal. The war crimes expert was Gary Solis at West Point, I said. And yes, Klann had flown to New York and had come to the CBS studios wearing his SEAL tie with a blue pin-striped suit. In the darkened studio, he recounted to Rather the same story he had told me at the German club in Pittsburgh, never changing the facts. He had such a strong presence and authentic manner that Anderson and the cameramen said afterward that they had never seen such a powerful interview.

Then Kerrey stepped over the line. He also wanted to know the name of the SEAL captain who had tipped me off to the story. I would have refused even if the captain hadn't spoken to me in confidence. Knowing that Kerrey was now going after Klann to undermine his credibility, I wasn't about to hand him another target.

I didn't know it at the time, but Kerrey was about to call in some formidable help in his defense. He spent $60,000 in

old surplus campaign funds to retain one of the most controversial yet influential public relations experts in the country.
John Scanlon was a hired gun who had represented clients
with some unsavory agendas. When it was accused of stealing
hundreds of millions of dollars deposited by Jews during
World War II, the Swiss bank Credit Suisse had retained
Scanlon to control the damage. He preferred to call himself a
"strategic counselor," not a "paid liar." Yet Scanlon was caught
passing "demonstrably untrue" information about Brown and
Williamson chemist Jeffrey Wigand who went to *60 Minutes*
with charges that the tobacco company had conspired to
make cigarettes more addictive. Scanlon gave the *Wall Street
Journal* a 500-page dossier peppered with erroneous facts on
the whistle-blowing Wigand.

Now Kerrey, whose maverick image in Washington rested
in part on his supposed contempt for that city's "spinners,"
was about to hire the ultimate "spin artist" to once again go
after CBS and *60 Minutes II*.

Kerrey seemed to be following the same script Scanlon had
successfully used for his other clients. Just as Scanlon tried to
destroy Wigand's reputation, it was his aim to discredit
Pham Tri Lanh, the Vietnamese eyewitness, and smear the
man Kerrey said he wished no harm, Gerhard Klann.

While Scanlon went to work, Kerrey continued his own
counteroffensive. He was calling me often now, sometimes
several times a day, asking questions and dropping hints
about Klann's credibility. "He was part of Phoenix," Kerrey
said in one call. Klann's previous tour in Vietnam, according
to Kerrey, had been with the CIA-run assassination teams.
(Records of Klann's previous tours show otherwise.) His
implication was clear: Klann was the one responsible for the
killings in Thanh Phong, not Bob Kerrey. Another call was
about Klann getting into "some kind of trouble" in Latin
America as a member of SEAL Team Six. It seemed obvious

that he wanted me to think that Klann was not only a professional assassin but also a rogue operator, a loose cannon who
didn't follow the rules.

Klann's account may have been independently corroborated by eyewitnesses, but he was still a faceless Pennsylvania
steelworker on the graveyard shift. Kerrey, the university
president and ex-senator, had almost limitless access to the
editors of the world's most powerful newspaper. On Easter
Sunday, he called Adam Moss, the editor of the *Times Magazine*, and asked if they could meet for breakfast the next
morning in Greenwich Village. Far from angry, Kerrey's tone
was almost confessional. He said he was not trying to talk
Moss out of the story, scheduled to be published in two
weeks, but that Gerhard Klann had a drinking problem. Kerrey also invited Joseph Lelyveld, the *Times* executive editor, to
a party. Kerrey did not miss the opportunity with the *Times*'s
men. He called Klann not just a "drunk" but a "delusional
drunk."

It was not something that could be easily ignored. Adam
Moss asked me to dig some more into Klann's background.
We needed to know if alcohol had been a problem in his life,
if it had impaired his memory to the point where his story
was subject to question.

As it turned out, there was a problem. Not a large one, but
it nearly unraveled three years of work. Court records in Butler, Pennsylvania, revealed Klann had been stopped in 1999
by a state trooper and held on drunken driving charges.
Because he had no previous convictions, he was allowed to
enter a program that put first-time offenders on probation for
two years. If he stayed clear of alcohol-related problems,
Klann could petition to have the matter dropped from his
record. There were no other incidents, and in late April he
was applying to have the record expunged when I told him
that the *Times* would have to disclose his problems with the
police. He blew up and threatened to disavow his version of

the Thanh Phong killings. What made matters worse was that Klann had made his threats to recant not just to me but to Adam Moss as well. The *Times* believed it had no other alternative but to include them. Klann was angry, embarrassed, and devastated by the *Times*'s decision. I was irked that he hadn't told me, that I had had to dig it up. Still, I tried to find some humor. George W. Bush had been stopped for drunk driving, I said, and *he* became president. If you pull out of the story now because of this, you will be thought of as a crazed old Vietnam veteran. "Stick it out," I said, "you're doing the right thing." Then Klann finally confided why he was so upset. On the day of the incident, he had spent the day with his best friend, a fellow Vietnam veteran who was a counselor at the local veterans center. After Klann left him, the man committed suicide.

That night, Klann said, "I just went a little overboard."

Walking from the university to his new Greenwich Village apartment, Bob Kerrey punched my home telephone number into his cell phone. It was a few days before the magazine would be published, and he was calling with more of the same questions. His friends were mad as hell, he said, and they wanted to sue *The New York Times* and CBS. This couldn't be serious, I thought. He knew what it meant to open up the history of the SEALs to pretrial discovery.

"Go ahead," I said, "you'd be putting the entire SEAL community on the stand." He'd open the floodgates, I said, on every SEAL abuse ever committed.

"I don't want to do it," he said, backing off. He explained the idea was floated by people who weren't thinking straight. And besides, Kerrey had cooperated throughout the process and had gone far in acknowledging his own role in the events at Thanh Phong. He had even said some things that were personally damaging. As he walked down the street in New

York, he said he should have followed the advice a fellow SEAL had given him about reporting their missions in Vietnam. "You should have done what we did," Kerrey said the retired officer instructed, "never put anything in writing."

It was advice that Kerrey would ignore again. On April 17, the day before he was to give a speech at the Virginia Military Institute, Kerrey e-mailed me. "Can we talk one more time?"

My intention with Kerrey was to always keep things civil and never turn down an opportunity to listen to what he had to say. "Please call at your convenience," I replied.

When he did, Kerrey said he was going to acknowledge publicly his Vietnam misdeeds in a speech the next day at VMI. Would I read the speech and give him my advice? he asked. Flattery was a tool Kerrey employed well. I had fallen for his charm before, but this time it was clear what he was up to. He was going to leak the story far enough in advance to make it appear as if he wasn't trying to undermine my article on him in the *Times*. Would any reporters be attending his speech? I asked. When he said there would be no press, I e-mailed back, "I will look at it now. Thanks and good luck."

I felt conflicted. I was investigating Kerrey for a story on possible war crimes. Advising him on a speech about his role in the killings was, I felt, not entirely appropriate. But, then again, as a journalist, I wanted to know what he planned to say. I decided I'd read the speech but offer little in the way of advice.

Kerrey wanted to inspire the cadets by talking about leadership. He began by speaking of meeting Nelson Mandela, Lech Walesa, and Vaclav Havel. He called General George Marshall "one of America's greatest heroes," and told baseball stories about Willie Mays and Warren Spahn.

Near the bottom of the speech, he wrote, "Allow me to tell you an unhappy story about myself and a choice I made while serving in Vietnam." What came next was a grossly selective interpretation of what happened amidst the thatched hooches inside the small confines of Thanh Phong. The victims whom Kerrey's team killed were not unarmed women and innocent adolescents—they were "enemy sympathizers." He said nothing about the knifing of the family in the first hooch, only that they took fire from men who then ran away, with the intention of "drawing our fire." Under this scenario, the "missing men," as Kerrey described them, would have to have roused the women and children, gathered them into a group in the middle of the village, retreated to safety, and then fired a few shots at Kerrey's squad. Kerrey sought to portray himself as a victim. "Though it could be justified militarily, I could never make my own peace with what happened that night."

He was anxious to hear from me and sent off two late-night e-mails asking if I got the speech. I didn't reply until the next morning. "I have my thought(s), but I'm not sure you would want to hear them," I wrote. He persisted, and I told him it was a good speech and that "I understand you want to get out in front of this story."

It was true that there would be no reporters at the speech. What Kerrey didn't tell me was the other part of his media strategy. He'd decided to leak his story to David Kotok of the *Omaha World-Herald* and *The Wall Street Journal*'s Dennis Farney. Kotok, who had covered Kerrey since he'd been elected governor, could always be counted on to write a positive story. That Farney would do the same was uncertain. Both were capable reporters who had traveled with Kerrey to Vietnam but hadn't spoken to him in years.

"I was surprised he called me," Farney later told press critic Seth Mnookin. "Since the '91 trip we've scarcely talked more than three or four times. But he said his motive was to give David and myself a heads-up on the story he knew was coming. Now, you can argue that it was also a way of introducing

to the public something he knew was coming, and so a certain amount of calculation went into it."

Kerrey's damage-control team, including Harrison Hickman, his 1992 pollster and now a CBS News consultant, felt
they could depend on the two reporters to set a positive, or at
least understanding, tone for the rest of the media's coverage.

Their plan backfired.

Chapter Twenty-one

A FEW MINUTES PAST midnight on April 25, Harrison Hickman logged onto his computer to read Dennis Farney's article. While the *Omaha World-Herald*'s David Kotok would, as predicted, give Kerrey long (2,025 words) and uncritical front-page treatment ("Haunted Memory: Civilian Deaths in 1969 Assault Still Pain Kerrey," read the headline), *The Wall Street Journal*'s prestige and circulation made Farney's piece the one that mattered.

The article ("Former Senator Bob Kerrey Discloses His Role in Civilian Killings") was short (598 words) and placed deep inside the paper (A-22). That was no doubt fine with Hickman. It began:

> Former Sen. Bob Kerrey, a possible Democratic presidential candidate in 2004 and a decorated Vietnam War veteran, has publicly acknowledged his role in a previously undisclosed incident: the killing of Vietnamese civilians by a Navy SEAL unit he was leading.
>
> "I went out on a mission and after it was over I was so ashamed I wanted to die," the Medal of Honor winner said in an interview last night.
>
> "This is killing me. I'm tired of people describing me as a hero and holding this inside."

So far, so good. But Hickman's hopes quickly sank. Without mentioning Klann by name, Farney said Kerrey denied another SEAL's account that the squad rounded up women and children and executed them. The *Journal* story also spelled out Kerrey's motive for coming forward: two other news organizations were planning more damaging accounts.

> **The disclosure comes at a time when the 57-year-old Mr. Kerrey, who sought the presidency in 1992, is believed to be weighing another try.... He said he was approached recently about the other Navy SEAL's account by two news organizations. He has included the incident in a partially completed memoir; divulging it now could also help inoculate him against future attacks.**

Hickman knew that the strategic leaks had failed. "We were trying to make chicken salad out of chicken shit. And it didn't quite work," he said.

That morning, my phone began ringing off the hook. My father-in-law had heard a news break about Kerrey on the radio. Other friends, who knew about my investigation of Kerrey, had heard news snippets, too, and called wondering if my story was finally out. Of course, it wasn't. I'd been scooped, and I had a sinking feeling in my stomach.

On one level, I felt angry and betrayed. I had been working with Kerrey for three years on this story and had never deceived him. On another, I expected something like this. You don't work "with" a politician on a story this explosive. Over the last few weeks, it had become plain that his instinct for self-preservation was going to trump any sense of loyalty or friendship. And in the end, what did he really owe me? From our first conversation in the corridor at *Newsweek*, we had been adversaries. For a while, at least, I'd lost sight of that. In the end, at least, he didn't.

I hit bottom when a friend telephoned with the news that C-Span was interviewing Kotok. When I turned on the radio, he was holding forth on how he had broken the story, and how a national magazine had rejected the initial article on Kerrey because of problems. It was obvious that Kerrey had provided Kotok with his own twisted account of what happened at *Newsweek*. Again, I shouldn't have been surprised.

But that afternoon, the *Times* intervened and took the story in an unexpected direction. Lelyveld, Moss, and Managing Editor Bill Keller decided to post my article on the newspaper's web page—four days before it was to hit the streets in the magazine. This was unprecedented, and the impact was enormous. Within hours, the story had become the hottest news event in the nation. That night, on the evening news, CBS ran a clip of Dan Rather's *60 Minutes II* interview with Kerrey. Other networks and cable channels carried their own accounts, most of which were sympathetic toward Kerrey. But by posting the article, we were clearly able to add to the next day's coverage. Almost every daily newspaper in the country had run something about the story, including Klann's more critical account.

Kerrey's efforts to spin the news spiraled out of control. Among the first to turn against him were students at the New School, angry about having an accused war criminal as their new president. More than a thousand students and faculty members crowded into a campus auditorium to hear Kerrey explain himself. In the first of several encounters at the school, Kerrey preached the need for healing and reconciliation. He even brought with him former *New York Times* reporter David Halberstam, who won a Pulitzer Prize for his work in Vietnam. Halberstam told the crowd Kerrey was operating in "the purest bandit country. By 1969 everyone who lived there would have been third-generation Vietcong." His defense wasn't persuasive.

One group of students even took a vote on whether Kerrey

should be fired. They overwhelmingly said he should go. But Kerrey was central to a large fund-raising campaign for the university, and a prepared statement by the trustees left little doubt about his future: "The Board of Trustees stands solidly behind him."

That only infuriated the faculty. They drafted a resolution critical of Kerrey: "Given all the testimony so far, we believe that there is a distinct possibility, though surely not beyond all reasonable doubt, that war crimes, crimes against human-ity, and criminal violations of U.S. law have been committed. Until the facts of the matter are clarified and, as we hope, President Kerrey exonerated, we are concerned about our president's ability to represent effectively this University's historic commitments to human rights and international jus-tice. We therefore ask Bob Kerrey to support our call for a thorough, complete, and impartial investigation of the events by Congress, as well as the United States Department of Defense."

At a faculty meeting called to discuss the resolution, Ker-rey "showed up to answer questions—effectively derailing any subsequent debate," said Jim Miller, a professor who helped write the resolution. The dean of the graduate faculty, Ken Prewitt, asked Miller not to put the resolution up for a vote, pointing out that there were other ways to deal with the Kerrey crisis at the school. Miller reluctantly agreed.

As the tide began to turn against Kerrey, he moved quickly to regain control of the story. He called a press conference for Thursday, April 26.

That morning, journalists packed into a Manhattan hotel's conference room waiting for Kerrey to arrive. An ABC televi-sion correspondent was doing a stand-up amidst photogra-phers and television cameramen who were jockeying for position by the door Kerrey was soon to enter. The story was a hot one for the New York press. Kerrey may long have been a creature of Washington, but, as president of the New School, he was now a New Yorker and in the backyard of the world's toughest tabloid newspapers.

Photographers snapped his every movement as he entered with his new wife, Sarah Paley, and stepped up to the podium. Kerrey smiled nervously at them, then asked, "Is that enough?"

Usually long-winded and improvisational in a setting like this, Kerrey instead took out some prepared remarks, buttoned his dark coat, and began. "Every person who has gone into war has struggled with the question, 'Did I do it right?' And I've struggled with that question privately since February 1969. For more than three decades I have carried this deeply private memory with a sense of anguish that words can not adequately convey. But I will also not let the shame I feel prevent me from saying these sets of facts."

He said the SEAL unit had been operating in a free-fire zone, implying that this gave it the authority to shoot at anything that moved. He told the reporters that intelligence reports had indicated there would be soldiers in Thanh Phong for a meeting and that there were not supposed to be civilians in the village. "We did not go on a mission with the intent of killing innocent people," he said. "We fired because we were fired upon."

Kerrey said he had chosen to talk about the raid because "it helps me heal." He recounted how he had finally told his two children. "They told me that they still loved me. Their love heals and makes me glad that I've begun to tell this story."

He was trying to win public sympathy by describing his emotional suffering. But the roomful of reporters wasn't buying. "Senator Kerrey, according to international law, it's not just people like you who pull the trigger and kill civilians who bear different levels of responsibility, but it's the architects of a war like in Vietnam," one reporter began. "What do you think of setting up a war crimes tribunal that would bring people like you, but more importantly, the architects [before a tribunal]?"

Without revealing his idea for a truth commission, he said, "I'm not prepared to talk about where this is going to go or where this ought to go. I'm really not."

Despite Kerrey's confessional tone, he was misleading with the facts. When grilled over his acceptance of the Bronze Star, Kerrey said he never wore nor mentioned the medal. It is, however, listed in his official Senate biography. Asked if his operational reports mentioned that his team had killed women and children, he answered dishonestly: "Women and children were unquestionably mentioned," he said. In response to a similar question later, Kerrey replied, "I don't know that it says exactly 'women and children' but it was not a secret what happened that night." Why were the dead all in a group, one reporter asked. "I can't explain it," Kerrey answered.

The press was courteous but forceful in wanting to know why he was only now revealing the raid. "I don't think it's fair to say I've kept a secret for thirty-two years," Kerrey said.

The next day, the *New York Daily News* stripped "Kerrey's Massacre" across its front page. His media advisers cringed when they saw it. Yet despite the tabloid headlines, the overall coverage was at first favorably disposed to Kerrey. Pete Hamill wrote a sensitive piece on the travails of Vietnam. Some pundits, notably Alex Beam, wondered what all the fuss was about. "Where do these peace-time Charlies get off?" he wrote in the *Boston Globe.* "What a laugh. The only rule of war is kill or be killed."

But as the disturbing findings printed in the *Times* began to sink in, sentiment began once again to shift against Kerrey. And the *60 Minutes II* piece, "Memories of a Massacre," was scheduled to air Tuesday night.

Kerrey was worried and wanted to keep things civil between us. He sent me an e-mail: "Greg, after Tuesday, I hope we can talk." What he didn't tell me was that John Scanlon was hatching one last operation for Fire Team Bravo.

Scanlon launched a clever counterattack. He had Bob Kerrey quietly bring his SEAL squad to New York (minus Klann) so they could compare notes and release a statement. On Friday evening, they met at the home provided to Kerrey by the New School and, for the first time, talked as a group about what happened more than thirty years ago in Thanh Phong. The meeting didn't break up until 2 A.M. Later that morning, a one-page statement, signed by the six men, was faxed to *The Washington Post*, where it landed on the desk of veteran defense correspondent Tom Ricks. It was Scanlon's view that the *Post* was the only newspaper with the prestige to give the Raiders' collaborative version any clout. The paper also had a strong incentive to run the statement, Scanlon reasoned. Since it had been scooped by its arch rival, *The New York Times*, it was certain to play up news about the SEAL gathering in New York. Not coincidentally, the statement was released in time for the Sunday morning talk shows.

> Last evening six members of the SEAL team came together for the first time in 32 years to talk about what happened in Thanh Phong—up to this point a private memory. Our reputations have been challenged about the events of February 25, 1969. We feel compelled to respond. Here is what happened.
>
> On February 25, 1969, our SEAL team squad went on a mission to eliminate the local leadership of the South Vietnamese Communists in the area.

Our intelligence sources told us they would be meeting in the village of Thanh Phong. We expected the meeting to be well protected by enemy security. Thanh Phong was behind enemy lines in what is known as a free-fire zone.

From the beginning the mission did not go as expected. We have individual memories of a night that was a defining and tragic moment for each of us. These individual memories have been made worse by individual emotion and the advance of time. We will never know all the details of that night but we do know these for certain.

At an enemy outpost we used lethal methods to keep our presence from being detected.

At the village we received fire and we returned fire.

One of the men in our squad remembers that we rounded up women and children and shot them at point-blank range in order to cover our extraction. That simply is not true. We know there was an enemy meeting in this village. We know this meeting had been secured by armed forces. We took fire from these forces and we returned fire. Knowing our presence had been compromised and that our lives were endangered we withdrew while continuing to fire.

When the *Post* story ran on Saturday morning, April 28, Kerrey got the positive bounce that Scanlon expected. Most of the television producers and the reporters who followed the story for the next day's coverage didn't closely examine the statement, which raised as many questions as it tried to answer. Kerrey and his teammates glossed over the killing of Bui Van Vat's family, calling their hooch "an enemy outpost." The "lethal methods" they used to keep from being detected was a euphemism for killing with knives. And if there were men inside, as Kerrey first asserted, why omit this critical fact now?

The Raiders described being in a firefight. Yet Kerrey said in previous statements they took only a few rounds from one hundred yards away. Why the difference now? Previously, Kerrey had recalled walking into the village and finding the women and children dead in a heap. In the team's official spot report after the raid, they said they counted the bodies. Now, according to the statement, they had to withdraw under fire, never making it into the village. One document had to be wrong: the spot report filed right after the action three decades ago or the middle-of-the-night communiqué orchestrated by John Scanlon. Which version was true?

I was surprised that Tucker, Knepper, Schrier, and Peterson had signed on to the statement. When I spoke to them over the course of my research, three of the men were trying to keep the memories locked away. Tucker, though still pained, talked freely about the mission.

Kerrey must have pushed Tucker and Knepper hard. I had spent two nights in November 1998 talking with Tucker in Dallas. Tucker had confirmed the deaths of the women and children but said he didn't want anything to do with backing either Kerrey or Klann. He said he had previously avoided most contact with his former teammates. Tucker was the only one who didn't show up when the team had gathered to plant a tree on Capitol Hill for the thirtieth anniversary of Kerrey's Medal of Honor. "I don't go to the SEAL Team reunions," Tucker told me. "I've got no interest in them."

Knepper had no interest in getting involved in the story either. We spoke by telephone several times, and I mentioned I would like to see him on one of my reporting trips to San Diego. He was noncommittal, but said to call him when I arrived. Assuming the answer would be "no" when I called again, I planned to show up unannounced on his doorstep. When I pulled up to his home in Bonita outside of San Diego, nobody was there. But as I drove away, I saw Knepper and his wife pull into the driveway. I parked so I could see him and waited a few minutes. Rather than ambushing him, I rang him on my cell phone. "You said to call you when I got to San Diego. I'm here," I said, not mentioning that I was across the street just a few feet away, able to see him through his window. Knepper became upset, not angry, but it was clear from his voice that he still carried tremendous grief about Vietnam.

I had to give him the opportunity for fair comment, so I laid out the entire story—Klann's version and Kerrey's different account. "My time in Vietnam was too hard," he said. "Please leave me alone." He was literally begging me, and I didn't have the heart to confront him. I wished him well, hung up, and drove away.

Based on my last conversation with Knepper, I was surprised that he had signed on to any one version of the events. In addition, Kerrey had told me on several occasions that Knepper didn't remember anything about the massacre. Now, it seemed he had better recall.

I did ambush Peterson. After my encounter with Knepper, I showed up at the Los Angeles Police Department precinct where Peterson was a juvenile detective. The cop at the desk told Peterson he had a visitor. He came out to a small waiting area wearing a tight short-sleeved shirt, with a revolver tucked into a shoulder holster. I introduced myself. "I've got nothing to say," Peterson responded defiantly.

"Please hear me out," I said. Not waiting for an answer, I laid out Klann's story—that Kerrey's team had slaughtered unarmed villagers. Peterson said he did nothing wrong. But he did acknowledge that civilians had been killed, only he tried to put the blame on Coast Guard cutter. "The *Point Comfort* had clearance to fire into that area," he said.

Schrier had nothing to say. I made sure he knew what was about to be printed concerning the SEAL raid and asked him for a comment. "Well, I sure don't want to make anything I did in SEAL team public. I don't care if it has to do with training, whether it has to do with going down to the city of Coronado and getting shit-housed. I just made up my mind that I don't want to deal with the news people. I'm not apologizing, I'm just not gonna do it."

As for Ambrose, he was one of Kerrey's closest friends in the SEALs and had even helped out in several political campaigns. I had interviewed him three times, the last shortly before the *Times* article was complete, so he had the opportunity to comment again on Klann's allegations. Ambrose wholeheartedly denied Gerhard's account, but the one he offered me was quite different from what he signed on to in New York. Though he said his memory had dimmed, Ambrose told me that he remembered bursting into one of the hooches to find only women. When he left the hooch, he said, "We took a round somewhere near the back by Knepper and Peterson. Somebody yelled, 'Incoming.' Once we received fire, we immediately fired." Then things got out of hand. "It got ridiculous pretty much once the guns got going. I was in survival mode. It was dark, you're not seeing much but movement. You couldn't tell if they were women or men." Ambrose recalled the team shooting from twenty to fifty feet, and when they stopped, he realized the dead were all women and children.

Now Ambrose was signing on to another, contradictory version that Scanlon had orchestrated. Later, he sent me a bizarre e-mail in which he said, "We have never met."

As quietly as the men had slipped into New York, they left without going before reporters to defend their statement.

Klann was stunned. These were his friends, people he had fought with in the war. Two days before the New York gathering, Klann said that some of his former teammates called to say they were backing him. Now they had turned against him and were supporting Kerrey.

Several of the men would later take steps to make amends with Klann. They telephoned to apologize. And Peterson sent an e-mail explaining why they did it. Klann was convinced that Kerrey had told them they would all go to jail for war crimes if they didn't refute his story.

On Saturday, April 28, the same day the Raiders issued their statement, Kerrey got a jolt. The Vietnamese government had allowed foreign correspondents to travel to the remote village of Thanh Phong to conduct interviews. Now, the first press reports were trickling in from Reuters, the *Los Angeles Times*, and the Associated Press, all of which were at odds with what Kerrey was saying about civilians being killed. The most damning came later on May 7 in the *Washington Post*, a lengthy and detailed account that reported the claims of Vietnamese eyewitnesses that there had been an unprovoked slaughter.

Around noon on Saturday, a stringer for *Time* magazine weighed in with a short sidebar in which the correspondent questioned the veracity of Lanh's account: "What isn't yet clear is whether villager Pham Thi Lanh is an honest witness, a propagandist, or just an old woman with hazy memories." The correspondent claimed Lanh had changed the story she had given to *60 Minutes II*. She had not seen the killings. Rather, she was an "ear witness" who heard them.

Kerrey's media handlers were buoyed by the news and quickly moved to discredit the old woman. They believed they had found a hole in the story, and they were going to open it up as wide as they could. Kerrey gave a statement saying Lanh had no credibility. Then he went after *The New York Times* and CBS. "It's disgraceful. The Vietnamese government likes to routinely say how terrible Americans were. The *Times* and CBS are now collaborating in that effort." (He later apologized in letters to both organizations.) Pundits trying to bolster Kerrey's version of events began to assail Lanh. How could she be trusted to tell the truth? She was an uneducated peasant, a woman, she didn't speak English, she was Asian and a Vietcong sympathizer, as well. Therefore she didn't exist. It was vicious stereotyping and it almost worked.

But soon enough, other reporters had found a witness who backed up Lanh, a development that the *Time* stringer had failed to report. Living in a nearby fishing village with her husband and five children was Bui Thi Luom, who as a young girl had been sleeping in a bunker when Kerrey's Raiders quietly arrived.

In 1969, Bui Thi Luom was the oldest of eleven children who were all in the bunker. The youngest was three years old. "That night I was sleeping inside the shelter," she told foreign reporters. "My grandmother woke me up, calling everybody in the shelter to come outside."

When she appeared, the Americans stood just a few feet away and after a few minutes they began to shoot at the villagers she said. Luom escaped unnoticed by fleeing into a nearby dugout shelter.

Thirty-two years later, her anger at the Americans, who she said killed twenty of her family and friends, still raged.

"At the time I was too small, but if I could get revenge, I would. If I could have killed them, I would."

On Tuesday evening at eight o'clock, Bob Kerrey turned on his television and sat down with his wife, Sarah Paley, to watch *60 Minutes II.*

Kerrey had already made arrangements with his hometown

newspapers to have two reporters available for his comments to be published the next day. David Kotok would talk with him from Omaha, and Don Walton, a longtime Kerrey watcher for the *Lincoln Journal Star*, had flown in to see the broadcast at Kerrey's home.

When Walton arrived, he bumped into Kerrey and Paley, who were out for a walk on this first night of May. The trio strolled through lower Manhattan for a while longer, then headed back to Kerrey's apartment to watch "Memories of a Massacre." Inside, Paley nestled next to Kerrey on a living room couch so she could hold on to him. Well into the hourlong *60 Minutes II* segment, neither Kerrey nor Paley had uttered a word. And during commercials, when Paley muted the sound on the small television, the three sat in silence. "I found it rather tense, and I think they did, too," Walton said.

About a third of the way into the show, when Klann began describing in graphic detail how the team had slaughtered the villagers, Walton glanced at Kerrey and saw that he was visibly agitated. Then Kerrey rose from Paley's embrace and walked out of the room and into the backyard. Walton wondered if he was going to come back in. A few moments later, Kerrey returned to his place beside his wife.

Afterward, Walton began to question Kerrey.

"Did you hear anything that has reminded you of things you haven't yet spoken about?" Walton asked.

"No," Kerrey said.

Walton passed on Kerrey's offer of a beer, excused himself, and went back to his hotel to write his story.

When Kerrey spoke with Kotok of the *Omaha World-Herald*, he was forceful and critical of the broadcast. "It was presented in a very dramatic and sensational fashion," Kerrey said.

Kotok asked if the show would end the week-long controversy about the raid into Thanh Phong.

"I have no idea," Kerrey said. "The truth is, I'm afraid it

won't end until the last Vietnam veteran is dead and in the grave. We are going to be in a free-fire zone the rest of our lives," Kerrey said. "They will go back and keep second-guessing what the soldiers did instead of the decision the politicians made."

John Scanlon could not have come up with a better script.

Epilogue

Three weeks later, Bob Kerrey was in the CNBC studios for an interview with Washington's top celebrity journalist, Tim Russert.

He could not have picked a friendlier forum for his first attempt at rehabilitating his tarnished image. Russert, who had worked for Pat Moynihan, Kerrey's Senate mentor, was eager to help and had prepared an upbeat show complete with archival tape of past political triumphs. Normally a combative and tough questioner, he gently guided his guest through virtually an entire hour without once mentioning that Kerrey had acknowledged committing an "atrocity" in Vietnam. Indeed, when Russert addressed Thanh Phong at all, it was with euphemism and code, using words like "incident" and alluding to the "anguished stories" written about Kerrey. He spent perhaps a few minutes, if that, on the subject.

But toward the end of the hour, while commenting on Bill Clinton's honesty, Kerrey pulled the pin from a rhetorical grenade and rolled it toward Russert. Even by Kerrey's cosmic standards, it was a surreal moment.

"Look, who doesn't lie?"

"Right," Russert replied weakly.

"Show me somebody who doesn't lie, and it's not somebody I want to hang out with," Kerrey said.

But rather than ask if Kerrey was lying about what actually had taken place on the SEAL raid, Russert—perhaps not believing what he'd heard—told his national audience, "We have to take a quick break."

When he returned, Russert switched the subject as if the previous conversation had never occurred. "You're on a new chapter in your life," he said to Kerrey, "a new wife, a new baby coming in September."

Russert's coddling typified establishment Washington's treatment of the Kerrey story. On *This Week*, the ABC Sunday morning talk show, Sam Donaldson and Cokie Roberts hosted four U.S. senators decorated for their service in Vietnam: John McCain, Chuck Hagel, John Kerry, and Max Cleland. They dismissed the allegations against Kerrey and all but McCain said they would oppose any investigation. McCain would let the Pentagon decide. It was a meaningless concession. While the Defense Department had a mechanism for investigating whether the Bronze Star—which Kerrey won for Thanh Phong—had been awarded under false pretenses, it had no intention of beginning a probe unless directed to do so. And that wasn't about to happen. "To talk now about an investigation, it seems to me, is just the wrong way to go," said Senator John Kerry. If Bob Kerrey was to be judged, then "you'd have to investigate the whole war." Cleland added, "There's no point in it."

The creaking sound audible in the background was the circling of wagons. Few of Washington's elite journalists and politicians seemed capable of believing that one of their own could have committed the terrible deeds alleged. Even fewer appeared ready to seek the truth. Rather, the point of departure for any discussion of Bob Kerrey was that he was innocent. Excuses were made: He was young and scared, operating in the jungle and at night; those really at fault were the leaders who put him in harm's way. What his defenders overlooked was that the Bob Kerrey of 1969 was not some kid GI fresh from the cornfields. He was a Navy SEAL, painstakingly trained to penetrate enemy lines in the middle of the night and quietly, cleanly, kill whoever was considered to be the enemy. "We were instructed not to take prisoners," Kerrey emphatically told me. (That, according to Samantha Power of Harvard, is a war crime under international and American law.) Bob Kerrey was not forced to do these things—he volunteered.

Why was Kerrey so believable—both to Washingtonians and the country at large—while Gerhard Klann's self-implicating account caused many to recoil in disbelief? "Americans like to believe that atrocities are committed by others, but we are not immune from such things. We like to think we are, but we are not," wrote Edwin H. Simmons, a retired Marine general in the foreword to Gary Solis's book, *Son Thang, An American War Crime.*

Had Klann's claims been made in 1969, they would likely have been viewed in a dramatically different light—placing Kerrey on a roster of accused war criminals like William Calley. Certainly, press exposure at the time would have forced the Pentagon to investigate and, if the evidence supported it, led to court-martial proceedings against Kerrey and his Raiders. Today, such a move would cut directly against the political and cultural mood of the country. So dramatically have attitudes toward the use of military force changed in the last thirty-plus years that it would take an extraordinary act of barbarism for Americans to question the battlefield conduct of their troops.

Vietnam was a mistake and is considered by many to be a national shame. But the perceived national impotence of the early post-Vietnam years (the Iranian hostage crisis, Desert One, the unraveling of morale and discipline in the military) triggered its own backlash. The Reagan-era defense buildup, widely believed to have accelerated the collapse of the Soviet Union and the end of the Cold War, combined with the creation of an all-volunteer force and its televised prowess in the Persian Gulf, created a new "warrior class" that had Washington as its Sparta. The Reagan and Bush administrations' sophisticated use of the military as political propaganda (reinforced by Hollywood, which followed the national mood with a string of patriotic films like *Saving Private Ryan* and *Pearl Harbor*) let Americans feel good about the use of military power.

One major casualty of this change in sentiment was human rights, which President Jimmy Carter had established as a cornerstone of U.S. foreign policy. In the ensuing years, however, that commitment, as the timidity over Bob Kerrey illustrates, has slowly been dismantled by policy makers whose only concern is that U.S. troops do "whatever it takes to get the job done."

This is why the story about Bob Kerrey is more than just a tragic piece of history. More and more, our military model, especially in dealing with terrorism, is going to be closer to the SEAL method of operation than the conventional-forces model. The next generation of young men on antiterror ops are inevitably going to find themselves in a village where their map is bad, where their intelligence is bad, and where they've been compromised. They may or may not comport themselves properly. If they do not, they will likely be haunted for years to come in much the same way as Bob Kerrey has. If this happens, will we excuse their behavior the same way we excused Kerrey's?

Washington is still quick to condemn other nations (and rightly so) for crimes against humanity, as in Serbia's recent atrocities in Kosovo. "But how different everything becomes when our own countrymen are the wrongdoers," Jonathan Schell wrote in an essay on Kerrey for the *Nation*. "Whereas before we seemed to be looking at the events through a sort of moral telescope, which brought everything near and into sharp focus, now we seem to look through the telescope's other end. The figures are small and indistinct. A kind of mental and emotional fog rolls in. Memories dim."

Thanh Phong is only the latest example of American myopia. Though the majority of the United Nations' member states have already signed on to or signaled their intention to join a permanent international criminal court—an idea first recommended after Nuremberg—President George W. Bush has steadfastly refused to support the court or accept its jurisdiction. In Afghanistan, there have been credible reports and numerous allegations that civilians were tortured, even killed by U.S. troops or by the Afghans they operated with during the war against the Taliban and Al Qaeda. The Pentagon "investigated" and, not surprisingly, exonerated its troops in a quick, internal investigation. Congress remained silent, and, in much the same way it reacted to the Kerrey story, the public just shrugged its collective shoulders—a discouraging and demoralizing act of ambivalence, says Aryeh Neier, a respected investigator of war crimes.

Missing is any public-spirited effort at national self-criticism. In its place is a nationalist fervor and an environment of fear in which anyone who seeks to hold our soldiers to standards of conduct risks being bludgeoned as unpatriotic.

In the Senate, Kerrey was among the most vocal of a chorus calling for action against despots like Saddam Hussein. But when he found himself on the other side, that of the accused, he claimed ignorance of the very laws to which he used to hold war criminals like Milosevic accountable. "The first time I read the rules of war," Kerrey told Russert, "was four weeks ago at West Point." (Other SEALs who went through Officer Candidate School flatly dismiss Kerrey's claim. "We had instruction in that," said one.) That a United States senator would claim to be so unknowledgeable about what constitutes a crime against humanity is breathtaking in itself.

There is another reason that Kerrey was able to evade an inquiry with such ease. People were simply in love with the idea of him rather than the reality: hero from the heartland, boyfriend of a movie star, governor, senator, and presidential candidate. It was a script that everyone, including me, for a while, was invested in.

When I first confronted Kerrey about Thanh Phong, I was surprised that he didn't deny the raid. Had he done so, it might have derailed the whole project. That he chose to play along and admit to at least part of the story was immensely intriguing. Was there a need to finally, after all these years, clear his conscience? How was a very public official able to keep such a dark secret? And what was it like living a double life? To answer these questions, I had to delve deep beneath the surface. To do that, I needed to get close to Kerrey. That was easy; Kerrey was readily available for drinks, dinners, telephone calls, interviews in his office or on the steps of Capitol Hill and in e-mail exchanges. The hard part was keeping the charismatic power of his personality from clouding my journalistic judgment.

For some time, I was not very successful.

Kerrey's account of his grief and years of emotional distress saddened me. I was left with strong feelings of sympathy and, at times, a desire to protect him by giving him the benefit of the doubt in my reporting. As I moved deeper into the research, forces from my own past also came into play. Years earlier, I had uncovered the Tailhook scandal, a sordid story about naval aviators sexually assaulting women in a Las Vegas hotel. A lot of people, including admirals and the secretary of the Navy, had their lives ruined by public exposure.

Some deserved it; some did not. And the experience left me with a desire to infuse my work with a greater sense of forgiveness. I wanted to treat peoples' misdeeds less in black and white and more as part of their fallability as human beings. In essence, I wanted to love the sinner and hate the sin.

Even after Kerrey's brazen performance on CNBC with

Tim Russert, I still felt the need to comfort him. "Saw you last night on Russert," I e-mailed. "You looked pretty tired, but there seemed to be a real calm within you. I hope that is true. You are in my thoughts and prayers (honest)."

He wrote back: "Thanks. You are in my thoughts and prayers, too (honest). And I am not tired; I am exhausted. Be well."

That was the last time I communicated with him. In the months that followed, and in the process of writing this book, I realized that I had at times ignored my first obligation as a journalist—the pursuit of the truth. When we swapped personal stories over dinners and drinks, I was acting more like Kerrey's friend than a reporter. Like much of Washington, I was enamored with the idea of Kerrey rather than reality.

I believe in the power of forgiveness, and I think it's important to forgive Kerrey but not forget what he did in Thanh Phong. But I have also come to terms with another disappointing truth: He is not a hero, and he can be, as many politicians become, a user and a person who does not have enough of a conscience to be a truth teller. On the surface, he appears to be a man of integrity. Beneath his public persona, however, I saw a devious side: when he and his handlers called my *Newsweek* editors to try to kill the original piece, when he hired John Scanlon to trash the reputation of Gerhard Klann who cradled Kerrey like a baby and gave him morphine as he lay seriously wounded on Hon Tam Island. Instead of simply expressing horror at the events of that night in February 1969, Kerrey has cast himself as the victim.

His selective and misleading recall continues to this day. In his recently released memoir, *When I Was a Young Man*, he provides yet another version of what happened to the Vietnamese women, children, and babies whose lives were snuffed out thirty-three years ago. Only three sentences in the book vaguely describe what happened to Bui Van Vat and his family. In recounting events at the second hooch, Kerrey is equally brisk. He takes all of two paragraphs to discuss the killings:

> At the village, we approached the house where the meeting was to take place," Kerrey wrote. "One man entered the building while six others remained outside to provide security from all angles of approach. We waited, spread out with one man on point, and from my position I did not see any security. Our point man came out of the house and whispered excitedly that the men were not there. No meeting was taking place and all the men were gone. He said their sleeping places had been recently abandoned. He went into other houses and reported the same thing. When he came out of the second he had a look of real fear on his face.
>
> "The women and children in each of the three houses woke, gathered outside and began to talk loudly in high sing-song voices. We knew we were in trouble. The absence of men told us we had been compromised. We were certain there were armed cadre in the village now on full alert. We had two choices: withdraw or continue to search houses in the dark. Before we could make the decision, someone shot at us from the direction of the women and children, trapping them in a crossfire. We returned a tremendous barrage of fire and began to withdraw continuing to fire. I saw women and children in front of us being hit and cut to pieces. I heard their cries and other voices in the darkness as we made our retreat to the canal.

This new explanation sharply contradicts the account that Kerrey and his men had carefully constructed in New York at

Scanlon's behest. It is Kerrey's tacit acknowledgment that the post-midnight statement was nothing more than a public relations countermeasure to throw the hounds off.

Whether Kerrey intended it or not, this latest attempt to recall the events of that tragic night places him closer to Klann's version. I can only wonder if, in his own tortured way, he is inching toward a new truth. One day, perhaps, he may even embrace Klann, and the complete story will finally be known. In the meantime, when Kerrey's multiple inconsistent stories are coupled with the available evidence, the only conclusion I am able to draw is that Klann has provided the more accurate version. It may also turn out to be flawed, to some unknown extent, but until the United States government uses its powers to conduct a full and independent investigation, including the exhumation of bodies to examine bullet and knife wounds, it will have to stand.

Klann, for his part, is at peace with his decision to speak out. While he has been a target for SEALs angry that he violated their culture of silence, he's also received high-level support. Three top SEAL commanders e-mailed their congratulations for doing the right thing. Klann wants to put in five more years at the steel mill, then pack up his camper and retire to New Mexico.

Kerrey is planning no such disappearance. This spring, he cut a television ad for the Sierra Club. In June, *Roll Call*, the Capitol Hill newspaper, reported that a year after the "biggest crisis" of his public career Kerrey "is beginning to reemerge on the political scene." In addition to a nationwide book tour, he's hosted fund-raisers for Democratic candidates and recently donated $40,000 to the Iowa Democratic party. *Roll Call* deemed it "enough of a whirlwind of activity to start a buzz" in party circles about his plans for a presidential run in 2004 or, more likely, 2008—two years after his New School contract expires.

That's assuming he makes it to the end of his contract.

Kerrey has fallen on hard times in his new life. After September 11, enrollment declined, forcing him to freeze the budget. His handpicked choice for deanship of the school's prestigious graduate faculty of political and social science, Kenneth Prewitt, resigned after just a few months.

Prewitt's departure captures with perfect clarity why Kerrey is not likely to change. This year, Kerrey told *The New York Times* that he had increased the New School's endowment by 20 percent in just over a year. At a faculty dinner at Prewitt's house a few nights later, he was asked why that increase hadn't translated into a larger academic budget.

Kerrey replied with a laugh: "You can't believe everything I tell the *Times*."

Notes on Sources

This book arose from my coverage of Bob Kerrey for *The New York Times Magazine* and for *60 Minutes II*. Nearly all of the material in these pages comes from interviews with a wide range of individuals: political operatives, congressional staff members, military officers, academics, SEALs who served in Vietnam and the naval officers who trained them, CIA and State Department men assigned to the Mekong Delta in 1969 and 1970, and antiwar activists. I spoke to each member of Kerrey's SEAL team and the officers in their chain of command, sometimes on several occasions. Kerrey and Gerhard Klann sat numerous times for lengthy interviews. I also interviewed members of Team 88, the army advisory unit responsible for the Thanh Phu Secret Zone and members of the Swift boat that transported Kerrey and his teammates to Thanh Phong. I relied on the videotaped interviews my colleagues Tom Anderson and Derek Williams of *60 Minutes II* conducted with eye witnesses and family members of those massacred in Thanh Phong. In addition to the oral interviews, I combed through thousands of pages of documents at the Navy's historical center and at the National Archives to review records pertaining to SEAL operations in Vietnam, including Kerrey's. Finally, I used media reports and books when it helped to clarify or expand on information from primary sources. Included among the books I reviewed were those written by SEALs on training and operations in Vietnam; the only biography on Kerrey, *Waltzing Matilda*, by Ivy Harper; and Kerrey's own memoir, *When I Was a Young Man*. Media coverage by journalists on Kerrey's youth, his political life, and his Medal of Honor mission was so widely reported that there are only a few sources that warrant attribution. Much of the prologue, with the exception of my interviews with Kerrey and the Richard Nixon presidential papers, fall into this category. Two exceptions: the anecdote of JFK's image in Kerrey's laptop comes from Jake Thompson's March 23, 1998, story in the *Omaha World-Herald*, and Colin Powell's reaction to Kerrey's comments on the Medal of Honor come from Sally Quinn's "Party Protocol" in *The New Yorker*.

CHAPTER ONE

This chapter was reconstructed using several sources of information: interviews with family members of those killed in Thanh Phong done by Tom Anderson and Derek Williams; my interviews with Kerrey, Klann, Michael Ambrose, and William Tucker; Swift boat crew members William Garlow, William O'Mara; Team 88 advisers James Cook and David Marion as well as senior military advisers familiar with the area; other SEALs who had a working knowledge of the habits of villagers in the Mekong Delta; and official records that had to be declassified at the Navy historical center. Garlow also provided internal documents. In addition, I drew from press dispatches by reporters who visited Thanh Phong after my story in *The New York Times* broke. The most authoritative were written by *Washington Post* foreign correspondent Rajiv Chandrasekaran on May 7, 2001, and Richard Paddock of the *Los Angeles Times* on April 29, 2001.

CHAPTER TWO

I have kept the name of the Navy captain who tipped me off about Gerhard Klann confidential. I interviewed Roy Boehm, who wrote about the renegade squad of SEALs in his memoir, *First SEAL*. The material in this chapter on Kerrey's youth in Nebraska comes primarily from my interviews with Kerrey. Martha Sherrill's January 1996 *Esquire* article, "Grave Doubts," came closer than anybody up to that point of understanding why Kerrey was such an iconoclast.

CHAPTER THREE

Kerrey told me that he used to jog to the Vietnam Wall early in the morning. A naval officer I interviewed, jogged the same path as Kerrey and frequently saw him in the early morning hours. Sherrill described Kerrey in *Esquire* as "astronaut size." Kerrey wrote how his wounds left him different in *The Vietnam Reader*, edited by Walter Capps. I interviewed Kandra Hahn, Ed Howard, Tom Fogarty, and Dick Herman, among others, on Kerrey's fickleness and political career. Herman, an editorial writer at the *Lincoln Journal Star*, provided a brief history of Lincoln. I also read a number of historical articles on Nebraska that described Bethany's early roots. The material on James Kerrey and the relatives who cared for him comes predominantly from my interviews with Kerrey. There are secondary sources: newspaper articles, Harper's work, and Kerrey's memoir. *The Daily Nebraskan*, University of Nebraska's student newspaper, ran a number of stories in the winter of 1965 on the discount card investigation.

CHAPTER FOUR

Since late 1997, I have interviewed or communicated by e-mail with several SEALs and UDT team members who trained with Kerrey in Class 42. Some did not want their names mentioned, others like Bill Hemming, Steve Frisk, Donald Crawford, Frank Czajkowski, Tom Lawson, and Earl Courtney did not request confidentiality. In addition, I spoke with Barry Enoch, who was one of Kerrey's SEAL instructors, and Larry Bailey, who was responsible for SEAL training in the 1990s. Much of this chapter on SEAL training and ROTC course work comes from Kerrey. The *Daily Nebraskan* ran articles on October 24, 1964, and May 11, 1964, on Kerrey's efforts to change ROTC requirements. For a good understanding of the UDT training culture, I relied on the following books: *Teammates: SEALs At War*, by Barry Enoch; *The Element of Surprise, Navy SEALs in Vietnam*, by Darryl Young, which includes an excellent introduction by Nicolas E. Walsh; *The Making of U.S. Navy SEALs, Class-29* by John Carl Roat; *SEALs in Action* by Kevin Dockery; and Douglas Waller's *Commandos*. I interviewed many SEALs who went through training and watched portions of Hell Week, including activities in "The Grinder" as a reporter in San Diego. The quote about Kerrey's "drive" from a teacher in high school and the passage on Kerrey changing his doctor's certificate are from Ivy Harper. The quote from Kerrey's brother "last in the swims," was reported in the *Lincoln Star*, December 9, 1982. I interviewed a number of officers who went to the Navy's Officer Candidate School in Newport. Kerrey wrote about becoming "severely nauseous" in the foreword of *Teammates*. "It took balls," comes from an October 16, 1998, e-mail from Frank Czajkowski. The recruit with the instructor's boot on his head comes from Czajkowski. It was so forceful, "that it removed his upper teeth." Besides interviews with SEALs who were present during the drowning of McCall and Greco, the local papers, the *San Diego Union* and *San Diego Tribune*, carried short stories about the tragedy.

CHAPTER FIVE

The material for this chapter comes from Kerrey, Klann, Tucker, Ambrose, and Roy Hoffmann. The information on Robert McNamara's memorandum and increase in U.S. forces comes from Neil Sheehan's *A Bright Shining Lie*.

CHAPTER SIX

Interviews with Kerrey, Hoffmann, and Paul Connolly were used for this chapter. In addition, Ambrose, Garlow, and other officers under Connolly and Hoffmann's command provided information. I also used official Navy records such as Hoffmann's monthly report, daily intelligence reports on

Vietcong activity, and internal communiqués found at the Navy's historical center.

CHAPTER SEVEN

Interviews with Kerrey, David Marion, James Cook, William Garlow, and other members of Delta Platoon were the primary sources for information in this chapter. I also found helpful records kept by Team 88, such as the Phoenix ledgers, and the daily operational reports for the Thanh Phu District and the Kien Hoa Province at the National Archives. Marion read me his journal entries from 1969. Barry Enoch, who was a respected SEAL instructor and who operated extensively in the Mekong Delta, wrote about the Vietcong being driven out of the Delta by late 1968 primarily because of losses incurred in the Tet Offensive. On April 26, 1971, then Congressman Ronald Dellums held "unofficial" hearings on Capitol Hill which were published a year later in the book *On War Crimes in Vietnam*. Witnesses who served in the Army and under General Julian Ewell's command testified to his statements about the need to kill more enemy.

CHAPTER EIGHT

Interviews with Kerrey, Klann, Ambrose, Tucker, Cook, Marion, Hoffmann, Connolly, and official Navy documents were used for this chapter. The number twenty seven comes from five people at Bui Van Vat's hooch, fourteen villagers at the second hooch (one who was pregnant), and the seven who were killed (according to the records) when trying to flee. My source for Tran Van Rung was Rajiv Chandrasekaran's May article in *The Washington Post*. *60 Minutes II* also interviewed a man who claimed to be at the meeting of Communist leaders on February 25, 1969, in Thanh Phong.

CHAPTER NINE

I interviewed Kerrey, Ambrose, Klann, and Hoffmann for this chapter and used documents on the Hon Tam raid, including after-action spot reports, Hoffmann's monthly summary, naval operational and intelligence reports, and commendation reports used for awarding medals for heroism to the SEALs involved in the raid. Some of these were located at the Navy's historical center. Klann provided me his award citation which says: "He was instrumental in keeping the sappers from overrunning his element's position and in quickly suppressing the hostile fire." Other SEALs provided secondhand information on the mission.

CHAPTER TEN

In several interviews, Bob Kerrey and I discussed his stay in the hospital, his parents' visit, and the decisions he had to make concerning the amputation of his leg and the treatment of his injured hands. In addition to Kerrey's memory, Lewis Puller's Pulitzer Prize–winning memoir, *Fortunate Son,* contains the best description of life on SOQ 12. I have relied on the book and its wonderful anecdotes, like Kerrey's jelly bean episode, to provide a better understanding of this period in Kerrey's life. There are also numerous media reports on Kerrey's hospitalization and rehabilitation. In interviews with Kerrey he discussed the letters he wrote home from Vietnam and when he was in the hospital. In his memoir, he also refers to his first letters home after his injury, which I have drawn from. Navy records reviewed at the historical center report how Kerrey did not want his family notified about his injury. This time in his life was covered extensively by the local and national press. Kerrey's quote "I sat in the hospital with a wounded guy," comes from the *Lincoln Star,* October 25, 1976. I also interviewed Navy doctors from the Vietnam era who told of the horrible conditions, from overcrowding to rush decisions regarding care, at hospitals like Philadelphia. On Kerrey's trip back to San Diego, I interviewed Barry Enoch and several other SEALs, including Joseph Quincannon, Kerrey's replacement as squad leader of Fire Team Bravo, who saw Kerrey at the SEAL compound. Kerrey's quote about Enoch comes from the foreword of *Teammates.* Klann never told me he should have received a higher decoration for the raid on Hon Tam, but clearly he would have liked to have been recognized for saving Kerrey's life. I interviewed several of the members of Delta Platoon, including Dwight Daigle, who lived outside New Orleans, about their trip there. Roy Boehm's comments come from my interview with him.

CHAPTER ELEVEN

This period in Kerrey's life, when he was trying to adjust to returning home after the hospital, was one of great struggle and deep despair. Again, the majority of the quotes and information—such as his thoughts of suicide, confiding in his mother and minister—come from lengthy interviews with Kerrey. I also interviewed others in Nebraska and elsewhere who provided wonderful insights into Kerrey's transformation from wounded veteran to active member of the community and eventually to politician. June Levine, Paul Olson, Marilyn McNabb, Kandra Hahn, Paul Douglas, Tim Renne, Ed Howard, Tom Fogarty, Dan Ladely, and Oscar Pemantle were especially helpful as were Tim Butz and Tod Ensign, who were very knowledgeable about the antiwar movement and the Vietnam Veterans Against the War. I also used official divorce records from Kerrey's first marriage and drew background information from the *Omaha World-Herald*, the *Lincoln Journal* and the *Lincoln Star*. John Gottschalk's remarks on Kerrey were first reported in the *World-Herald* and used by Ivy Harper in *Waltzing Matilda*. Gottschalk is the president and chief executive officer of the *World-Herald* and a longtime friend of Kerrey; he declined to be interviewed. Kerrey discussed his nightmares in several interviews with me. He also wrote about them in his memoir, which adds the detail that he saw the faces of his victims. Remarks from his sister Nancy, "We were a little nervous," appeared in *Waltzing Matilda*. "Slightly Angry Young Man Who Appears Alienated," *Lincoln Journal*, January 2, 1970. I interviewed Oscar Pemantle about Kerrey's correspondence to him and his visit to Berkeley while governor. The letter was also cited in Karen Tumulty's in-depth profile on Kerrey in the *Los Angeles Times* on February 10, 1992. "Those who feel it mocks Vietnam veterans," comes from the *Lincoln Journal*, November 13, 1981. "President Nixon should not be re-elected," comes from the *Lincoln Star*, June 7, 1971. "It didn't take much convincing," comes from UPI in the *Lincoln Evening Journal*, August 3, 1971. Kerrey often talked about being enamored of World War I veterans in his speeches and in my interviews with him. I use the quote "drawn to that era" from Craig Winneker's story on Kerrey in the June 1998 issue of *Capitol Style*. The "What you've got" quote comes from the *Lincoln Star*, October 23, 1977. On his May 2001 appearance on Tim Russert's show, Kerrey said: "I thought I might enjoy it, thought I might be good at it." I also reviewed the incorporation papers for the businesses Kerrey and his partners were involved in; these are on file with the Nebraska secretary of state's office.

CHAPTER TWELVE

"Uh oh, we got a battle here." The description of Governor Charles Thone's impression of Kerrey comes from Karen Tumulty's February 10, 1992, profile. Those interviewed for this chapter include June Levine, Paul Olson, Marilyn McNabb, Kandra Hahn, Paul Douglas, Dick Herman, Tom Rinne, Ed Howard, Tom Fogarty, Bill Hoppner, and Dan Ladely. "I shall never forget" comes from the text of Kerrey's announcement for governor. "Find a sense of place and a sense of time" comes from the *Lincoln Star*, December 16, 1981. "I'm a little embarrassed" comes from a December 3, 2001, e-mail from Don Walton. I also interviewed Don Wright, the cameraman, who said Thone's campaign was looking for "dirt" on Kerrey. Press coverage of the May protest march was extensive. Both the *World-Herald* and the *Journal* and *Star* covered it and the ensuing controversy about Kerrey's actions that day. "God, was I dumb," comes from Kerrey's appearance on Russert's CNBC show. "Woody" comes from an interview with Howard as well as the *World-Herald*. "Blew our chickens all over the yard" and the story of Rod Bates comes from the *World-Herald*.

CHAPTER THIRTEEN

Those interviewed for this chapter include June Levine, Paul Olson, Marilyn McNabb, Kandra Hahn, Paul Douglas, Dick Herman, Tim Rinne, Ed Howard, Tom Fogarty, and Bill Hoppner. "I became a Democrat" is from Morton Kondracke's January 20, 1992, *New Republic* article "Careless Kerrey." Kerrey also addressed his party affiliation at a press conference. Kondracke wrote about the savings and loan scandal; this was also covered extensively in the local press. I also reviewed the incorporation papers for Kerrey and his business partners on file with the secretary of state's office to check for affiliations with the Copple family and Kerrey's relationship to William Wright. Wright's problems were written about extensively in the Nebraska papers. The information on Kerrey's relationship with Debra Winger comes from interviews with Kerrey, Ed Howard, Tom Fogarty, Bill Hoppner, Marilyn McNabb, and Paul Douglas. In addition to these interviews, Kerrey and Winger were covered extensively in the state and national papers. Winger appeared on KLIN radio. "It was just love," comes from Kerrey's appearance on Tim Russert's CNBC show. Ivy Harper also has a good chapter in *Waltzing Matilda* on Winger and Kerrey's tenure as governor of Nebraska.

CHAPTER FOURTEEN

Interviews with Kerrey are the primary sources of information—from his stay in Santa Barbara to his political career in Washington—for this chapter. Kerrey and I spoke about his "kittens" article, which appeared in *The Vietnam Reader,* edited by Walter Capps. He said it was an allegory for his actions in Thanh Phong. His short stay in Santa Barbara and his singing "Waltzing Mathilda" in the classroom there, was covered extensively by the national press. Kerrey and I spoke on several occasions about his forgiving Richard Nixon. Sidney Blumenthal's *New Republic* story appeared on January 20, 1992. The Department of Labor investigation and his speculating in cattle futures were also widely reported in the national and Nebraska media. Martha Sherrill's "Grave Doubts," with its references to female reporters and Kerrey's telephone calls, irked him.

CHAPTER FIFTEEN

I interviewed Gerhard Klann at length three times in visits to his home in Pennsylvania and numerous times over the telephone between 1997 and 2002. In addition, he sat for a taped interview for *60 Minutes II.* I reviewed material he had—including a diary, memorabilia, and the application his former executive officer filed nominating Klann for the Medal of Honor—concerning his covert operation inside Iran. I also interviewed other SEALs who knew or operated with Klann to verify his military record and bonafides. I also used SEAL after-action reports on Kerrey's team found at the Navy's historical center for this chapter. In addition, Clint Major provided me an operational diary kept by a SEAL team Klann previously was on in Vietnam. The diary shows that the team had interrogated civilians then let them go.

CHAPTER SIXTEEN

"Like a drill sergeant," comes from *Time*. Kerrey's fund-raising efforts on behalf of the Democrats are listed in Federal Election Committee reports I reviewed. I uncovered the story about Gore's daughters and the CIA and asked Kerrey about it. The CIA confirmed the story as did Porter Goss, the chairman of the House Intelligence Committee. A Kerrey staff member tipped me off to the senator having a bootleg copy of Gore's "Practical Idealism" speech and Kerrey's anger over it. The scene in Kerrey's car comes from Greg Weiner. Kerrey's relationship with Clinton was widely covered by the national media. In my interviews with Kerrey, he commented on the chance of being Clinton's vice president and his belief that Hillary Rodman Clinton probably nixed the idea. Kerrey said Clinton gave him a copy of *Blackhawk Down* and one night after dinner, he cut into Clinton, calling him a "liar." "I don't intend to enter a race to cause anybody any difficulty" comes from David Kotok's November 22, 1998, story in the *World-Herald*. A videotape of the February 2000 exchange with McNamara was sent to me. Kerrey's office provided me copies of his speeches on patriotism. "The people of Vietnam" comes from Fred Barnes in *The American Spectator*, October 1995. My first interview with Kerrey, on December 7, 1998, took place in his Omaha office and lasted nearly four hours.

CHAPTER SEVENTEEN

Kerrey's dropping out of the 2000 presidential race was widely covered by the national media. "If Bob were a Republican" comes from Fred Barnes. "I'm going to the floor" comes from a Kerrey staff member. "I do not come to the floor" comes from the *Congressional Record*, September 3, 1998. "In that case" comes from columnist Robert Novak, *Chicago Sun-Times*, October 4, 1998.

CHAPTER EIGHTEEN

The information in this chapter comes primarily from my interviews with Kerrey. Kerrey spoke admiringly of McCain on several occasions. A McCain staff member also recounted the senator's respect for Kerrey and how he stood whenever the Medal of Honor winner entered a room. "Zinged her?" he said, "I put a flamethrower on her." Kerrey used this remark with me and other reporters like Fred Barnes in *The American Spectator*, October 1995. He also told me "it would have been hard not to support" McCain. "This isn't going to be a hatchet job, is it?" comes from Tom Anderson.

CHAPTER NINETEEN

I spoke with Derek Williams while he was in Vietnam about what he had found in Thanh Phong and later reinterviewed him. Those in attendance at the April 4, 2001, interview in Kerrey's office were Tom Anderson, Kerrey, and me. The comments on Klann and his concern about resigning from the New School came when we were waiting to board the Metroliner from New York's Penn Station. Seymour Hersh's comments come from a brief conversation we had at the International Consortium for Investigative Reporting awards ceremony. The attacks on Quang Ngai and Jonathan Schell's reporting on the area come from Neil Sheehan's *A Bright Shining Lie*. I also spoke with Schell about Quang Ngai. The statistics on war crimes were tallied by Gary Solis from military records. The 3.8 million figure for dead Vietnamese comes from Robert McNamara. The rear admiral in charge of the SEALs in 1991, George Worthington, told me that the name of the camp was switched because of dislike for Kerrey. "Nobody would sit with him," comes from an interview with Larry Bailey. The information on SEALs involved with other possible war crimes comes from interviews or records.

CHAPTER TWENTY

Gary Solis invited Kerrey to West Point to talk about the incident of Thanh Phong. It was during this visit that Kerrey said he first read the rules of land warfare. Federal election commission records show Kerrey used $60,000 for expenses related to Thanh Phong. The *Omaha World-Herald* also reported this. *The New York Times* and Seth Mnookin's article on me and Kerrey in *Brill's Content* both reported the hiring of John Scanlon. I found the records on Klann at the court recorder's office in Butler, Pennsylvania. "I was surprised he called me" comes from Seth Mnookin's article in *Brill's Content*.

CHAPTER TWENTY-ONE

The information on Harrison Hickman comes from the *Brill's Content* article. Mnookin also interviewed me on several occasions for his article. David Halberstam's remarks were reported in *The Village Voice* on April 27, 2001. I reviewed a videotape of his press conference. In an interview in 2001, Klann said some of the SEALs called him to make amends and that they

were sorry about the turn of events. I interviewed Don Walton about his
visit to New York to watch "Memories of a Massacre" with Kerrey. Kotok's
story in the *World-Herald* ran on May 2, 2001.

EPILOGUE

Kerrey's exchange with Tim Russert comes from a transcript of the May 23,
2001, broadcast. Comments from John Kerry and Max Cleland on ABC's
This Week come from a transcript. Kerrey made the comment to me, "We
were instructed not to take prisoners," on the train ride to Philadelphia. I
interviewed Samantha Power of Harvard, Jim Miller of the New School,
Jonathan Schell, and Aryeh Neier for the epilogue. The story about Bob
Kerrey's possible presidential ambitions appeared in *Roll Call* on June 6,
2002. Kerrey's comment "You can't believe everything I tell the *Times*"
comes from an interview I did with a participant at the dinner party. It also
appeared in a May 20, 2002, article by Scott Stossel in *The American Prospect*.

Index